What people a
If You Passed Your Ba

In his usual manner, Dr. Stecker gets straight to the point . . . don't quit too soon and finish strong. The entire book points out that many times those who pass the baton too early often find themselves missing their greatest opportunity for impact and often losing their sense of purpose and self-worth.

I am thrilled with this book, as I often speak on the subject of "Finishing Well" using Paul's farewell statement: "I have fought a good fight, I have finished my course, I have kept the faith" (II Timothy 4:7). Hundreds of times I have told people nearing retirement age, "Don't retire, refire."

This is a powerful and dynamic book for all ages and a must read for those reaching what our culture calls the senior years. I believe If You Passed Your Baton . . . TAKE IT BACK *will give you an entirely new perspective on the importance of the senior generation.*

—Dr. Neal Weaver
President
Louisiana Baptist University and Theological Seminary

I am so excited for this book to be published and reach the hands of people young and old. As someone approaching those years (quicker than I would like), I have given much thought to what I will continue to do, where I will serve, how I will find fulfillment.

In my years of ministry, I have observed there is great value pairing a younger generation volunteer with a more seasoned volunteer. I believe there is always something we can learn from others, and we need to be open and willing to hear what God might speak to us from someone else.

Each generation needs to pick up its baton and pour into the lives of others; share your story, the things you have learned, the changes you have seen, the insights you have gained, and then stop and listen to someone else share his or her perspective, his or her story. We can learn so much from each other if we will stop and take the time to listen. This book will serve as our guide.

—Kathy McShane
Community Liaison
Shiloh House

Dr. Stecker has developed an incredible resource accompanying the ACG seminar with the same name. Chuck has brought together an outstanding group of authors to add to and enhance the reader's understanding that we must become an intergenerational church and we desperately need everyone to assume his or her role in the body. I cannot recommend highly enough If You Passed Your Baton . . . TAKE IT BACK *not only as an excellent read but a guideline to we 2ndhalfers that we are to reintegrate ourselves in the body and accomplish what God has called us to do.*

—Loyd Hoskins
Director
2ndhalf Adult Ministries, RMMN of the Assemblies of God

Most all of us will one day become a senior in our life span. Dr. Chuck Stecker and the forty plus authors in this book give an ultimate insight why it is important to never stop growing spiritually as a Christ follower and serving. God only wants the best for each of us in our family and our daily walk of life. If You Passed Your Baton . . . TAKE IT BACK gives every senior a path to continue to grow spiritually and not settle for anything other than God's best in what could be the greatest season of your life.

—Darrel Billups, Th.D.
Executive Director
National Coalition of Ministries to Men

Dr. Chuck Stecker has strategically gathered over forty knowledgeable authors, ministers, and teachers from different age groups to give a compelling insight on the importance of our "Mature Believers" completing the race and not standing on the sidelines, handing out water to the seemingly faster and younger runners. This revelatory and interactive must-read book shows all generations that our "Mature Believers" are not antique pieces of China that are placed on a shelf to be looked at, but rather are effective people needed to serve the Kingdom of God.

—Vanessa Sander
Co-Pastor
Miracle Temple Ministries, Alexandria, LA

As the president of one of the most significant ministries to men in Germany and Hungary, I believe the issues presented in this book are very important to all our men and churches. We are working to help men understand the need to become Spiritual Fathers and to impact younger generations. This book will be vital to the pastors and families we are serving. In any language, this book is needed greatly to bring the generations together and help our seniors find their God-given identity in their senior years. We are anxious to translate this book into the German language for greater impact.

—Rainer Osterloh
President
Christian Men's Training
www.cmt24.de
Germany

FOREWORD BY DR. GENE GETZ

IF YOU PASSED YOUR BATON . . .
TAKE IT BACK

GENERAL EDITOR: DR. CHUCK STECKER

SEISMIC
PUBLISHING GROUP
Denver

AN INTERGENERATIONAL RESOURCE

IF YOU PASSED YOUR BATON . . . TAKE IT BACK
© 2017 by Charles W. Stecker, Jr.

Published by Seismic Publishing Group (seismicpg.com)

Second Printing, 2018
Printed in the United States of America

The Web addresses (URLs) recommended throughout this book are solely offered as resources for the reader. The citations of these websites do not in any way imply an endorsement on the part of the author(s) or the publisher, nor does the author(s) or publisher vouch for the content for the life of this book.

Cover Design By: Genesis Design, LLC
    genesis.1@juno.com

Page Layout By: Pat Reinheimer
    pat.reinheimer@reagan.com

Library of Congress Cataloging-in-Publication Data
Stecker, Chuck, 1947 –
    If You Passed Your Baton . . . TAKE IT BACK / Chuck Stecker
p. cm.
    Includes bibliographical references (p.) and Index
ISBN 978-0-9843866-3-5 (alk. Paper)
Seniors. 2. Church Activities. 3. Mentoring – Christian. 4. Coaching. 5. Encomentoring.
6. Fathering and Grandfathering. 7. Mothering and Grandmothering.

To the pastors, churches, and ministry leaders who have captured the vision and are excited about re-engaging an incredible generation of seniors who will invest their lives in the generations that are following them to change the world and influence even generations yet to be born.

To the board of trustees, staff, and faculty of A Chosen Generation, who more than anyone have captured the vision of restoring an intergenerational culture in our churches. Without them, this project never would have been completed.

CONTENTS

Prelude   11

Foreword: God's Grace, Mama's Genes *(Gene Getz)*   13

Acknowledgments   17

Introduction: To Finish Well, We Must Get Back in the Race
(Chuck Stecker)   19

Chapter 1: RED—*R*efired *E*xtremely *D*angerous *(Chuck Stecker)*   23

Part 1: Who Stole My Church?

Chapter 2: Finally, Someone Said It! *(Ward Tanneberg)*   29

Chapter 3: You Can Stay, Pray, and Pay, but You Can't Play!
(Roger Shaffer)   35

Chapter 4: We Did Not Steal Your Church *(Hannah Harder)*   41

Chapter 5: Any Chance We Could Do This Church Thing *Together*?
(Noah Addis)   45

For Personal Reflection or Group Discussion   49

Part 2: Reconciling with Your Past and Present

Chapter 6: Your Next Best Day *(Sid Overton)*   53

Chapter 7: Do Not Let Your Past Determine Your Future
(Athena Dean Holtz)   59

Chapter 8: You Don't Even Know Who You Are *(Angie Fouts-Hyatt)*   65

Chapter 9: I Must Fix the Mess When You Do Not Reconcile
(Jessi Chrisp)   71

For Personal Reflection or Group Discussion   75

Part 3: If My Phone Is So Smart, Why Do I feel So Dumb?

Chapter 10: Sorting Out This Generational Mess *(Pete Menconi)*   79

Chapter 11: Now, More Than Ever! *(Phil Schneider)*   87

Chapter 12: Learning to Live Your Best Story *(Cheryl Eichman)*   91

Chapter 13: It Is Not Your Church—It's His Kingdom *(Terry Hoggard)*   97

For Personal Reflection or Group Discussion   102

Part 4: I Just Can't Drive at Night

Chapter 14: Your Incredible Third Calling
(Richard and Leona Bergstrom)   107

Chapter 15: YES—Young Enough to Serve *(Wes Wick)*   113

Chapter 16: Think of It as Your Home—There Is Plenty for All of Us
to Do *(Kathy Addis)*   119

Chapter 17: Your Entire Life Has Been Getting You Ready for This
(Scott Haima)   125

For Personal Reflection or Group Discussion   130

Part 5: Find Your "Jason Stevens" and Change the World

Chapter 18: Your Character Really Does Count *(Rod Handley)*   135

Chapter 19: A Shared Vision to Change the World
(Pastor Jamey Bridges)   141

Chapter 20: Goofy Kids Can Become World Changers
(Kip McCormick)   145

Chapter 21: Create a Common Ground *(Truman Abbott)*   151

Chapter 22: Community. It's What We are. It's Where We Are.
(Molly Ramirez)   157

Chapter 23: The Cry for Spiritual Fathers and Grandfathers
(Dan Schaffer)   163

Chapter 24: The Cry for Spiritual Mothers and Grandmothers
(Julie Thomas)   169

For Personal Reflection or Group Discussion   175

Part 6: For Generations Yet to Be Born

Chapter 25: Your Legacy Foundation: The Family Blessing
(Rolf Garborg)   179

Chapter 26: Taking The "Blur" Out of Your Legacy *(Clarence Shuler)*   187

Chapter 27: Can You Help Me Think About My Legacy?
(Maddison Hardin)   193

Chapter 28: They Are Listening *(Chuck Stecker)*   199

Chapter 29: Filling the Legacy Void *(Greg Bourgond)*   205

For Personal Reflection or Group Discussion   210

Part 7: Finishing Strong

Chapter 30: Resilience: The Key to Finishing Strong *(Bob Dees)*   213

Chapter 31: Faith: The Path to Finishing Strong *(Peggy Fulghum)*   221

Chapter 32: Intellectually: You Are Never Too Old to Learn *(Russ Counts)*   227

Chapter 33: Physically: God Made It, You Maintain It! *(Toby Quirk)*   235

Chapter 34: Overcoming Our Loss *(Cathy Erickson)*   241

Chapter 35: Helping Our Family Overcome Our Loss *(Ross Holtz)*   247

For Personal Reflection or Group Discussion   253

Part 8: Where Do We Go from Here?

Chapter 36: The Starting Line Is Today *(Jeff Baxter)*   257

Chapter 37: God Rested, but He Didn't Retire *(Marni Mrazik)*   265

Chapter 38: It's "With," Not "For" *(Joel Thomas)*   271

Chapter 39: Overcoming the Roadblocks *(Amy Hanson)*   277

Chapter 40: Just Do Something *(Chuck Stecker)*   283

For Personal Reflection or Group Discussion   287

Part 9: For Pastors Only

Chapter 41: Repairer of the Breach *(Pastor Andy Addis)*   291

Chapter 42: Jethro: A Grandfather Pastor Who Saved a Nation *(Pastor Jerrel Gilliam)*   299

Chapter 43: The Lost Treasure *(Pastor Chad Stecker)*   305

Chapter 44: Who Gave the Command to "Stand Down"? *(Pastor Craig Kirkpatrick)*   311

Chapter 45: Well Done! *(Pastor Apolonio "Sonny" Castilleja)*   321

Chapter 46: Leading Seniors to Live Out Their Callings *(Reverend Kristi Lemley)*   325

Chapter 47: Until We Draw Our Final Breath *(Bruce Fong)*   331

For Personal Reflection or Group Discussion   336

Appendix A: Additional Reading   337

Appendix B: Ministries and Resources   344

Appendix C: A Chosen Generation Ministry and Seminars   351

PRELUDE

When I thought of someone to write the foreword to this book, I thought of Dr. Gene Getz. He's been a friend and mentor for many years. Furthermore, I believe there are few individuals who understand the book's message better than Gene.

Gene became a member of the faculty at Moody Bible Institute in 1956, at the age of twenty-three. In 1968, only thirteen years later, he was invited by Dr. Howard Hendricks to become his associate professor at Dallas Theological Seminary. And in 1973, Gene left the sacred halls of learning to start the first Fellowship Bible Church, which in turn launched the Fellowship Bible Church movement, with local assemblies now numbering in the hundreds.

In 2004, after thirty years serving as a church-planting pastor, Gene, at the age of seventy-two, turned his lead role over to his successor. But then came his greatest surprise. He was invited to work on a study Bible using a translation just completed by Broadman and Holman. By that time, he had already written more than sixty books, but this would be his greatest literary challenge. The opportunity resulted in a full-time process for seven years authoring the *Life Essentials Study Bible*.

This Bible contains over fifteen hundred principles to live by embedded in the biblical text and is the first multimedia study Bible. With each of the principles is a QR code enabling the reader to access more than fifteen hundred videos of Gene teaching these fifteen hundred principles from Genesis to Revelation. Today, people all over the world are freely accessing these videos on YouTube.

But since the study Bible's first publication, Gene has stayed busy sharing his Biblical teachings and insights to pastors all over the world who have not had formal training. For these servants of the Lord, the *Life Essentials Study Bible* is a seminary in a box!

Gene has not stopped his efforts in making this Bible current. He has been redoing all the videos using high-definition cameras. "Chuck," he said, "it will take me approximately two or three more years to complete this process! If it's the Lord's will, I'll be near ninety and praying that I'll be able to complete this project before God takes me home."

So, I've just shared with you *why* I asked Gene Getz to write this foreword. He's living proof of continuing to carry the "baton of engagement."

Chuck Stecker

GOD'S GRACE, MAMA'S GENES

When my good friend Chuck Stecker asked me to write the foreword for this exciting book, I soon figured out why: I'm old! (Eighty-five, to be exact, and when this book comes off the press, I'll probably be eighty-six.)

Yes, I passed my pastoral mantle of leadership to my successor more than fourteen years ago. And, of course, I have not "taken it back." But in the spirit of all the authors of this book, I never gave up the "baton of engagement." In some respects, I've never been busier and more fulfilled, thanks to God's grace and Mama's genes!

Needless to say, when we grow older, both God's grace and Mama's genes are involved. My mother entered heaven's gates at age ninety-eight and for at least ninety-six of those years was a very active woman. Life was difficult for her. When Mom was eighteen, her mother died and she had to step in to "mother" her younger sisters. About the same time, her older married sister died, and she had to step in and mother her children as well. She then married and mothered me and my three brothers and two sisters.

However, what I saw in my mother was not only good genes that gave her strength but also God's grace to endure some very difficult situations. She was a great model to me, and it appears I've been a recipient of her genetics, but it's a fact that I've been blessed with God's grace. As each day goes by, I realize more and more that without Jesus, I can do nothing (see John 15:5).

When God called me from my role as a lead pastor at age seventy-two, I knew it was time for a new voice and a unique opportunity for my successor. But I also knew it was *not* the time to stop serving Jesus Christ. As Chuck reminds us, retirement is not in the Bible. Consequently, I've stayed active in the ministry, and I hope to continue on into the future, realizing, of course, that my time is in God's hands.

Years ago, I was deeply moved by Moses's words in Psalm 90. He wrote,

> Our lives last seventy years
> or, if we are strong, eighty years. . . .
> Teach us to number our days carefully
> so that we may develop wisdom in our hearts.
>   (verses 10, 12, HCSB)

I actually preached a message on these verses, and at that time I shared something like this: "If I live to be eighty, I'll have this many days to do God's will," and I actually calculated the number of days I had left *if* I were to reach that age.

As I recall, I also went on to say, "If I live to be eighty-five, I'll have this many days to do God's will," and again I calculated the number of days.

Well, today I'm eighty-five, and if I live to be ninety, I'll have approximately 1,826 days to do God's will!

For me, staying active and serving Jesus Christ was and still is my goal. But please understand. This does not mean not spending quality time with my precious wife, who by God's grace and her own mama's genes has shared my vision. And, of course, should she need more of my time and energy, it's definitely God's will that she be my priority!

Furthermore, my goals include spending quality time with my grown children, their children, and hopefully grandchildren. Let's not forget Proverbs 17:6: "Grandchildren are the crown of the elderly" (HCSB)!

This, of course, is *my* story, which is written with the words of James ringing in my ears:

> Come now, you who say, "Today or tomorrow we will travel to such and such a city and spend a year there and do business and make a profit." You don't even know what tomorrow will bring—what your life will be! For you are like smoke that appears for a little while, then vanishes.

> Instead, you should say, "If the Lord wills, we will live and do this or that." (James 4:13–15, HCSB)

The principle to live by from James's instruction is clear no matter what our endeavors: Jesus wants us to stay busy about our Father's business, but we're always to do so realizing we have a sovereign God!

Your story, of course, is different from mine—and unique! But as we age as believers, we should have one thing in common: to always desire to do God's will. We also know that to those God gives much, He expects much (see Luke 12:48)! And certainly the word *much* includes our time, talents, and treasures, as well as God's grace and our genetic structures.

So as we grow older, let's pray for one another, encourage one another, and serve one another, "keeping our eyes on Jesus, the source and perfecter of our faith" (Hebrews 12:2, HCSB).

I firmly believe that this book, written by various authors representing many ages and various walks of life, will help all of us serve God faithfully until Jesus takes us home.

Dr. Gene A. Getz
Professor, Pastor, Author

ACKNOWLEDGMENTS

This book represents the hearts and minds of a great number of very talented men and women of all ages. It is a dream come true for me personally as well as for the Board of Trustees of A Chosen Generation, who are constantly working to ignite this ministry.

Very special thanks to:

Ray and Mary Morgan, who have been part of A Chosen Generation from the beginning. They have never hesitated to invest their time, talents, and treasure to increase the impact of this ministry.

The authors. These men and women, who have contributed, responded in record time to submit their chapters.

Dr. Gene Getz for contributing the foreword. You are a friend, mentor, and hero to me and countless others.

The Board of Trustees of A Chosen Generation, past and present, including the incredible group now serving: our chairman, Wendell Morton; vice chairman, Rob Zavaglia; treasurer, David Ifflander; and trustees, Loretta Abbott, Pastor Andy Addis, Lori Antone, Pastor Jerrel Gilliam, Ray Morgan, and Troy Reichert. This would not have been accomplished without your steadfast leadership, encouragement, and passion for intergenerational ministry.

Pastors and ministry leaders across the nation and around the world for your faith and trust in A Chosen Generation. Your support for this ministry cannot be measured.

Dr. Neal Weaver, president of Louisiana Baptist University and Theological Seminary, for capturing the vision of intergenerational leadership and including significant courses of instruction at every level of education.

The remarkable staff and auxiliary staff of A Chosen Generation, especially Margo Beasley, our administrative assistant, who compiled the manuscript as the chapters were submitted and worked on the "additional reading" list.

Tim and Amber Tomlinson for guiding this project and being part of my and Billie's lives.

Billie, my wife, for forty years of marriage in which she always has placed me and her family before herself. She has been my constant source of inspiration and encouragement. During our military years and more than twenty-three years of vocational ministry, Billie has been a rock for me and our entire family.

Our children, their best friends (read spouses), and our grand-kids. I love you, and each of you is a part of anything I could ever accomplish.

Finally, the men and women who have inspired and encouraged me and A Chosen Generation to complete this project!

TO FINISH WELL, WE MUST GET BACK IN THE RACE

— Chuck Stecker —

I consider my life worth nothing to me; my only aim is to finish the race and complete the task the Lord Jesus has given me—the task of testifying to the good news of God's grace. (Acts 20:24)

Several years ago, my wife and I were visiting a longtime friend when he decided he would take us to Atlantic City, New Jersey, which we had never visited before. We had both heard of the famous boardwalk and knew there were several casinos located there.

Although we had no intentions of gambling, we both thought it would be an interesting experience. As we approached the casino area, we could see lines of buses parked. Neither of us was prepared for what we saw as we entered the first casino. On a Tuesday afternoon, the casino was filled with seniors gambling.

It was not just the fact that the casino was filled with seniors; it's that they were lifeless. Their faces were almost catatonic. They had no emotions. They were not happy or sad. They were sitting at the slot machines with blank stares as they entered the amounts to be wagered.

In a very short amount of time, Billie and I both felt sick to our stomachs, and we went outside to sit on a bench facing the ocean.

When we talk about the wealth of a nation, it is so easy to be grieved when we see the untapped wealth of experience of our seniors who go to the casinos and sit with blank stares because they do not realize they still have great purpose remaining in their lives.

If You Passed Your Baton . . . TAKE IT BACK is more than a book; it is our attempt to help change the culture of our communities, churches, and nation. It is the heart of every author included in this project to reverse a diabolical trend sidelining the greatest resource we have in our nation and the world today: our seniors.

Before a great change can take place in our culture and the world, we must first change ourselves.

We have bought into a terrible lie. The lie is there is a time to "pass the baton" and step away.

We have confused the "baton of engagement" with the "mantle of leadership."

Passing the baton refers to when one runner in a relay race passes the baton to the next runner. What is rarely considered when the runner completes the passing of the baton is he or she must quit running, step off the track, and stay out of the race. In summary, that person is *finished*!

In the United States, we have two generations of seniors who feel they have been told their time was over. They have been told to pass the baton, quit running, and get off the track and made to feel that they are no longer needed in the race.

We must have a shift in our thinking. As seniors, we must embrace the concept of pouring into the next generation, passing the mantle of leadership, and staying in the race until God calls us home.

I would like for you to travel with me back to the casino in

Atlantic City. What I initially saw were men and women sitting lifeless, without emotion, gambling. Although that was sad, I came to realize that what caused me to be sickened was a casino filled with incredible experience, in every area of life, remaining untapped by the communities who saw them as retired and having passed the baton.

I also saw a casino of men and women who shared the blame in that they had bought into the lie and "checked out."

This is more than a book to be read. It is a resource to call a generation of seniors to get back in the race and finish well. Our communities and churches need our seniors now more than ever. It is a resource to help pastors and ministry leaders better understand the incredible possibilities if they will tap into the wealth of experience and availability of their seniors.

I would like for you to imagine forty-six male and female authors who have contributed to this book ranging in age from nineteen to eighty-five from across the United States and Canada. Authors include pastors, ministry leaders, military personnel, housewives, mothers and grandmothers, fathers and grandfathers, educators, students, husbands and wives, widows and widowers, counselors, denominational leaders, community leaders, and CEO/directors of nonprofits. Some of the authors have been published extensively, while others have not been published prior to this book.

In short, I am deeply honored and greatly humbled by the men and women who have given their hearts and minds to this project.

It is important to know that this book parallels the "If You Passed Your Baton . . . TAKE IT BACK" seminar from A Chosen Generation. A Chosen Generation is a Christ-centered ministry that exists to equip and train leaders for intergenerational ministry.

The title of each part of the book is the same as the title of the corresponding session in the seminar.

Finally, the apostle Paul stated in 2 Timothy 4:7, "I have fought the good fight, I have finished the race, I have kept the faith."

As a generation of seniors who want to finish the race and finish well, we must get back in the race. Today is the day and now is the time. If you passed your baton, take it back!

CHAPTER 1

RED—REFIRED EXTREMELY DANGEROUS

— Chuck Stecker —

In 2010, the movie *RED*[1] was released, starring Bruce Willis, Morgan Freeman, John Malkovich, Helen Mirren, and Richard Dreyfuss. It is a fast-paced movie about a retired CIA hit man who is lonely and bored with his life. His only connection with anyone after his retirement is by phone with his caseworker at the pension-processing center. To have contact with her, he would regularly call and claim that his check was missing. His life is turned upside down when a team of professional assassins are sent to kill him. As the movie continues, he assembles a team of other CIA hit men/women from his past to determine why assassins would want to kill him and who sent them.

Frank (Bruce Willis) discovers that his personnel file, as well as those of his friends, has been stamped "RED." He would then be told *RED* was an acronym for "Retired Extremely Dangerous."

As I watched the movie unfold, I had this desire for my spiritual personnel file to be stamped "RED." For me, however, RED would mean "*Refired* Extremely Dangerous."

---

[1] *RED* (2010) © Summit Entertainment, LLC. All Rights Reserved.

I want to be more dangerous in my senior years on behalf of the King and His kingdom than at any other time in my life.

On many occasions, I have had the privilege of speaking to seniors. I will normally begin by saying that I will make two statements. I warn them that if they stay and listen to the first statement, they must remain to hear the second. I give them the opportunity to leave and again warn them that if they listen to the first statement, they must also listen to the second.

I begin by telling them I love them and I have earned the right to say what they are going to hear next.

Statement one is "The greatest problem in the local church today is the seniors." Never have we had a more self-centered, narcissistic, and "It's all about me" generation than today's seniors. All too often, our seniors demand that the church remain unchanged until they die; after their magnificent funerals, the church leadership has "permission" to change anything in the church. To be sure you heard me correctly, we seniors can be the biggest problem in the church. But remember, I love you!

Then I pause before moving to statement two.

I can tell you that after this first statement, the faces of many of the seniors look angry. Some look as if they wished they had left before hearing anything from me.

Next comes the second statement. I again begin by telling them I love them and have earned the right to say what they are going to hear next.

Statement two is "The greatest hope for our churches and communities today are our seniors." Never in history has there been a generation like this generation of seniors. We are living longer and healthier lives. We have the greatest availability of any senior generation before us. Seniors can and should be the foundation of the church in reaching all the younger generations. We must learn to get over looking at only ourselves and look at His kingdom for His glory.

Before you start to think this is just a great halftime locker-room speech like "Let's win this one for the Gipper," I want you to consider this as a mandate from our heavenly Father.

Repeatedly, we are instructed in the Bible with the phrase "From generation to generation" (for example, Exodus 3:15; Psalm 79:13; Isaiah 34:10).

I can find no verses telling us we have earned the right to sit back and do nothing.

There can be no "generation to generation" if we, as seniors, quit before a time appointed by God.

Retirement is not a biblical word. I do not find the word *retirement* in the Bible. In fact, I often ask seniors if they have read about the glorious retirement ceremony in God's Word. As they respond with puzzled looks, I suggest to them that God's retirement party in the Bible is called a funeral.

Before you launch into the following chapters, take a moment to consider Psalm 78:5–7:

> He decreed statutes for Jacob
>   and established the law in Israel,
> which he commanded our ancestors
>   to teach their children,
> so the next generation would know them,
>   even the children yet to be born,
>   and they in turn would tell their children.
> Then they would put their trust in God
>   and would not forget his deeds
>   but would keep his commands.

In verse 5, take notice of the words *commanded* and *to teach*. In verse 6, read again carefully the phrases "even the children yet to be born" and "they in turn would tell their children." Consider God's specific items to be taught written in verse 7: "*trust*," *remember* ("not forget"), and *obey* ("keep his commands").

Seniors, our work is not done until God calls us into his presence.

I am a big fan of the television show *Blue Bloods*. There are several reasons for my affinity with the show, including the fact that nearly every show has a scene at the dining room table with four generations seated together. In addition, every episode seems to honestly present the family as not being perfect. In one of the episodes, Frank Reagan, played by Tom Selleck, admonishes the family with loving sternness and states, "This family never stands down." My heart longs to hear God say that about our generation of seniors: "This generation never stands down."

Get to Know the Author:

Dr. Chuck Stecker is executive director and founder of A Chosen Generation, which he and his wife, Billie, launched in 1997. After twenty-three years in the US Army, he served on staff of Promise Keepers as regional director in field ministry division for south-central region. Chuck and Billie have three children and nine grandchildren.

Questions:
- How did you feel when you read statement one?
- How did you feel when you read statement two?
- What is needed in your life for you to go from "retired" to "refired"?

WHO STOLE MY CHURCH?

PART 1

WHO STOLE
MY CHURCH?

What to Expect

In 2010, Dr. Gordon MacDonald wrote the book *Who Stole My Church?* Although it was written as a novel, the book tells the story of many churches in existence today. Gordon creates characters in their fifties, sixties, and seventies who meet regularly to talk about their churches. They discuss the past, present, and future of their churches, and during the conversations, one individual expresses what everyone else is feeling when he asks, "Who stole my church?"

In these first few chapters, you can expect to be challenged to examine your true feelings regarding your church. You will read the thoughts of and hear the hearts of four authors who love the church. They range in age from nineteen to seventy-six.

The real issue is very simple: If we cannot deal honestly with "the elephant in the room," then very little of what follows will really matter to any of us.

CHAPTER 2

FINALLY, SOMEONE SAID IT!

— Ward Tanneberg —

Okay, maybe they didn't *steal* it, but on Sundays it feels like my pockets have been picked and I come away with nothing to show for it. So I report the robbery to the new sheriff/pastor in town, but he just pats me on the shoulder and says, "It's not all about you. The ones you think picked your pockets need what was in them more than you do. Get over yourself and you'll be all right."

"But I don't like the music or the special lighting effects, and the sound system is too loud."

"Just get on board and go with the flow. It's a new day (and you're an old person)."

"What did you say?"

"Oh, nothing really. Just thinking out loud, I guess. By the way, we need the room at nine thirty, the one all you seniors have been meeting in. You see how the church is growing. Lots of new families with kids and we're running out of space. The community college is only a mile from here. Maybe they will rent space for your class. Yes, there is a risk there'll be no parking spaces left when you come for the worship service, but your inconvenience is just something we have to live with for a while. I'm sure you understand. After all, you've been here forever. Of course you do. Oh, and we need it starting next Sunday."

Did this really happen? In truth, it's a composite conversation, linking events that really have happened. Maybe this is your story, or part of it. Maybe you sacrificed financially, helped build the church building, and volunteered hundreds of hours working with children, teens, and young adults. Maybe you were all these people years ago.

But First Church of Wherever isn't First Church anymore. Even the name may have changed to something more cool. You love it still; you just don't like it right now.

And was that your pastor apologizing to the guest speaker for so many "gray hairs this morning in the congregation"?

No one seems to need us like they did before, when we were really engaged. Before our kids went away to college, got married, moved out of state. Before we kind of lost interest for a while. Now it's hard to find a reason to stay. Still, it is our church. At least it was once.

I was scheduled to speak to a group of Jesus followers age fifty and older in a large church in the Bay Area. Snow and ice were keeping all airplanes on the ground at our airport. I finally caught a commuter plane leaving for Portland, Oregon. From there I could catch a flight to the Bay Area, so I did.

I was late getting in. A driver met me at the gate and as we rushed to the meeting site, he explained what had come down the Sunday before. Their senior pastor had had it with older adults' complaints about the current worship style. He made it clear in his sermon that instead of fielding further complaints, there were several churches nearby he would be happy to recommend to them. It hadn't set well.

I was saddened at the story and wondered how I could (a) honor the lead pastor (with whom I could empathize, having spent the biggest share of my ministry life being one) and (b) also serve as an emergency room doctor repairing a fresh spiritual wound.

I entered the chapel, stepped onto the platform, was introduced by a very relieved host, and said hello to more than two hundred fifty-plus-aged men and women gathered there. They didn't care that I was still in travel clothes; they just wanted to know if I might have something of value to give them. I did my best.

The next morning, I attended a leaders' breakfast to listen to and dialogue with their volunteers in the ministry. Of course, the previous Sunday comments came up. I was asked point blank, "Pastor, what would you do in our situation?"

I recalled an event from years before in my own life in which I accepted a call to a small church in California. After a couple of years, the church began to grow. I was persuaded in my heart that I had heard from God as to how this church was to be led, but it was a stretch for me. Exciting? Yes, but still a stretch. It was something different from what I was used to.

As we grew in numbers, some of my colleagues in the surrounding area complained to the presbytery about my not being faithful to the traditions of our denomination, so I was called to appear before this body of gentlemen to answer their questions.

Some were not easily persuaded, so at last I said, "Brothers, as I see it you have two options. One, you can have your church back and I will return to where I came from. I was well thought of there, with a good reputation. I don't really know anyone here other than the good folks who called me to be their pastor. Or two, you can allow me to be me and lead in the manner in which God has spoken to my heart. I'm confident in being directed by the Holy Spirit, but I'm also under your authority, so it's up to you to decide. Do I go or do I stay? I'm not changing how I lead because of innuendo, and I'm not leaving the church unless you tell me to leave."

I did not leave, the church continued to grow, and there came a day when my ministry colleagues even elected me to represent them as their presbyter.

I said to these wounded leaders sitting around me, "You all are old enough now. You can cross the street by yourselves. You don't need permission. You may need forgiveness. But later. You know in your hearts the right thing. Don't leave the church unless you are told to leave. And don't trouble your pastor. Give him grace. He's got lots on his mind. Just do what God wants you to do, and the Lord will honor it. When you are successful, your pastor will love you for it. If you fail, he just might say, 'I told you so,' and you can live with that. You've been told worse. Meanwhile, you will have honored the Lord and your pastor, even though you've been hurt. There is something bigger at stake here. You are Jesus's followers. The question is, will you be His influencers?"

When it comes to changing the world, what most of us lack is not the courage to change things but the skill to do so. As followers of Jesus, even when wounded we must see ourselves as influencers.

Whoever believes in me . . . rivers of living water will flow from within them. (John 7:38)

Go and make disciples of all nations. (Matthew 28:19)

Pastor and author Eugene H. Peterson wrote, "Exile (being where we don't want to be with people we don't want to be with) forces a decision. Will I focus my attention on what is wrong with the world and feel sorry for myself? Or will I focus my energies on how I can live at my best in this place I find myself? . . . Daily we face decisions on how we will respond to these exile conditions."[1]

The serenity trap, seeking solace instead of solutions, is a dangerous one. You don't see it coming, and then it caves in on

---

[1] Eugene H. Peterson, *Run with the Horses: The Quest for Life at Its Best* (Downers Grove: InterVarsity, 2009), 150–151.

you. Life in the second half is about more than feeling good, isn't it? It's about solving problems no one else is solving, and caring for people no one else cares about. It's about being mentored by someone twenty years older and mentoring someone else twenty years younger.

Maybe it's not the church leaders who will make change happen. Maybe it's up to you to seek the help of others, not turn your church upside down but see beyond the surface behavior and hear the hearts of the young. Diverse. Conflicted values. No objective truth. What is it like to be in their skin? When you listen to understand as you come alongside those you want to influence, you're emulating Jesus's style.

How can you be salt and light? It's a great question, and the answers are not easy. Still, they are what Jesus called us to be, are they not?

There is a world out there. What does the world mean to you? How often do you think about things outside your church? Your town? What does the world or the church expect of you?

NOTHING.

You are too busy, but not forever. One day you'll be free. Retired! And someone will ask, "What do you do with all your time now?" And you will answer defensively, "I'm busier than ever [playing, traveling, living the dream]."

There are so many things wrong—things you don't like. What if the world, after one reaches a certain age, is just a big disappointment? Too old to make a difference. Stuck in a rut. Gazing wistfully across the generation gap. Knowing you could help, possessing the tools and materials to build bridges, but lacking the will. Sinking in serenity.

Get to Know the Author:

Drawing from a lifetime of ministry, Ward Tanneberg speaks today in churches, at adult retreats, and at ministry conferences on transformational living, learning, and leading in life's second half. He began ministry as a young evangelist in 1959 and has served as a denominational youth director, Christian-college public relations director, guest lecturer and adjunct professor, and writer and novelist. He also has been a pastor in three churches, which included five years as pastor of the Assembly of God in Forks, Washington; twenty-three years as senior pastor of Valley Christian Center in Dublin, California; and seven years as executive pastor of the nondenominational Westminster Chapel of Bellevue, Washington. He served as executive director of CASA 50+ Network from 2008 to 2014. Ward lives in Washington State and is a widower who has two married children, seven grandchildren, and two great-grandsons. His interests and ministry have taken him to more than fifty countries of the world.

CHAPTER 3

YOU CAN STAY, PRAY, AND PAY, BUT YOU CAN'T PLAY!

— Roger Shaffer —

Seniors (you know, the ones who built their churches, are dedicated to them, and know how to spell *tithe*) are moving to heaven in record numbers. On average, ten thousand baby boomers turn sixty-five years old every day.[1] Their knowledge, wisdom, money, and influence are valuable resources, but these folks are treated as if they are passé. They are not valued in our culture. They are seen as technologically outdated, living in the past, and unwilling to change. We tend to ignore seniors or abuse their goodwill by focusing our resources on accommodating the young out of a fear of losing them and because of a desire to reach them. Seniors are simply ignored and face ageism, which is the stereotyping of senior citizens and is often fraught with error. How the younger members of society feel about seniors is one thing, but how seniors view themselves is even more important. It affects

---

[1] Glenn Kessler, "Do 10,000 Baby Boomers Retire Every Day, *Washington Post*, July 24, 2014, https://www.washingtonpost.com/news/fact-checker/wp/2014/07/24/do-10000-baby-boomers-retire-every-day/?utm_term=.9469837da34e.

how they engage younger people and how useful they become. No one wants to be considered too old to be an active, vital part of church or society, yet those of retirement age are often seen that way. Is this unavoidable? Is this right? Perhaps the best question is, is this God's intention for His church? How should seniors view themselves in relation to their churches? Is there a healthy and biblical way to involve the senior population in the church (those fifty years old and above)? I have written at length about this in my forthcoming book, *Re-Engaging the Lost Generation*.

Some churches "do church" for the seniors simply by getting them a special pastor and program as they do for their youth. This is separation of the ages, and separation is wrong. We are to be unified and intergenerational. Others simply excoriate seniors for being what they are and demand they change to become like the younger ages. Their old music is seen as invalid because it doesn't fit with younger tastes. Their experiences are not applicable to youth. They must change! Often because of being devalued, seniors check out of the church. But is senior change to accommodate youth the only way? What should they consider changing and how? What does God say? What works? What do we do as the "lost generation"?

There is no doubt a different and fractured culture in America and its churches. We see fatherless generations, abused by neglect. We see young people with no parents near and no one with whom they feel welcome to share their lives. Couples reject marriage commitments and simply live together, causing their children to sense this lack of commitment and suffer in their security. Let's face it: some parents and grandparents are not worth the powder to blow them up. Some are enablers of youthful addictions to drugs and sex and are not good or effective at parenting. So many parents are in their second or third marriages and cannot help their own children be faithful because they don't know how to themselves. They are unacceptable role models. Who is there that can become role models to the younger generations? Those over fifty in the church are a block of available mentors, but they do need to adapt to God's model.

"In order to become an integral part of the generations, the lost generation will need to reevaluate themselves as they relate to the church as a whole and specifically to younger generations. They also will need to retool a bit as they try to understand the position and needs of younger ones. They will need to find and institute a rite of passage into adulthood for children so that these newly made adults can find themselves and fit themselves into the church and so successfully interact and meld with older generations. This is a key to the intergenerational life and to re-engaging the lost generation."[2] So we have some work to do. Are we free to retire (an American invention) and enjoy ourselves? Do we instead have a responsibility in our church?

The reason that we "can't play" is that we are sometimes unwilling to change. But if simple accommodation to youth is not the only or right way or is simply not working for all, what shall we do? In the Great Commandment to love God and our neighbor, there is a clue: emptiness is found in serving ourselves. But retiring from working often leads to living for only ourselves and our families. We need to repent of this idea and stay devoted to God and His purposes in the church. The Great Commission shows the way. We who are discipled are to disciple younger ones in the faith. Period. No excuses. This is God's way for the church to serve Him to the end of this age! We are to make disciples of all nations, baptizing and teaching (discipling) them to observe (live out) everything that Jesus commanded us to do (see Matthew 28:19–20). The apostle Paul described the same method when he commanded that the same things he taught were to be committed to faithful men who in turn were to commit to others. It

---

[2] Roger K. Shaffer, *Re-Engaging the Lost Generation* (Shreveport, LA: Doctoral Dissertation at Louisiana Baptist University, 2017), 5.

is spiritual parenting done in the church because of love—love first for God and then for others. Mentoring and coaching in the church means discipling.

How is it done? Do we start a new class? No. One way it can be accomplished well is by multiple generations serving together. The young observe the older and learn what it is to follow God and serve Him. Mission trips and camping experiences and such are useful if we remember to love and engage younger ones. Another basic way that also must be used is individual engagement. Much if not all of discipling is best done one on one. It occurs at coffee shops and by texting, calling, e-mailing, and writing letters. It does not occur in classes or with group activities. It is based on the older taking interest in the younger. Trust is gained by intentional, loving involvement of an older person in the life of a younger one. Discipling is best done by showing interest in their lives and problems first and then praying with them and (after gaining their trust and respect) guiding them by the Word and godly advice. Jesus did this and asks us to do it as well. The younger ones need someone to trust and show them love. They need someone fully functional as a believer. They need someone who is sound psychologically from living the Bible to guide them to the way to live. Jesus reproved, rebuked, and exhorted His disciples and pastors to preach this way and calls on seniors in the faith to also do so to the babes in the faith.

Discipling, of course, starts in the home. Parents are to bring up their own in the care and teachings of the Lord. It is then to be continued by the church. We are to teach (literally, disciple) them to do everything we have been commanded. This takes a lifetime, doesn't it? How shall we as a church be involved in discipling? The answer lies first in acknowledging their development from child into adulthood and in serving their need for recognition in their passage from the one into the other. Chuck Stecker's book *Men of Honor, Women of Virtue* discusses this in detail.[3] Young people see the church as their parents' church. In their own minds, they were not a part of it as adults really. They were the youth who graduated out of it as they went on to work or college. They need a rite of passage that the church recognizes and believes in to establish them as a real part of the church. Then the church must take responsibility for discipling them in the matters of the church and its ministry. Here is where seniors become really valuable.

This question remains for us to answer: Can we do it? We are old, we are unvalued, and we are not specially trained. How can we? This is how. God has given us His Spirit, His Word, and His command. He also gives us His grace to perform that which He has commanded. He does not mock us by commanding without giving us His power to do it. He who said, "My grace is sufficient for you" (2 Corinthians 12:9), proved it in His servants who said, "When I am weak, then I am strong" (verse 10). God delights in using the weak to confound the mighty. He shows himself strong in those who obey Him.

Is anyone discipling the young successfully? Yes, says one church. "Research . . . shows that it takes five adults with consequential faith to be involved in a young person's life in order for their faith to become real to them. . . . Students long for the kinds of conversations the seniors offer, to learn from what they've been through, their daily walk with God. Seniors also find a sense of belonging by mentoring our youth."[4] That church keeps most of their youth—much more than the 3 percent that many churches retain. Discipling meets the needs of seniors for significance and a sense of doing God's will. It answers the desire of young people for a loving guide "in the flesh." It provides someone to care about

---

[3] Chuck Stecker, *Men of Honor, Women of Virtue: The Power of Rites of Passage into Godly Adulthood* (Seismic, Littleton, CO. 2015).

[4] *"Young at Heart" Seniors Mentoring Youth, Back to God*, January 22, 2016, https://backtogod.net/stories/young-at-heart-seniors-mentoring-youth.

them the way we say God does. With regard to my doctorate study, a pastor told me that "no one makes it who doesn't have a mentor." How much more important is a disciple in the spiritual life of a young believer? You can stay, you can pay, and now you know that you can play a big and needed part in the life of some needy young person who will love you back for eternity!

GET TO KNOW THE AUTHOR:

Dr. Roger Shaffer is an accomplished Bible teacher, singer, and former pastor. He served churches in South Carolina, Ohio, and Colorado and has written a forthcoming book on intergenerational ministry titled *Re-Engaging the Lost Generation*. A recent PhD graduate of Louisiana Baptist University in executive leadership, Roger has a passion for the Lord Jesus and serving His church and for reaching young people and involving seniors in discipleship ministry. He and his wife, Cathey, live in Green Mountain, Colorado, and are active in church work. They are proud to be parents of three grown children and eight grandchildren.

CHAPTER 4

WE DID NOT STEAL YOUR CHURCH

— Hannah Harder —

The times are changing constantly, and we are in an interesting period in both the world and the church. When we are supposed to be united, it seems as though division is on the rise. That is to be expected of the world, but it should not be said of the church. We have generations colliding in a clash of fear and hostility when it should be a beautiful collision of grace, understanding, and truth. There is a gap in age, a gap in time, but why does there have to be a gap in our spirituality and in our churches? I think if we rearrange our thinking, we might come to see we are more alike than we think and together we can debunk a giant lie that divides us: millennials hijacked the church.

I have had the awesome opportunity to be around elderly, middle age, millennials, and youths in the church. Each generation brings something to the table, and when one group does not share or contribute, the absence is felt in the church and ultimately in the whole body of believers. To get across this generational bridge and thinking that millennials are taking over the church, we need to get some things straightened out. Millennials are not changing the message, but they are putting to use other gifts. They are navigating their way through a dark time and are calling for generations to come together to grow in wisdom.

To start off, millennials are not changing the message of the Bible. Sure, I cannot speak for every millennial on the planet, but my experience with those I have been around, gone to school with, worked with, and worshipped with is that most of them desire to hold fast to truth and crave a holy awakening of the world around them.

They are, however, changing the methods by which the message is portrayed. It is no secret that we are in an instant culture. The world moves quick, and the church needs to keep step. We are not to be of the world, but we are in it and must know the side that is fighting us. It would be unwise for any soldier to enter a battle without knowing the enemy. He needs to know his tactics, what makes him attractive and successful, and how he will fight in the war. The church is the same way. I think too often we have tried to hide from culture and divide ourselves from the world around us and have actually isolated ourselves in a way that has turned many off from entering the church. For the first time in a long time, millennials are engaging the culture and taking it head on.

There are many avenues in which millennials are getting the church outside of the four walls of a building. You will find millennials doing Christian street art to share the message, holding worship nights in their houses, creating films, and a plethora of other avenues to engage people. More than ever, the church is meeting the desires of the culture without compromising the truth of the gospel.

When I think of my generation, one of the first words that comes to mind is *creative*. In my friend group alone, I am surrounded by those who are gifted photographers, videographers, storytellers, and musicians. They are not just being creative for no reason; they are donating their time and talents to the church. This generation is all about what catches the eye, and Christian millennials are capitalizing on the God-given gift of creativity to spread the gospel. Oftentimes you will walk into a church and see a video to start the service, aesthetically pleasing graphics in the lobby, or a deep kick drum from the stage. These newer avenues in the church are not a millennial invasion, nor are they perverting Scriptures, but they are giving movement to the church and reaching some who might never step foot in a church.

The times are hard. With the rise of technological advances and an ever-growing population, problems come up all the time. When people are going through struggles, they naturally look for someone who can relate. That is why my generation needs the older generations to walk the course with us. There is knowledge and insight that older folks have that can actually be applicable and help our current predicament. We can greatly glean from their experiences. There is wisdom in not having to suffer through an issue because someone else has heeded the advice of another. There are many hiccups we could avoid on our walks of life if we heard an older generation's heart and life stories.

We can be from different eras and generations, but one thing must be true: we have to be unified. Over and over again in the New Testament, unity is mentioned, and it is crucial to the body of Christ. We can disagree on the little things, but at the end of the day, we have to be unified on our understanding of Jesus Christ and His Holy Word.

We could argue with each other until we are blue in the face, but that would get us nowhere. We could segregate and go our separate ways, but that would only create isolation and a host of other problems. What must start is the conversation. We have to come together, and I think we would find that we are not that different. Putting all desires and aesthetics aside, I think we would find that our intentions are the same: we want a broken world to meet the Savior of the world. Let us fight the battle together, for that is when we are the strongest.

Get to Know the Author:

Hannah Harder is a senior at Colorado Christian University studying communications. She is a follower of Jesus, a writer, a speaker, an adventurer, and a lover of all people. She was an intern at Red Rocks Church and Altitude Sports Radio. She is the author of a devotional called *Exposed: The Raw Thoughts from an Ordinary Life*, which is a daily devo of quick reads that leave you with a thought to ponder. She launched her own ministry, called Purpose Generation, which is a company that seeks to propel people into their God-given purpose. Once a month she leads Purpose Nights, a gathering of young adults and older generations in a time of food, fellowship, worship, and a message. This is just one aspect Purpose Generation. You can learn more about it and Hannah Harder at thepurposegeneration.co.

CHAPTER 5

ANY CHANCE WE COULD DO THIS CHURCH THING *TOGETHER?*

— Noah Addis —

My name is Noah Addis. I was born in Fort Worth, Texas, but I've grown up in Hutchinson, Kansas. Correction, I've grown up in the church. My dad has been a pastor since I was born, so I've become intimately familiar with the church and all its goods, bads, and uglies. Growing up in the church, I spent a lot of time around church people; they became my second family. One group of people in the church I'm especially thankful for is the elders. I'm so grateful for everything the elders in the church have taught me and how much they've invested in me. I cannot even begin to express how important these people are.

I'm saddened by the rift that is growing in today's church between the elders and my generation. Thankfully, our church has been mostly unaffected by this problem. I can't even count the amount of times our elders have stepped up to support the youth and children of our church. The Bible tells us that one of the most important things in fellowship is unity: "Most of all, let love guide your life, for then the whole church will stay together in perfect harmony" (Colossians 3:14, TLB). We as generations cannot let this rift continue to grow.

I remember when I was in grade school, I would spend a lot of time in my dad's office. Generally, I was a nuisance, but he loved that I was there. He even got a PlayStation and some toys to keep in his office so that my brother and I would have stuff to do when we were there. One of my favorite memories of goofing around at the church was a game my friends and I would play out in the parking lot in a giant tree. Now, this tree was massive and its branches were just five or six feet off the ground, perfect for climbing. So my friends and I would gather around the base of this tree, and there was one limb in particular that ran parallel to the ground about four feet up. It had to be thirty feet long. One of us would climb up onto this branch, and the others had a really long stick we found lying around and would try to knock the person on the branch off! This game was obviously dumb and we could've gotten seriously hurt.

So why do we play similar games in the church? We run around trying to do good and help where we can, and there are people jabbing at us, trying to knock us down. But how often are we the people with the sticks? How often do we try to knock other church members off the branch? We all have our sticks; we all have our complaints; we all have our manipulations; we all do it. How much better do you think the church would be if we all put down our sticks and let each generation play?

I remember just about every weekend going out to eat with a bunch of adults from church. They would buy us lunch and offer to help us however they could. It was obvious they wanted me there even though I was just a kid, but where did I fit? I think that's one of the most important questions to ask if you start to see yourself drift from the church and its people. If you don't find where God wants you in the church, you'll never be able to experience fellowship. Every member of the church has a crucial part to play; you can't just be a casual bystander. I believe one of the reasons the rift between generations is growing is that too many of us are content with sitting on the sidelines watching everyone else do their part. I also believe that one of the best ways to bring unity is to work together, generation beside generation, to help each other, encourage each other, and spur one another on toward love and good deeds.

I remember becoming part of the youth group—doing the youth activities and joining a small group with a few other boys. This is where I finally started making my faith my own. This was also around the time I went on my first mission trip. I spent a week in Jacmel, Haiti, running a Vacation Bible School and building a kitchen and playground for the church there. It was during that trip that I was inspired by God to find my place in the church. Unfortunately, I'm not perfect and I have a habit of procrastinating, so I put that off for another few years.

Eventually, I went through a rite of passage in our church. Evidently, this is when God had had enough of my procrastination, because things really started to change in my life. I had a renewed excitement about my relationship with Christ. I went back to Haiti later that year, and I was finally able to call my faith completely my own. This was also around the time I was first asked to help lead worship for a weekend service. I had found my place in the church.

Looking back, I have noticed a common thread. I know that I never would've found my place, never would've claimed my faith, never would've become the man I am today if not for the support, encouragement, and prayers of the elders in our church.

Thank you. You shared your church service with me. You shared your service opportunities with me. You shared your prayers with me. You gave me expectations that made me a stronger believer. You gave me a place in our church. So, any chance we could do this church thing *together*?

Get to Know the Author:

Noah Addis was born in Fort Worth, Texas, and moved to Hutchinson, Kansas, when he was four years old. He still resides in Hutchinson, where he is now a freshman in college. He has grown up as a pastor's kid in the same church for fifteen years and understands the importance of serving in a local church. Noah enjoys helping lead worship at his church, and once he's finished with college, he hopes to be involved in full-time worship ministry.

For Personal Reflection or Group Discussion

- What do you find to be the hardest challenge with millennials in the church? Why does it bother you? How can we work through it together?
- What is one way you have seen millennials benefit the church?
- Where is your spot in the church? What are you doing to interact with other generations?
- Take an honest look at where you are in life right now. Teens in your family and your church are on a quest for identity, autonomy, and purpose—relevant issues at any age but dialed way up during adolescence. Young-adult singles and marrieds are facing issues in life seniors have already had to work through. Do you wish for meaning and purpose? Are you whining or winning? Seeking solace or finding solutions? Are you a captain on life's ship, steering a steady course through troubled waters? If you are, then you are needed by all those on board with you.
- Here is your assignment: think of an idea to change the world and get some friends who agree and will join with you in it. Then put it into action!
- What is God's way of building His church, and who should do it?
- Do you have what you need to be part of this?

RECONCILING WITH YOUR PAST AND PRESENT

PART 2

RECONCILING WITH YOUR PAST AND PRESENT

What to Expect

As I (Chuck Stecker) ate breakfast with a great friend, Sid Overton (author of chapter 6), I listened intently as he talked about the need to reconcile with our past and present before moving forward to the desired future God has for us.

Sid is an attorney who specializes in helping individuals make end-of-life decisions regarding their assets. He explained to me that most people he helps come in with regrets about mistakes they have made or about things they failed to do in the past. In every case, the past was a stumbling block to seeing great possibilities for the future.

In part 2, four authors are going to help you consider how you may move forward from where you are or have been to get to a new starting point.

You are also going to be challenged by two of the authors to consider how your failing to reconcile with your past and present might have negative effects on the future and destiny of those you love.

CHAPTER 6

YOUR NEXT BEST DAY

— Sid Overton —

As you begin to read this, try to imagine a green park in the middle of America. Then imagine that I am sitting on a bench in the park, reading a book. You approach me and sit down on the bench beside me. We exchange greetings. We are both senior citizens, and after some light talk, we begin to discuss life issues. Our conversation soon turns to spiritual matters, and we quickly discover that we are both followers of Jesus Christ.

You briefly share your personal story with me, which includes some of the victories and some of the defeats in your life. Likewise, I also share with you part of my life story. We then end our conversation with the farewell "Have a great day" and go our separate ways, with no plans to ever meet again.

About two weeks later, by sheer coincidence, we happen to be walking in the park and meet again at the park bench. We both realize that we have been ruminating about our previous conversation, and we decide to talk further. You tell me that you have retired from your employment, you and your spouse are "empty nesters," you spend time with your children and grandchildren as often as possible, you are in fairly good health for your age, but you feel that you are out of the mainstream of life and moving toward irrelevancy. You notice that our American culture has a tendency to segregate society by age groups and that perhaps youth and physical fitness trumps old age, experience, and wisdom.

Shifting from imagination to reality, there are some thoughts and ideas that I would like to share with you. Let me begin with my childhood.

I was born and grew up on a farm near a small town named Cando, North Dakota, just thirty-two miles from Canada. The population was approximately fifteen hundred people, and almost everyone knew everyone else. As youth of the community, we had the "can do" spirit. There was a prevailing community attitude that, as young people, we could accomplish any task we set our minds upon. There were fleeting moments when we believed that our future achievements, for good or for bad, were limitless. However, I didn't realize until much later in my life that for me, this attitude was coming from the Lord. All the credit regarding any good things that may be happening in my life, and perhaps in your life also, belongs to the Lord. I also realize that even the bad things in my life are allowed by God to test me, humble me, get my attention, and direct me toward repentance. As I have traveled through life so far, I have observed some universal principles and values relating to seniors, which I would like to share with you.

If we were to obtain a bird's-eye view of all the retired people in America, we would notice that "retirement" comes in all shapes, forms, and sizes and often has an economic component. Financial planners, investment brokers, trust officers, insurance agents, and other economic advisors fill the senior communities with programs to provide financial security as well as other forms of senior services. However, there is seldom a program directed at the mission and life purpose of seniors. Career retirement for seniors can come in many packages. Sometimes it is voluntary, and sometimes it is not. Sometimes it is planned, but sometimes it is unplanned. Often retirement candidates know, and will talk about, what they

YOUR NEXT BEST DAY

are retiring "from" but not what they are retiring "to." No matter how or when retirement from compensated employment arrives, the sad truth is that often it morphs into retirement from life. This subtle thinking process needs to be eliminated.

The Bible teaches us about the need to stay in the race (see Philippians 3:14). This verse is the antithesis of retirement from life. We live in a secular world where there is great emphasis placed upon the notion of winning and losing. With the exception of sports and politics and a few other arenas, life on this planet is not about winning and losing but about loving, serving, sharing, caring, forgiving, reconciling, and hoping.

The essential race of life is not a physical, economic, or social race; it is a spiritual one (see verses 12–14). Almighty God, who fully empowers us in this spiritual race, is not concerned about our destination but about our journey. He greatly desires for us to be in the right race and on the right road. If we are in the right race and on the right road, He will take care of the destination. He has already made full provision for our future, through the sacrificial death of His Son, but He commands us to "go and make disciples" (Matthew 28:19). There is no retirement from this command.

With all the temptations of our world, it is so easy to slip into the wrong race. Sometimes the race is so subtle that we can easily rationalize or justify our journey. We compare our journey with what we perceive to be another's journey, and in short order, we are right in the middle of the rat race of life. We must remember that when we are in the rat race of life, even if we win we are still a rat!

If we have experienced the rat race of life, we may be tempted to just quit and drop out of the race. This may well include isolation from the spiritual race as well. If we have substantial financial resources, we might be thinking, *I am old and I have gold, and I deserve to be enjoying the golden years of my life.* Or we may be on a limited income budget and therefore thinking, *I am not able to join in and get involved, because I can't afford to participate.* So with a little soul searching and quiet time with the Lord, we might come to the honest conclusion that entering and staying in the spiritual race is not conditioned upon financial ability or social standing. It is purely a matter of surrendering to a God-directed attitude, which leads to obedience. But surrendering is always in conflict with our selfish old nature.

We are taught that the second Greatest Commandment is to love our neighbor (see Matthew 22:39–40). What does it mean to love our neighbor? In the context as written, the word *love* is *agape* love, or God's selfless and unconditional love, which He freely gives to us. As written, it is not a noun but a verb, or action word. Jesus tells us that the greatest love requires action (see John 15:13), but so does all *agape* love. In this command from the Lord, "love" is more than just a wonderful and caring thought about another person or object. It is always coupled with some form of action. This action is referred to as service.

Who is our neighbor? A neighbor is anyone who comes into our daily lives. The questions we must ask and answer are "Am I available?" "Do I care?" "Do I know how I can serve?" When we answer these questions affirmatively, we are ready to enter the race.

It would be hypocritical and superficial to suggest that we, as followers of Christ, will ever sufficiently honor the Lord's command of obedience. Our old nature continually beckons us to a behavior of disobedience. Sometimes we even get puffed up and begin to think that we are less disobedient than we were in earlier days. The truth is that "our righteous acts are like filthy rags" (Isaiah 64:6). God has always known our imperfections, so we have been given the gift of forgiveness and reconciliation (see 1 John 1:9; 2 Corinthians 5:18–19), which we can appropriate each day of our lives. When we seek and receive His forgiveness and reconciliation, we are set free and ready to join the race.

It is true that many seniors are impaired with various health maladies. Adverse physical or mental conditions, or a combination of both, can limit the ability of a senior to participate in the race. There are many excuses for not participating. Excuses relating to factually based physical limitations that reduce the degree of participation must be honored, and empathy and compassion must be extended. However, capable seniors who do not enter into or who drop out of the race must be enlightened with the fact that everyone has been given one or more gifts with which to participate (see Romans 12:6–8; 1 Corinthians 12:4–11).

So, what is the race? In everyday basic language, it is the daily activity of the followers of Christ, of loving and serving God, and loving and serving our neighbor. There is hardly any limit to the number of daily opportunities we have to be in the race. Being in it may be the offering of physical or financial assistance to someone; a telephone call to a person suffering from pain or loneliness; a prayer with a family member, friend, or neighbor; a visit to a hospital or jail; service as a volunteer at a local church, museum, or library; voluntary service as a board member of a nonprofit organization; or caretaking for a family member, neighbor, or friend. The list of potential service is unending. However, in all activities, the Lord is the essential partner in one's service pursuit. Nothing of value can occur without Him.

When it comes to group participation in a younger group, a senior might be inclined to justify inaction by saying, "I don't feel needed," "Others can do the job better than I can," "I think they are looking for a younger person," "I think I would be marginalized," or "I don't want to be embarrassed." If those are your thoughts and feelings, you can ask the Lord to give you courage to step up and take your rightful place as a valued participant in the group. Do not forget that younger people "don't know what they don't know"! You have value and can contribute.

It is important to recognize that some senior groups, especially in the local churches, intentionally identify themselves with negative or self-deprecating names such as "The Snoozers," "The

Nappers," and "The Over the Hill Gang." Such a name sends a message that the senior group is insignificant, purposeless, and approaching irrelevancy. If we, as concerned seniors, desire to maximize our effectiveness as a group and believe that a group name is helpful, we need to select a positive group name.

Finally, my friend, as you get up and leave our park bench, I want to encourage you to recall the best day you have experienced in your life. It may have been your graduation day, or your engagement day, or your marriage day, or the day your child was born, or the day you believe you received a miracle. Whatever that day was for you, it is time to replicate that day as often as you can in the future. You won't ever achieve your next best day in the future on your own power, but with prayer and God's power and direction, all things are possible (see Philippians 4:13).

Are you ready, willing, and able to get in the race and seek the next best day in your life? If you are, begin today!

Get to Know the Author:

Sid Overton is a practicing real estate and estate planning attorney, and has served as a Board Member of more than 10 nonprofit organizations. He served as a founding board member and executive officer of Promise Keepers for eleven years. He and his wife, Karen, have a son, daughter-in-law, and two granddaughters who live in Houston, Texas. Sid and Karen live in Greenwood Village, Colorado.

CHAPTER 7

DO NOT LET YOUR PAST DETERMINE YOUR FUTURE

— Athena Dean Holtz —

We are products of our past, but we don't have to be prisoners of it.

—Rick Warren, *The Purpose-Driven Life*

If you're anything like me, you've made plenty of blunders and sinful choices, and if you're still breathing, you'll make plenty more. But what if you've struggled, stumbled, and sinned in ways that have destroyed lives, relationships, careers, or dreams—your own and those of others? How do you face the consequences after you've repented and taken steps to do what you can to make things right?

One thing I have learned over my thirty-plus years as a follower of Christ is that our past mistakes are meant to guide us, not define us. I have learned the hard way to ask, "Lord, what are You trying to teach me from this difficult situation?" And I've come to realize that He won't waste a thing. He can use the most horrific trauma and abuse, sins we've committed and situations in which we've been sinned against by others, and the fallout from our past

59

wounding to refine us and minister to others. True statement: we serve a Romans 8:28 God. And we know that God causes everything to work together for the good of those who love God and are called according to His purpose for them.

In my early twenties, with no Christian upbringing or foundational truths sown into my heart, I found myself drawn to important individuals and celebrities.

I am woman, hear me roar! I was offered a job working in the music industry as an assistant to Helen Reddy's husband and thrived on the thrill of being around famous people and jet-setters. It made me feel important in a strange way, which temporarily filled a need in my empty soul.

An actor friend and his wife invited me out to their estate in Santa Barbara and introduced me to Scientology as the "cool" spiritual experience. Looking back, I can see that it appealed to my pride, and it didn't take long before I had taken the bait, hook, line, and sinker. Little did I know that the Enemy would use this strategy on me again nearly twenty-five years later.

I ended up connecting with more "opinion leaders" at the Celebrity Centre in Hollywood and joined staff to be part of something larger than myself—the goal of "clearing the planet" and bringing goodwill on earth through the truths discovered by L. Ron Hubbard.

During this journey of finding myself and allegedly gaining control over my future, I married a Scientology "ethics officer." Those who were drawn to this position were attracted by the power they would have. Inside of a week after saying "I do," I made a snarky comment, only to receive a whopping shiner. Over the next four years, I became his personal punching bag. The final straw came when he broke my arm as I was nursing our six-month-old. I escaped with my life, my two kids, and a suitcase full of clothes.

Out of the frying pan and into the flame, twelve months later I married another Scientologist, whose main job was to sell

Scientology services. He was a Vietnam veteran with a healthy case of post-traumatic stress disorder, and I had no idea what I was getting myself into. About three years into that marriage, we found our way out of Scientology, receiving death threats as we left. Because we employed many Scientologists, our leaving was considered quite intimidating.

Fast-forward two years later to the brink of divorce. My veteran husband had rallied around the "Freeman" constitutional movement and was operating a fund-raising business outside state and county rules. He came under question by the charities division of the state of Washington and was indicted for fraud. This encounter threatened my position as senior vice president with a large insurance and securities company, so I'd had enough. We were done! After a few weeks in the pit of despair, he turned to Christ and I saw a new man. This drew me in and softened my heart, opening me up to a recognition of my need for forgiveness. After reading *Mere Christianity* at the age of thirty-three, I was drawn to Christ and prayed with one of my managers to receive Jesus. One of our first answers to prayer was the fraud charges being dropped and our names cleared.

What a transformation! My foul mouth laced with continuous f-bombs, cursing, and taking the Lord's name in vain was washed out with the cleansing soap of the Holy Spirit. I was a new person! It wasn't long before we were swept into full-time ministry working with Vietnam veterans and their family members. Our next five years were spent nonstop building an international network of small groups led by veterans who'd experienced the Father's love. Although it was an amazing experience with lots of fruitful ministry, it left us both vulnerable to deception, which ended up coming down the road when we least expected it.

Eight years into a highly successful publishing ministry, we ended up working on a book for a "pastor" who turned out to be a wolf. This one person was used by the Enemy to deceive, divide, destroy, and demolish my marriage, family, relationships with friends and colleagues, career in Christian publishing, and understanding of who God was. Twelve years later, I woke up and found I'd believed that a lie from the pit of hell was the truth. I'd been duped by someone who claimed to be a man of God but appealed, again, to my pride with a message of "spiritual insider information." He and his wife used Scripture out of context to control, manipulate, and talk me into divorcing my husband (in Jesus's name) and cutting off all communication with my four children when they challenged his doctrine. They then went on to steal my company, my house, my car, and my reputation in Christian publishing. A case of severe spiritual abuse and manipulation left me emotionally, mentally, relationally, financially, and spiritually bankrupt.

I easily could have walked away from God for good or stayed in a victim posture. As I began to receive counseling and healing from all the abuse, the Lord led me to ask, "How did I become vulnerable to this deception? How did I open the door to allow the Enemy to influence me? What was wrong with me that I could believe that a lie was the truth and be willing to give up everything for it?" He began to reveal to me many ways I'd become easy pickins for Satan and even red flags I ignored because of something I wasn't willing to let go of. He revealed the foolishness of going into full-time ministry without having built a strong spiritual foundation first. I had never become a Berean, learning how to discern the difference between Scripture being quoted in context or out of context!

There were so many things I needed to "own" in the devastation I encountered over those twelve years. I could not just blame others; I had to take responsibility for my part in the travesty that tore apart my marriage, my family, my business, and my life. Doing so allowed God to dramatically move on my behalf in healing and restoration.

What He has done in the last five and a half years to restore all that the locusts had eaten is truly a wonder to behold. He rebuilt every broken relationship, placed me back into publishing by establishing Redemption Press, and worked a breathtaking, modern-day Cinderella story as I became a pastor's wife to a man whose late wife of forty-nine years suggested me as her successor.

Had I stayed in that victim role, it would have been easy to allow my past to determine my future. Instead, learning valuable lessons about my own vulnerabilities and experiencing the faithfulness of God restoring my life enables me to comfort others who've made bad choices, trusted abusive and dishonest people, and been enticed into wrong decisions because someone flattered them and appealed to their pride.

I'm thankful that, along with the apostle Paul, I can proclaim, "All praise to God, the Father of our Lord Jesus Christ. God is our merciful Father and the source of all comfort. He comforts us in all our troubles so that we can comfort others. When they are troubled, we will be able to give them the same comfort God has given us" (2 Corinthians 1:3–4, NLT).

GET TO KNOW THE AUTHOR:

Athena Dean Holtz is the publisher and founder of Redemption Press and has enjoyed coaching authors through the book-publishing and marketing process for more than thirty years. She is president of the Northwest Christian Writers Association and is a member of the Christian Women in Media Association and the Advanced Writers and Speakers Association. Athena and her husband, Ross, live in the Seattle area and have a combined family of eight adult children and seventeen grandchildren.

CHAPTER 8

YOU DON'T EVEN KNOW WHO YOU ARE

— Angie Fouts-Hyatt —

Who am I? As I contemplated my new life, this question throbbed in my head, becoming louder as I packed boxes, gazed at photographs of my family, and tried my best to organize for the move to a new home. After several failed attempts to accomplish anything, I finally gave up and headed upstairs for a cup of coffee and some chocolate. For the record, chocolate is a definite must-have for anything life throws our way. I keep a steady supply in my closet for such times of contemplation. As I chomped through my third mini Snickers, it occurred to me that I had no good answer to "Who am I?" Worse yet, a new thought haunted my mind.

Had I ever really known who I was?

For the first eighteen years of my life, I went to school, got good grades, went to church, held a job, and set my sights on college. The "me" of those first eighteen years strived to please my parents, teachers, youth pastor, and friends. I tried with all my might to get my dad's attention and win his approval.

I yearned to go to college. The only people in my family who went to college was a distant cousin and my older sister. My dad wanted me to live at home and attend a university within thirty minutes of our house. When I refused, he reluctantly allowed me to attend a small university in the same town where my sister lived.

Then a handsome young man entered the picture. We met in a Bible study class, and he was charming, funny, and flirtatious. Our romance quickly grew, and as a small town girl who never had a boyfriend, I felt lucky to be pursued by him.

Our fun, lighthearted dates soon turned to talk of the future. With dreamy, starry eyes, I listened to him talk about his calling to be a pastor. The conversations then turned to what I would be like as a pastor's wife. I didn't like it one bit! A mousy, submissive, pretty little perfect woman who plays the piano, sings, and sits in the front row while her husband preaches was not at all who I wanted to be.

But I was in love and ended up becoming exactly what I did not want to be. I poured seventeen years into ministry. My identity became wrapped up in being the perfect wife, the perfect mother, and, of course, the perfect pastor's wife.

Then in one day, my life vanished as I discovered that the man I loved, admired, and respected wanted other women and a life completely contrary to a life of ministry. Suddenly I was a divorced single mom who had to start all over.

As I sat at my kitchen table, chomping on chocolate and drinking coffee, I felt a sense of hopelessness and despair. I could blame only myself for not being in control of my own identity. Sure, I could blame my ex-husband or the pastors who mentored us in ministry. I could blame my dad for not providing his approval. I could blame, blame, blame, and then what? Blame some more?

No. I think I will change the word *blame* to *analyze*. That sounds much more honorable and productive. The analyzing has been a constant work in progress for the past several years. I changed my focus from blaming to analyzing, which did prove to be more productive. Analyzing helped me face the reality of who I was.

Think of it this way. When we get up in the morning, we don't typically enjoy gazing at ourselves in the mirror. We have morning breath, messy hair, bags under our eyes, and hairy legs. It's much more pleasant to take that final glance in the mirror after we've spent an hour getting ready.

The morning version of me is what I felt like I was continually looking at during my analyzing process. It was ugly. I didn't like the reality of who I was. My ex-husband's addiction to porn and his affairs took their toll on my identity. When your husband intentionally chooses porn and other women over you, it's the ultimate rejection.

Rejection is a powerful and destructive emotion. It is difficult to recover from and warps one's rational thinking. When I was thinking rationally, I was appalled and angry at his indiscretions. But rejection warped my rational thinking, and for many years, I made excuses for why he deserved to view porn and seek out other women to fulfill his sexual needs. See? Warped.

Back to the identity crisis over chocolate and coffee. I grabbed a notebook and pen and began to jot down my new identity.

Single mom.

Ex-pastor's wife.

Broke.

Tired.

Sad.

Strong.

Smart.

Capable.

Determined.

Somehow the list went from negative to positive. As I wrote down words that described the new me, I became frustrated at the negative words. I thought, *I don't want to be that person!* That bit of frustration and anger fueled the motivation I needed to remake me.

That day began a new pattern of me, focusing on my identity.

Somehow I had to reconcile my past and begin the focus on my new life. Everything in me wanted to revert back to the pattern of being a people pleaser. I faltered but was determined to pick myself up and continue on to break the vicious cycle I had been in my whole life.

Today maybe you are in the middle of your own identity crisis. Whether you have experienced a trauma that sent you into the "Who am I?" cycle or spent your life pleasing people, you can learn to just be you. The path to that freedom takes work—a lot of daily, and sometimes hourly, work.

During the first few months of my crisis, I got up early every day. My morning ritual included coffee, my Bible, my journal, and a lot of crying and contemplating with God. I had to get grounded. I had to unravel and detangle the mess in my heart and in my head. There were years of tapes that played daily in my thoughts and drove my thinking and behavior. Spending that time each morning focused on who God wanted me to be was a lifeline and an anchor.

This type of lifeline and anchor is crucial for figuring out one's identity. Every day, people tell us what we need to be. Magazines tell us how skinny we should be. The media tells us we should be total sexpots in the bedroom and wear sexy underwear. Well-meaning people give their very best advice and squelch our attempts to be ourselves.

As I traveled my road to freedom, I was hit with triggers almost hourly that sent me right back to the questioning phase.

If only I had been a better wife, maybe he wouldn't have cheated.
Look at my stretch marks. Gross.
You aren't very smart, Angie. Look at the man you chose.
I don't deserve to be loved.
I need to lose more weight.
Why did God let this happen? I have served Him my whole life.
Despite the constant battle in my head, I forged on. Each

morning, I was intentional to recalibrate my thinking so it aligned with God's Word and what He said about me. By the time I had gotten up from my morning routine and hit the shower, the voices began to play in my head. I was determined to be who I was meant to be, so I persevered.

Perseverance takes dedication and hard work. If you're in a cycle where you have allowed everything and everybody to shape who you are, you have two choices: continue on in your pattern, or do the hard work and be you.

When we live in our God-given identities, we finally get to live out who we were meant to be. When we live out who we are meant to be, then we begin loving like He called us to love. The result of this healthy cycle is contentment, security, and a whole new pathway of dreaming that will lead us to be people who make a difference.

GET TO KNOW THE AUTHOR:

Angie Fouts-Hyatt is a wife and a mom to five beautiful kids. She is a licensed professional counselor and spends her days walking with people who desire to obtain healing and freedom from trauma. Her true passion is Flowers in the Desert, a treatment program that helps women who have experienced the devastation of their husband's infidelity find counseling, resources, and a road map for traveling a path to redemption (see www.revolutioncounseling.com). Angie wrote a book called *Nothing Compared*, which shares her story and strategies for healing from trauma and brokenness.

CHAPTER 9

I MUST FIX THE MESS WHEN YOU DO NOT RECONCILE

— Jessi Chrisp —

Let's be honest. We fall short in so many ways, especially in relationships. We find our value and identity in all the wrong things. We communicate poorly and hurt others. We have to start reconciling our past and our present to start the future that we want.

Reconciling the past must include forgiveness. There has to be an endless stream of honest communion with God about mistakes you've made and the ones others have made against you. Decisions have to be made about not letting the past define you and moving on to the present with intentionality. You have to process through it and dig deep into the good, the pain, and the things that don't make sense, even when doing so is horribly uncomfortable. Reconciling the present has to have equal parts acceptance of where you are, understanding of how you got there, and a refusal to let that be all there is. If seniors do not reconcile, there's a huge emotional and spiritual mess being passed on to younger generations, and my generation is going to have to clean it up.

I see this happening both personally and professionally. These are interconnected for me because I got into the field of counseling because of my own family's dysfunction. I wanted to understand how and why people do what they do. I felt that if I understood it better, I could have some sense of control over it. I wanted to help people because I wished desperately that someone would have helped me.

On the outside, my family looked so glossy and shiny. My parents paid off our house, my brother and sister and I went to the private school where my mom taught music, and my dad worked at a band instrument repair shop. We were all very musical, athletic, and well rounded academically. We had birthday parties and a big backyard to play in.

What you didn't see was the fear. My dad was constantly angry, and my mom cowered down to him. They eventually divorced. My mom scapegoated my dad, and my dad became pretty hands off. I had to sort through the muck of anxiety, an eating disorder, and lots of therapy in order to get a handle on myself. From the constant fear of being yelled at and having no control over the huge changes that were happening to me, I had to clean up the mess that my parents made in my life. I didn't ask for all that, but there it was, staring me in the face at just eleven years old. It wasn't fair. How would my life have been different if my dad's dad had been present in his life? What could have changed if my mom's mom would have been a little more nurturing instead of being so strict that my mom felt she couldn't have a voice? They didn't do the hard work of reconciling their past and present, so I was left with the mess without the tools or knowledge of how to do the deep cleaning.

As a mental-health professional, I see all sorts of generational messes. I've heard a mother tell her thirteen-year-old daughter, "You're the reason that I drink." If a child has that much control over your behavior, you've got some things to reconcile. This girl eventually ran away. I've seen a dad so anxious that his son will make the same mistakes he did, he drove his son away with his rigid rules and staunch control. His son is now doing exactly the things he was afraid he would do, just to explore his freedom. I've seen a mom who has had so many horrific things happen to her that she is nearly incapable of being in a healthy relationship. Her daughter was the product of a rape, and she can't even look at the girl. She blames her daughter outright for everything now going wrong in her life. This twelve-year-old is now in residential treatment for homicidal and suicidal ideation. I've seen a mom so afraid to be alone that she decides to be with any man who will "love" her. That's what she teaches her daughter—to accept the abuse, even sexually. Her daughter is left to accept a value far less than her true identity as daughter of the King. I realize that some of these may be extreme cases, but maybe not. If these parents would have deeply understood their value as children of Yahweh and their identity as the Imago Dei despite inevitable trials, they could have provided a completely different life for their children.

I know this is true, because I have seen it happen. I have seen reconciliation happen in relationships of my clients, and I have experienced it intimately. My first semester of seminary, I had one of the most important conversations of my life with my dad. Ironically, I was talking on the phone with him in the bandage-and-pharmaceutical aisle at a grocery store, and somehow all the wounds came pouring out of me. I told him all the ways he had hurt me (which was terrifying, because I knew I was opening myself up to be yelled at and blamed once again). I could hardly believe it. He took in everything I said and apologized for it. He acknowledged that he was once an angry young man and didn't know how to be a father and husband. He told me that he is not that same person, and I have since seen this to be true. Now we have a relationship that has much less resentment and hurt. My dad is not perfect, and he is admittedly still undecided about any sort of religion, let alone a relationship with Christ. But because of

Christ, I have been able to forgive him, and my heart has softened.

The point is that it's never too late! I pray every night over my daughter that anything that I have not reconciled from my past does not get in her way. I pray for the strength to move past my own issues to show her her true identity and value so that she can fully live it out in freedom. Now it's up to me to bravely clean up my own unreconciled messes so that she doesn't have to someday.

How might less of the mess and more of the joy get passed down? We are watching you, Seniors, and we are learning from you. We learn what is okay and what is not okay. We learn from you how to meet our needs. We learn how to treat people, how to communicate, and what our value is. The next generation needs to know that you are smart enough and strong enough to handle our questions and growing pains. Encourage us to be who the Creator has created us to be. We need you. It's not too late! It's never too late. Reconcile. Forgive. Apologize. Take responsibility. Soak in your true identity as the child of the King. You are forgiven. You are loved.

GET TO KNOW THE AUTHOR:

Jessi Chrisp is a clinical assessment specialist at a community mental health center in the Denver Metro area. She has worked in the counseling field for five years and has a seminary degree in clinical mental health counseling. She and her husband, Brandon, live in Parker, Colorado, with their daughter and black Lab.

FOR PERSONAL REFLECTION OR GROUP DISCUSSION

- Can you identify a few struggles or bad choices from your past that have left you hesitant to feel qualified to comfort others?
- Do you get bitter or better as you reflect on your past and the wounding you've experienced? If bitter, how can you fight that tendency?
- Maybe this sounds like a dreamy, foggy process. Grab a notebook and write down words that describe you. Some of your words might be negative, but don't be discouraged. Allow the negative descriptors to be fuel and motivation to bring you to a place where you begin writing down adjectives that describe who you want to be.
- Make and fill out a chart with two headers: "Who I Am" and "Who I Want to Be!" Contemplating who you are may be scary, but it's worth it! What do you really have to lose? Maybe a lot of baggage that has been weighing you down for years, and who wants more weight?
- What are some action steps you can take each day to reconcile your past and firmly live in the present?
- How might your life be different if you truly forgave and truly reconciled your past and present?
- How might your children's lives or your grandchildren's lives be different if you forgave and reconciled with your parents?

IF MY PHONE IS SO SMART, WHY DO I FEEL SO DUMB?

PART 3

IF MY PHONE IS SO SMART, WHY DO I FEEL SO DUMB?

What to Expect

Now would be a great time to just tell the truth. The problem is not our new phones. The real issue is that the culture is changing very rapidly and the older we are, the more difficult it is for us to change. Frankly, it is not only difficult to change; very often it is difficult to understand *why* we need to change.

Too often we live by the philosophy "If it ain't broke, there is no need to fix it." In our minds, so much of the world around us is not broken. We are doing just fine. The problem is others who want to change things just for the sake of change.

The harsh reality is that much of our world is changing and the smartphone is just an indicator. It is not the problem.

As you begin to read this part, remember this: as seniors, we did not live this long by being stupid. We are very capable of handling change and helping others manage it.

CHAPTER 10

SORTING OUT THIS GENERATIONAL MESS

— Pete Menconi —

The opening lines of the 1989 hit song "The Living Years" by Mike and the Mechanics goes like this: "Every generation blames the one before. And all of their frustrations come beating on your door." Generational tension and conflict is as old as mankind. But today the new longevity with people living longer has created a generational phenomenon unique to modern times. Generational relationships are more complex because there is the possibility of six generations being alive today in the same family.

The local church is one of the few places where these six generations can gather under the same roof, yet the different generations do not understand each other very well. Instead of offering an intergenerational experience, many churches are multi-generational with little substantive interaction between the different generations.

The current generations stretch from the GI Generation to Generation Z (yet to be officially named). These generations can span one hundred years, so imagine the differences in worldviews and lifestyles that exist between the generations. Most people are unaware of the ways that generational differences affect families, workplaces, schools, churches, and other places where the different generations relate.

Think about your family. How different are the youngest members from the oldest? Do any of your family members have tattoos or body piercings? How were these adornments received by older family members? How about music? Do younger and older members of your family share the same musical tastes? How radically do they differ? Does your extended family have members of other races? If so, how has this affected family dynamics? You get the point. The existence of multiple generations in our families has brought a greater range of life experiences and greater complexities.

Think about your workplace or church. How has it changed in the past ten to fifteen years? Does your workplace or church seem more chaotic today? Do you find yourself withdrawing at work because it takes too much effort to relate to younger or older people? Do you feel as if your church has been hijacked by younger people and you hardly recognize it anymore? These experiences are common among older adults because of generational differences.

In the Bible, we see that generations have always been important to God. For example, in Genesis 17:7, we read, "I will establish my covenant as an everlasting covenant between me and you and your descendants after you for the generations to come, to be your God and the God of your descendants after you."

If we are to stay in the game as we age, it is imperative that we understand the other generations. None of us, no matter what generation we are in, can overlook the fact that we are better together. But we will all need to work at it. Here is a matrix that will provide an overview that will help you understand other generations:

	GI Generation 1906–24	Silent Generation 1925–43	Boomer Generation 1944–62	Generation X 1963–81	Millennial Generation 1982–2000	Generation Z 2001–2018
Values	God, Family, and Country	Family, God, Security, Loyalty, Conformity	Competence, Consumerism, Excitement, Non-conformity, Relationships, Family	Self-Reliance, Freedom, Skepticism, Fun and Humor, Friends, Family	Image, Money, Fame, Success, Causes, Social Media, Friends, Family, Mentors	Pragmatism, Social Media, Friends, Entrepreneruial ship, Independence, Mentors
Work Ethic	Work hard, Do whatever it takes, Work is a duty	Work hard, Expect to be rewarded, Work is an obligation	Workaholic, The one with the most toys wins, Work is an adventure	Work to live, Not live to work, Work is a necessary evil	Work should be fun and fast, Work should have a social impact, Work should meet my needs	Work ethic not yet clear, but will probably be harder workers than Millennials
Play Ethic	Work before play	Work until retirement, then play	Work hard, play hard	Play hard, work only if necessary	Play even while working	Probably work and play all the time
Motivators	Sense of duty	Need for respect	Being valued and needed	Freedom for personal time	Flexibility, Social networking	Somewhat motivated by anxiety
Communication Style	Direct, Impersonal	Formal, Guarded	Informal, Face-to-face	Irreverent, Direct and short	Digitally, Constant, Not Face-to-face	Wireless, Constant
Leadership Style	Chain of command	Hierarchical Titles, Committee	Informal, networks of relationships	Everyone is on their own, Leave me alone	Non-hierarchical, Everyone is equal	Yet unknown
Technology	Radio, Black and white TV, Foreigners to technology	Transistor radio, Color TV, Immigrants to technology	Desktop computers, Walkman, Mostly immigrants to technology	Laptop computers, iPods, Mostly natives to technology	Smartphones, Tablets, Everything wireless, Natives to technology	All wireless technology plus constant change, Always-on restless natives to technology

© 2013 Peter Menconi

This brief overview of each of the generations will help raise your awareness of how and why we should pay attention to the differences and similarities. We are not all the same, and we need to learn to appreciate our differences. The church, the body of Christ, was always meant to be diverse and using the gifts of all.

But there are numerous reasons why the generations do not mix well in most local churches. Some of the major differences between the generations are triggered by values, music, dress, worship, work, and play styles. Often external appearances will keep older adults from relating to younger people, and vice versa. But many of the issues that keep the generations apart are about style and not substance; that is, many issues are superficial and need to be ignored.

If local churches are to be truly intergenerational, all generations will need to work at understanding each other better. The table on the next page will help you more fully understand the other generations in your church.

Intergenerational relationships do not have to be tense or in conflict. In fact, today more than ever, we need the different generations talking to each other. Life has changed significantly for both younger and older people, and many of us have lost our way. Healthy intergenerational relationships afford all generations the opportunity to learn from each other. If we relate exclusively to people in our generation, we miss the chance to give and receive wisdom that will better our journey through life.

Today, older adults have an excellent opportunity to develop healthy relationships with younger people. And contrary to popular opinion, most young people would like to have relationships with older adults they can trust. For example, many grandparents know that they have special relationships with their grandchildren even when the grandkids become adults.

Unfortunately, most young people will not initiate a relationship with an older adult, even when they need help or would like

	GI Generation	Silent Generation	Boomer Generation	Generation X	Millennial Generation	Generation Z
Worship Style	Formal/ Traditional	Traditional/ Predictable	Informal	Eclectic/ Artistic/ Informal	Eclectic/ Informal	Eclectic/ Informal
Worship Music	Traditional hymns	Traditional hymns/ choruses	Contemporary choruses	Newer emergent music	Variety of music styles	Variety of music styles
Preaching/ teaching	Practical	Professional	Relational	Interactive	Integrated	Personal
Community	Family-based	Collegial	Networks of Relationships	Tribes	Global/social media	Social media
Leadership Style	Chain of Command	Corporate/ committees	Teams	Individualistic	Three dimensional	Four dimensional
Theology/ Faith	Private	Propositional	Practical	Contextual	Global Post-modern	Postmodern/ Post-Christian
View of God	Distant father	Creator and truth-giver	Friend and ally	Compassionate healer	Global connector	Pragmatic helper
Worldview	God is in control of the world	The laws of the universe are at work	The physical, emotional, and spiritual worlds are all related	The world is chaotic and broken	The world can be "fixed"	The world is a dangerous place
Values	Family/ country/ security	Truth/ education/ security	Tolerance/ money/time	Genuineness/ acceptance/ fun	Options/ impact	Opportunity
Work Ethic	Do whatever it takes	Stable work/ loyalty/ longevity	Work hard/ play hard/ meaningful work	Work to play/ frequent job changes	Work should be fun and have impact/ Work should meet my needs	More pragmatic about work
Relationship	More formal and positional	Congenial with sense of propriety	Informal and competitive	Individualistic, private, tribal	Digital, social media driven	Wireless Relationships Social media
Needs	Acceptance, care and camaraderie	Inclusion/ stability and safety in the midst of chaos	Sense of purpose and opportunities to "change the world"	Sense of belonging/ opportunities to "heal"	Intergener-ational acceptance/ opportunities for impact	Mentors

Taken from
The Intergenerational Church: Understanding Congregations from WWII to www.com, by Peter Menconi

guidance. If an intergenerational relationship is to be established, it is usually the responsibility of the older adult to start it. Initiating an intergenerational relationship can be formal or informal; that is, it can be done through a structured mentoring program or as an outgrowth of a relationship that already exists.

Ideally, intergenerational relationships should be experienced in community and not in isolation. Although there is much talk about community among Christians, there is relatively little being experienced. The church was meant to be an intergenerational community. From the very beginning of Scripture, we see the various generations represented and acknowledged. But along the way, the church became more and more segregated according to age. Today, many local churches have age-based ministries that keep the different generations apart. Most churches are multi-generational but not intergenerational. A truly intergenerational church and experience intentionally involves all the generations in the life and activities of the community.

For a local church to truly experience intergenerational community, each generation must honor and love one another above themselves. Tolerance of one another will not get it done. All members of the church must learn to genuinely appreciate people in the body who are different from themselves. Simply put, as brothers and sisters in God's family, we are on this journey together. And we are better together. Here are some suggested steps that can be taken together:

- Challenge the stereotype of all the generations.
- Treat everyone in every generation with dignity; God does.
- Find common ground for meaningful conversations.
- Listen to each other with open minds.
- Appreciate and encourage the unique giftedness God has given each of us.
- Passionately seek the unity Jesus Christ has called us to.

- Allow people of all generations to contribute and lead.
- Expect all generations to learn from each other.

Even with the best of intentions, older adults might find an inter-generational relationship difficult to navigate. Generational differences are real and can often lead to misunderstandings. Even when a relationship is based on mutual respect and concern, the older adult may need to exercise an extra measure of grace. But despite the potential difficulties, intergenerational relationships are well worth the effort. In fact, if older adults do not step up to invest in younger people, our culture and society will be the poorer. We need more sages. Won't you be one?

GET TO KNOW THE AUTHOR:

Pete Menconi is a coach with Second Half Coaching, where he inte-grates his years as a dentist, pastor, counselor, and businessman into helping people fifty-five years and older navigate the remainder of their days. In addition, he is a consultant and speaker on intergen-erational issues, especially those affecting churches. He is the author of *The Intergenerational Church: Understanding Congregations from WWII to www.com* and the Aging Well Bible study series. He has been married to Jeanie for forty-eight years and they are parents of three adult children and grandparents of eleven grandchildren. Pete can be contacted at petermenconi@msn.com.

CHAPTER 11

NOW, MORE THAN EVER!

— Phil Schneider —

Though World War I ended in 1918, the squabbles of "The war to end all wars" continued as the European victors plundered Germany and the Central Powers. The US had spent millions of dollars on the war effort and gained nothing in return. Most of its loans were never repaid, and our citizens felt unappreciated and forgotten.

When Adolf Hitler was elected chancellor of Germany in 1933, Germany began re-arming itself in violation of the Treaty of Versailles. The war in the Pacific broke out in July 1937. By that fall, 75 percent of Americans believed that we should let the world fight it out among themselves and that we were totally safe, isolated from the war.[1] They believed that our nation had done its job in WWI and that it was now time for Europe to pay for and fight the war themselves. This isolationist policy was shared by our closest ally, Great Britain, and its policy of appeasement only served to embolden Germany and Hitler.

---

[1] William N. Denman, and Grant T. Weller. "U.S. Isolationism: How did U.S. Isolationism Contribute to the Cause of World War II?" *History in Dispute*, edited by Dennis Showalter, vol. 5: World War II, 1943–1945, St. James Press, 2000, pp. 288–294. *U.S. History in Context*, link.galegroup.com/apps/doc/CX2876500047/UHIC?u=imgacademy&xid=f07531c5. Accessed 3 Oct. 2017.

Three months before WWII broke out, a majority of Americans believed that staying out of it was the major issue our nation faced. Tragically, our policy of disengagement may have contributed to the deaths of more than sixty million people. The generation known as "The Greatest Generation" nearly missed its destiny when our nation passed the baton and refused to engage in warfare. Looking back, we can easily see the costs of passing the baton when war was ready to break out.

I can hear the comments of those who felt unappreciated and forgotten. "They only want our money. They don't remember all the work we did. They are so selfish. Well, let them do it on their own this time around!" May those words never be heard in the church.

The Lord says in Zephaniah 1:12 that He will search through His people and "punish those who are complacent." In James 2:14–26, He teaches that we are worthless, of no profit, if we give only lip service to the problems we see around us. We have a faith that is dead! We must not carry the curse of complacency. We must take up the baton.

A new war is brewing. The need for you to re-engage is greater than ever. We're experiencing a war of violence in our inner cities. Last year, Chicago averaged a shooting every two hours. All in all, two people are murdered every single day in Chicago. It would be easy to disengage and say, "That's their war," but know this: we are the ones who will pay the price.

It's a war of the sexualization of our children, poverty in rural America, and the acceptance of a drug culture. It's a spiritual war, and we must engage *now, more than ever.* God is laying out a "last days" plan in the hearts and minds of leaders around the world. For the first time in forty years of working in the church, I am hearing a cry to reach America through the building of rural churches.

Here's what our church is doing to prepare for war. We've appointed a "retired" pastor to mentor rural church boards and pastors. We've appointed a "retired" pastor to be a spiritual father to young pastors. And we've appointed a Chicago pastor to create a plan to lead our charge back into the city of Chicago! The Spirit of God is moving, being poured out upon a people willing to jump on board with all God is doing.

We can't afford for this generation of seniors to isolate and disengage. If you disengage, we lose our workers, warriors, wealth, and wisdom! Don't think of yourself as worn out, washed up, or worthless. Don't allow yourself to think you are retired, ready to rest, deserving of your time. Don't let others wage the war while you sit on the sidelines. Don't let them take the baton from you. Don't throw away the opportunity to serve God in a new capacity. We need you *now, more than ever!*

This generation of seniors knows how to work! You grew up without modern conveniences. You learned how to work with others. Like many of you, I grew up with a daily list of responsibilities. We learned how to jump in and get the job done. The church world desperately needs workers. You probably have time to do more around the church now than you've ever had in your life. We need spiritual mothers and fathers! That's the work God gives us in Scripture! This generation has grown up without intentional discipleship. We need you *now, more than ever!*

You are a generation of spiritual warriors. You are the last generation steeped in God's Word. We've gone from a Bible-based curriculum to a Bible-influenced curriculum. We need people who learned to wait at the altars, who practiced "praying through" until the answer came. The church can't afford its warriors to retire.

Do you realize that you are the generation of increasing wealth? A new study by Boston University says that our generation will transfer 59 billion dollars to the next generation.[2] And your wealth isn't limited to your finances. You are wealthy in time, influence, and God's favor. Don't waste your riches by sitting

---

2   Wealth Press Release 5-28-2014. Chesnut Hill, Mass. Boston College Center on Wealth and Philanthropy. Paul Schenish, Director.

down and watching to see if the next generation destroys what you've built.

Last, we need your wisdom. Your life experiences are a road map for those who follow you. You have a mandate from God in both the Old and New Testaments to pour your wisdom into the next generation.

Here's a truth that will surprise you: no one wants you to let go of the baton! The generations following you want you in the game. They respect you. Though they are different from our generation, there are things we can learn from them. If you let go of the baton, you'll never learn from them or teach them anything. They and the church need you. The kingdom of God needs you *now, more than ever!*

I'll finish with the story of *Little House on the Prairie*, the TV show based on the books by Laura Ingalls Wilder. On the show, Laura begins writing books about her family's experiences while a young woman in her late teens or early twenties. The truth is that Laura didn't start writing the "Little House" books until she was sixty-five years old! It's not too late for you to pick up the baton!

Get to Know the Author:

Phil Schneider served as pastor of a multisite campus church. In 2012, he and his wife, Renee, were elected regional overseers of more than 280 churches and 950 ministers. Phil has always been involved in the life of the next generation. Over the past thirty years, he served at youth camps for eighty-three weeks. He is on the board of two universities and Teen Challenge Illinois and serves as chairman of the board for New Life Media. Phil can be reached by e-mail at Phils@idcag.org or by calling 217-854-4600.

CHAPTER 12

LEARNING TO LIVE YOUR BEST STORY

— Cheryl Eichman —

"Dorothy, when I grow up, I want to be like you," I said half joking. "Oh no! No." Her eyes conveyed how serious she was about her next words. "No, Cheryl, you should want to be like Jesus." Dorothy is right. I should want to be like Jesus. I *do* want to be like Jesus, but I still kind of want to be like Dorothy too.

Here is why I want to be like Dorothy. Dorothy turned ninety this year and says she won't quit until one hundred. She gets her nails done every week, she faithfully cheers for the Denver Broncos every fall, and she can make anyone smile. Dorothy and her husband participated annually in our church's Trunk or Treat outreach and never failed to wear a great costume. Even at ninety, Dorothy is on Facebook regularly and posts things to make readers laugh, think, be encouraged, and be inspired. She is on oxygen, has a walker, and still sings worship songs with all her heart. Most important, Dorothy is an example of Christ to all around her, be it her family, those working and living at her assisted-living residence, people at church (young and old), or friends living miles away.

What Dorothy may not realize is that although I do love the spunky, fun-loving, never-give-up attitude she has, what makes me want to be like her when I grow up is her story. Her story is so clearly about becoming more and more like Jesus. Every day she strives to honor Jesus and love those He has put in her path, and in so doing, she changes the world one day at a time for however many days she has left.

There are a few books that are so good that I reread them every few years just so they stay fresh in my mind. One of those books is called *The Noticer*, by Andy Andrews. Its main character is a man named Jones. Jones has the gift of perspective. Partway through the story, Jones ends up sharing that gift with Willow Callaway, a widow, mother of four, and grandmother to many more.

Willow runs into Jones sitting on her favorite bench overlooking a canal, and the two of them end up chatting. Willow had truly loved her life. However, she's come to the conclusion that she's given all she could and there is nothing left. Willow confides to Jones, "I have outlived my usefulness. How in the world did I get so old?"[1] At this point, Jones begins to use his gift. Without trying to be rude, Jones gently disagrees with Willow.

After some joking around about their old ages, Jones asks,

"Should we let a number dictate how we feel? Besides, young lady—and I *do* consider you a young lady—who gave you permission to decide that you had nothing more to do, nothing more to offer?"

"Well," Willow said, "that is just an honest look at things. After Bobby [Willow's 47-year-old son] passed away, and with the children living lives of their own . . . " Willow trailed off, but then, as if trying to convince herself, said with an air of finality, "There is only so much bridge one can play, and after all, isn't it the duty of the old to make way for the young? I simply feel that my time has passed."[2]

At this point, Jones's gift of perspective comes out in all its

[1] Andy Andrews, *The Noticer: Sometimes, All a Person Needs Is a Little Perspective* (Nashville: Thomas Nelson, 2009), 79.
[2] Andrews, *Noticer*, 81.

beautiful colors as he shares with Willow the accomplishments of such people as Harland Sanders, known to most as Colonel Sanders, who didn't start his restaurant until age sixty-five; Benjamin Franklin, who invented bifocals at age seventy-eight; Winston Churchill, who wrote a Nobel Prize-winning book after many careers; Nelson Mandela, who became president of South Africa at seventy-five; pianist and conductor Igor Stravinsky, who was still doing concerts at eighty-seven; Grandma Moses, who sold her first painting at age ninety; and Michelangelo, who didn't even begin his work on Saint Peter's Basilica until he was seventy-four.

Jones's gift powerfully moves Willow to believe there may be more for her. At that moment, he challenges her one more time with the idea that all impacts are big impacts. Jones conveys that Norman Borlaug's Nobel Prize-winning impact of saving two billion lives never could have been done without a man named Henry Wallace, who could not have done it without a man known as George Washington Carver, who could not have done it without two people named Moses and Susan Carver. After Willow receives the gift of a changed perspective, she realizes there is still a story for her to live.

This might sound funny, but no matter how many times I have read this chapter, I want to scream out, "Hallelujah!" You see, I have a fear. I have a fear that in ten to fifteen years—as I get into my midforties, early fifties—there will be no one older to inspire me, mentor me, or challenge me. I have a fear that people older than me will feel as though there is nothing left for them, and therefore there will be no one who will show me how to keep living out every single breath to its fullest. I have a fear that I will not get to understand the fullness of verses that have wooed me since I was thirteen. I fear I won't see verses like Philippians 3:14, "I press on toward the goal for the prize of the upward call of God in Christ Jesus" (ESV), or 2 Timothy 4:7, "I have fought the good fight, I have finished the race, I have kept the faith" (ESV), lived out.

I have a fear that the older generation of God-loving, wise people will want to stop living their beautiful, powerful, God-written stories and feel the same as Willow, convinced they have outlived their usefulness. To me, this would be one of the greatest tragedies and worst nightmares I could ever imagine. I cry out for the older generation to show me what it's like to finish well. I yearn for them to engage the teens I work with and share their wisdom. I crave for them to give my kids hugs and show them God's love despite an eighty-year age gap. I beg and beseech the older generation to understand that their story is not done and to live in the hope that their impact will change the world, even if they may not live to see it.

In another great book, *A Million Miles in a Thousand Years*, author Donald Miller said, "If you watched a movie about a guy who wanted a Volvo and worked for years to get it, you wouldn't cry at the end when he drove off the lot, testing the windshield wipers. . . . Nobody cries at the end of a movie about a guy who wants a Volvo. But we spend years actually living those stories, and expect our lives to feel meaningful."[3] And it is true. Just the thought of this movie makes me want to demand my money back. Who would pay for such a story? It is also true that we live this way.

While I was in seminary, I heard about a youth-staff volunteer who was in her seventies. She couldn't play the games, she didn't know much of the teen slang, she may not have been the coolest, but she did make cookies every Thursday night for youth group. She was faithful to giving her time and baking talents to a group of youths. This youth volunteer was most beloved and had teens pour their hearts out to her. I think I would cry at the end of her life's movie. I imagine that when she passes away, there will be many crying. Her impact was little, but it was huge.

The story doesn't have to be as grandiose as Nelson Mandela's

---

[3] Donald Miller, *A Million Miles in a Thousand Years: How I Learned to Live a Better Story* (Nashville: Thomas Nelson, 2009), xiii.

or Winston Churchill's. Maybe it is baking cookies for youth group, maybe it is helping a neighbor kid with an Eagle Scout project, maybe it is learning to use FaceTime so you can say, "Well done. I am proud of you," to your grandkids at their first swim meet. Stories do not end at changing technology or a senior discount or retirement or even an oxygen tank and a walker.

I want to be like Dorothy. I want to yearn to be one hundred because I know that every day is a chance to let God keep writing his story. I want to be like Dorothy, who eats lunch with her generation, jokes around with and encourages my generation, and is on Facebook with the younger generation, all because she wants to love people with God's love. I want to be like Dorothy because she knows that while she still has breath in her lungs, God is not done with her yet. I want to be like Dorothy because she helps me understand a bit more tangibly what it means to be like Jesus, and in the end, Jesus really is who I want to be like.

GET TO KNOW THE AUTHOR:

Cheryl Eichman is a passionate follower of God who desires for people to understand and live out of the truth that Jesus loves them. She is an adoring wife, devoted mom, caring daughter, and faithful friend. When she is not writing, Cheryl can be found exploring the mountains with her family, grabbing coffee with friends, capturing beauty with her camera, or cheering enthusiastically for the Denver Broncos!

CHAPTER 13

IT IS NOT YOUR CHURCH—IT'S HIS KINGDOM

— Terry Hoggard —

Perspective is a powerfully important thing. Pay attention to perspective because it is a big deal. What we see drives what we believe, and what we believe will decide what we will or will not do.

So, I have a question for you. Are you ready? From your perspective, what matters most: the work of the church or the work of His kingdom? Think about it!

As one who has served with churches in America, Asia Pacific, Eurasia, Europe, and Northern Asia and been a missionary pastor in Italy, Belgium, Denmark, and Sweden, the answer to this question is resoundingly clear for me: what's most important is the work of His kingdom.

Now, I am a church loyalist in every way, and likely you are as well. However, it was not love at first sight for me—not at all. Like many in my generation, I saw a lot of glaring errors with the church. It seemed that in order to be an insider, one had to buy into the house rules and follow them, one by one, all the time. Discussion regarding differences was difficult, and freely expressing another point of view was painful.

Those were transitional years for me with the church, and things were clumsy at best. However, I came to love and joyfully support the church. I celebrate when the church succeeds, and as you can imagine, I stand up for the church when things go wrong.

As much as I love the church, I do recognize that its routines can often become adversarial to kingdom realities. For the most part, this is not intentional, but nonetheless our priorities often run counter to God's plans.

- We prioritize style when His plan is substance.
- We prioritize uniformity when His plan is unity.
- We prioritize staying the course when His plan is seeking His heart.

In reality, the church thrives when God's kingdom is the focus and is in great peril whenever that changes or shifts for any reason. These things I do believe, but more than that, these things I have proven.

My wife, Ruthanne, and I were honored to be at the center of an international church planting surge that was sovereignly birthed in the nations of Europe. Our experiences were thrilling, but they tested the depth of us on every level. Our churches were spontaneously launched, more dependent on Spirit inspiration than strategic intent, and the only clear master plan was indeed the Master's plan. Every church was a miracle in the making, and each one convincingly proved that when the focus was God's kingdom, the church thrived.

Let me tell about our first church plant. Our family arrived in Rome on June 17, 1986, with a dream to plant churches. I had crafted an intentional plan and came believing that God would find a way to help me know when and how to initiate the plan. Well, He certainly did, but not in the way we had planned. We came thinking with a church organizational view, but God filled our hearts with a kingdom vision.

Even thirty years ago, a great number of people from many nations were moving, for a multitude of reasons, to Rome. This migration of people was the result of tragic challenges, such as natural disasters, war, and poverty, as well as very unique opportunities to live, work, or study abroad.

This phenomenon, entirely unknown to us when we arrived in Rome, quickly became our driving passion. People from every tribe and tongue who we never expected to meet in a lifetime were in our city. Most saw them as only foreigners, but God inspired our hearts to see them as friends and understand that He saw them as family—His sons and daughters. Clearly, this was not a moment being driven by any church; it was a kingdom directive.

My friend Charles Sibthorpe said this: "God often does His supernatural work in such a natural way that only the discerning will perceive it." Very often we fail to discern His realities, so sadly we define things based on popular opinion. It is important that we develop the capacity to see and know what is not obvious or commonly known.

I believe that the movement of the world's people has rich, divine kingdom purposes that will bring blessing, yet others dismiss this movement as being of no divine value at all.

Here are three kingdom realities that we need to bear in mind:

- **The Redemptive Promise.** We know that it is not God's will that any would perish (see 2 Peter 3:9) and that He will go to extraordinary ends to fulfill this promise. In Rome, we had the opportunity to share God's redemptive purposes with people who in their normal life circumstances would never have that privilege. We saw people come to faith in Rome who originally came from nations with little or no gospel presence.
- **The Revitalization Potential.** We are warned in Galatians 6:9 that we must "not become weary in doing good, for

at the proper time we will reap a harvest if we do not give up." However, we do grow weary, so God seeks to revitalize us. In Rome, I was honored to meet ardent Christ followers who came from other nations and were mightily used by the Lord to bring spiritual renewal to Rome and beyond. In the eyes of many, they came unexpectedly, but to those who were discerning, there was a keen awareness that they were truly sent by the Lord.

- **The Restoration Possibility.** Many who came to us in Rome had suffered great loss on their life journeys. Their stories were heartbreaking, and seeing their agony was hard for all of us to process. Proverbs 13:12 says it best: "Hope deferred makes the heart sick, but a longing fulfilled is a tree of life." I believe that God sent people to Rome to have their hope restored. Seeing this glorious work being done in the hearts of so many is something that will change a person and stay in one's heart forever.

Let me share a very personal example of these things being actuated in the lives of just one of the many wonderful families who came our way. This family has a powerful redemptive story. They are change makers who greatly influenced those in their world, and they witnessed hope being restored, both in them and through them.

A seasoned US Army officer came to Rome in the nineties with his wife and two young sons to serve his country. This family blessed our church and our members in a wonderful way. They also brought the presence of His kingdom into our city and into their world, literally—every single part of it. It was such a joy to see this whole family thrive in their faith development while living far from home and outside their normal context.

Billie, Chad, Courtney, and Chuck Stecker were all this and more. The Stecker family is a big part of our Rome story and lived out all I am hoping to clearly communicate to you.

When God's kingdom is the focus of the church, we will enjoy His presence like never before and experience His power in ever-increasing measure.

Why am I so sure of this? Because it is for these things that He taught us to pray in the Lord's Prayer. Read these words again and make them a prayer from your heart:

> Our Father which art in heaven, Hallowed be thy name.
> Thy kingdom come, Thy will be done in earth, as it is in heaven.
> Give us this day our daily bread.
> And forgive us our debts, as we forgive our debtors.
> And lead us not into temptation, but deliver us from evil:
> For thine is the kingdom, and the power, and the glory, for ever. Amen. (Matthew 6:9–13, KJV)

Now more than ever before, we need you! We need you to accept the challenge of a lifetime of service, to advance His kingdom, to assure that His will is done in and through your church, and to acknowledge that it can not happen without you. It is to this end that I am praying! It is not just your church—it is His kingdom!

GET TO KNOW THE AUTHOR:

Terry Hoggard currently serves as vice president of international program for Convoy of Hope, leading the international team and developing partnership activities globally. He also engages with the leadership teams of Global International Church Network (www.gicn.org), which he launched in 2012, and with Fellowship of European International Churches (www.feic.org), a network he founded in 2004. Since 1986, he has provided pastoral leadership for European international churches and has served in Rome, Italy; Brussels, Belgium; Copenhagen, Denmark; and Malmö, Sweden.

FOR PERSONAL REFLECTION OR GROUP DISCUSSION

- What are your attitudes toward people in the other generations? How might you adjust those attitudes to reflect a more Christlike spirit?
- What relationships do you currently have with people of other generations that can develop into mentoring relationships?
- What posture do you have about where you are in your story? Do you feel like Willow Callaway, like the youth volunteer who made cookies, or like something altogether different?
- What things can you do, what technology can you learn, and what people can you invest in as you continue to live your story?
- When you first came to Christ, was there an elder who engaged you, befriended you, and encouraged you along the way? Who are you serving in that same capacity?
- Take an inventory. Can God show you a need, a gap in the wall (see Ezekiel 22:30), where He needs a warrior to pray? How can you support that situation with your giving? Could you ask God to give you wisdom about the situation that no one else has shown? How can you work to see that situation resolved?
- What are the greatest causes of the church and the kingdom conflict?
- What dynamic things have you seen in the church that inspire and encourage you to believe that kingdom focus matters?

I JUST CAN'T DRIVE AT NIGHT

PART 4

I JUST CAN'T
DRIVE AT NIGHT

What to Expect

After I had taught a seminar on intergenerational ministry at Louisiana Baptist University and Theological Seminary in 2014, one of the students approached and told me she wished her former pastor could have heard this teaching.

Some phrases grab my attention. One of those is "former pastor." In this specific instance, the student referred to a pastor of a church where her parents and two brothers had attended for quite some time before leaving to find another church. As she unfolded her story, I learned that four entire families had changed churches. They had all left a church, but not just any church. It was the church her parents had grown up in and where they'd met. It was the church her parents were married in and raised three children. It was the church the three children were married in and raised their families. Wow!

The student explained to me that her father had worked very hard all his life and arrived at a season where he could "retire" from his lifelong work to do what he always wanted, which was devote the rest of his life serving his church.

He told his pastor the time had arrived and he could work full time for the church without needing any salary or pay. He told the pastor he could do anything the pastor needed, but he just could not drive at night. The church apparently could not find anything for him to do. In a few weeks, he again approached the pastor with the same offer. And again, nothing for him to do.

All four families found a new church.

I asked the student what her father was doing. She smiled and said, "Everything!" His main job was as a small-group leader for the middle school boys. She told me that her dad and mom look younger and happier than they have in years.

He still can't drive at night, but God is using him mightily.

What you can expect in this part is a clear challenge for you to think about what you can do in this season of your life, not what you cannot do.

CHAPTER 14

YOUR INCREDIBLE THIRD CALLING

— Richard and Leona Bergstrom —

Moses, leader of the Hebrews, exemplifies our dreams and goals for the ministry of Re-Ignite. You might say he is our poster child.

Who else has ever stood barefoot beside a bush engulfed in flames and heard the voice of God? At age eighty, he was probably considering retirement; maybe he'd sit under a palm tree and eat figs or putt a few balls into the desert dust. But God had other plans. He spoke in fire and re-ignited Moses's purpose and passion in life. He gave him directions for what we've termed his "third calling."

In our signature book, *Third Calling: What Are You Doing the Rest of Your life?*, we identify three seasons of life. We named them callings. The first calling is a time for preparation. It includes growing up, pursuing education and training, and building a foundation for life. It is a season full of possibilities and abundant questions. The second calling is a time for accomplishment. It might include establishing a career, marrying, starting a family, and acquiring things. It is a season filled with opportunity, but there are also times plagued by failed relationships, financial stress, and occupational disappointment. Around the sixth decade of life, we tend to experience an event that propels us into what we call the third calling. It might be the death of a parent or spouse, the arrival of an AARP card, retirement, the kids leaving home, or a health related wake-up call. Something arouses a deep need to understand our purpose in life. There may be another season that follows: the fourth calling, the final season, one after the work of life is complete. Eternity beckons. It is a sacred and powerful time.

How do we live each season, or calling, to fulfill God's purpose, especially in those later years of life? It benefits us to consider the seasons and transitions Moses experienced.

We first encountered Moses, the infant son of a Hebrew family, living in ancient Egypt. When Pharaoh ordered the murder of every Hebrew child under the age of two, Moses's mother placed him in a protective basket and hid him near the riverbank. He was discovered, rescued, and later adopted by Pharaoh's daughter. Raised in the royal courts and hailed as the prince of Egypt, Moses had a first calling replete with the finest education, training in warfare and management, and extravagant living. He was a man of power and authority.

Increasingly curious about life and heritage, Moses began exploring the plight of his kinsmen, the Hebrew slaves. Some scholars believe that he knew in his heart that someday he would be the one to redeem his people. Alas, he took matters into his own hands when observing an Egyptian mistreating a Hebrew. Moses killed him, realized the impact of his action, and fled from Pharaoh's court and kingdom. It is in exile, in the desert of Midian, that Moses entered his second calling.

Moses married, raised a family, and spent forty years shepherding livestock on his father-in-law's property. It's hard to say what Moses thought about during those years, but it is probably safe to guess he had moments of regret, disappointment, and grief and overwhelming questions about the purpose and meaning of life. His daily reality was what we commonly refer to as a backside-of-the-desert experience.

And then something happened that catapulted him into yet another season of life, another calling.

It had been an ordinary day of work when, without warning, a strange breeze whipped around Moses's shoulders. He sensed something unusual yet powerfully familiar. A commanding presence pierced through his solitude and prompted him to spin around. With eyes wide open, he scanned the desert horizon, witnessing a most unusual sight. Although no one was within earshot, he announced his intentions out loud. "I must go over and look" (Exodus 3:3, HCSB). What he found transformed his life.

Imagine him staring into a bush that is clearly on fire but not consumed. At that sacred spot in the wilderness, Moses heard the voice of God giving directions for the next chapter of his life. He heard God calling, and after considerable reluctance and rebuttal, Moses followed His instructions. Moses followed his third calling. His assignment was huge and fraught with political, physical, and emotional danger. It was also filled with opportunity and potential as he took on the burden of leading the children of Israel to the Promised Land. His third calling would involve forty years of adventure, risk, trust, and purpose.

Many of our lives run parallel to Moses's first and second callings. We've had opportunities to grow and establish ourselves. We've known careers, families, and marriages and have accumulated our share of goods. Most of us have had a major failure or two along the way. Often, like Moses, we are resigned to living out our later lives conforming to society's expectations. A new purpose, a third calling, seems out of the question. Not so! Re-Ignite, as a ministry devoted to helping baby boomers and older adults discover purpose and passion in life, boldly proclaims that you have an incredible third calling awaiting you! Like Moses, you need to "go and look" (see Numbers 27:12) and stand in awe of the God who speaks in both fire and whisper. He has an assignment for you!

Certainly, a third calling doesn't maintain its luster forever.

Eventually, something comes to pass: a diagnosis, a debility, or simply the harsh realities of aging. We begin to anticipate what is ahead as we face our final days—our fourth calling. What does Moses teach us about this incredible period of time? How did he navigate being a senior facing the final ascent? What footprints did he leave for us to follow?

We know Moses obeyed God's directions in living out his third calling. He led with clarity, forbearance, and faithfulness as the children of Israel made their way through the wilderness. He knew God personally by talking with Him both on the mountain and in the tent. He understood the importance of the Law. Moses's journey through life and into his fourth calling gives us several directives:

1. Always be willing to do the next thing God asks, even it it's crossing a desert, climbing a mountain, or loving a group of stubborn people.

2. Remember that God has eternity in mind. When he bids us to come up the mountain to die, we can have faith that He will be there to greet us. Moses, at age 120, climbed Mount Nebo with the strength of a young man. He was ready to meet his God.

3. Leave a message to the next generations. Moses actually sang his, and the lyrics were anything but catchy. In fact, they were harsh words of warning and rebuke, but they were vital. He was sure of the importance of the message: "They are not just idle words for you—they are your life" (Deuteronomy 32:47).

4. Recount God's faithfulness; share your journey of faith. "Remember the days of old; consider the generations long past" (verse 7).

5. When the time is right, be ready to pass the baton of leadership and heritage to the next generation. Moses laid

hands on his assistant, Joshua, and anointed him as the next leader. He blessed him with these words: "The LORD himself goes before you and will be with you; he will never leave you nor forsake you. Do not be afraid; do not be discouraged" (31:8).

Moses was invited to the mountain to enter eternity with God. Before he died, God showed him the vastness of the Promised Land. His faithfulness was rewarded even though he was not allowed to enter. The Scripture says he died on Mount Nebo and God buried him; no one knew the location. The Israelites mourned his death.

Whatever season you are in, whether you are actively pursuing your third calling and serving in purposeful and meaningful ways or slowing down in your fourth calling, God has a purpose for your life. He is calling you to know Him, to love Him, and to bless the next generations with your story and faith.

That's incredible!

GET TO KNOW THE AUTHORS:

Dr. Richard Bergstrom is the founder and president of the non-profit organization ChurchHealth (doing business as Re-Ignite) and has served more than forty years in pastoral and church-related ministries. Leona Bergstrom has worked in the field of gerontology for thirty-five years, planning, implementing, and managing a variety of social and health-care programs for older adults and their families. For the past twenty years, they have focused on helping mature adults realize their callings. They have lived in the Pacific Northwest for more than forty years and have two children and six grandchildren.

CHAPTER 15

YES—YOUNG ENOUGH TO SERVE

— Wes Wick —

An obvious benefit of being older is the ability to pull from a broader array of personal life experiences. Rather than relying solely on my current experience as director of YES! Young Enough to Serve, allow me in this chapter to circle back a couple of decades and pull out something I learned while serving as a certified rehabilitation consultant.

PEPPERING THE SULK SHAKER

Let's focus on the "I just can't drive at night" sentence at this section's beginning. I know that the statement implies the capacity to do pretty much everything except night driving, but it places immediate focus on inability rather than capabilities.

Personal identity and a healthy self-image are, of course, critical in our moving forward in life. Even how we introduce ourselves to others matters.

In vocational rehabilitation, I learned that I was not working with disabled workers; my clients were workers with disabilities. Workers first. The physical challenges, although real, came second.

This may sound like an inconsequential stab at politically

correct speech, but when we immediately emphasize what's off limits, we sell ourselves short, even within our churches, where we're likely offering our time and talent for free.

So, let's reshape this intro by starting with what we can do. "I'm available daytime hours. I'm a good driver and am open to serving any way I can. I have specialized skills in _____. I have a passion for _____."

Yes, we are in the second or last half of our lives. But we don't do ourselves a favor by hanging our heads and complaining about being second, last, or left out.

Let's shut down the pity party and celebrate. We're still here, and God has wonderful plans for the remainder of our lives. Sure, others will misunderstand and overlook our potential, but that's part of the adventure. We'd fall asleep if it weren't for a few bumps in the road.

Think back to your teenage years. Did others misunderstand you and perhaps fail to see your potential? Let's talk to ourselves as we would talk to that overlooked teen. Do we reinforce the teen's victim identity, or do we look for ways to build up and encourage? Do we commiserate by focusing on people around us who *just don't get it*, or do we zero in on the unrealized, God-breathed potential lurking within, anxious to break through?

I can guess which track you'd take in advising a teenager. Let's step forward with our strengths, gifts, time, and other resources and then deal later with the night driving obstacle and other limitations, if they ever come up.

DECLARATION OF *INTER*DEPENDENCE

First Corinthians 12 is a fabulous New Testament chapter that talks about the church as the interdependent body of Christ: "The eye cannot say to the hand, 'I don't need you!' And the head cannot say to the feet, 'I don't need you!'" (verse 21).

In this verse, it's common for some to correlate older adults with the forsaken foot and hand. And we assertively follow up with, "Don't let anybody tell you you're no longer needed—even if you can't drive at night!"

But the targets in this verse for changed behavior are the head and the eye. Let's break from our victim role and adopt the head-and-eye vantage point, in need of a good tweak. To whom do *we* say, "I have no need of you"?

As my wife, Judy, and I began working with multiple churches about ten years ago, we quickly saw a troubling pattern. Second-half adult ministry had too often become a closed generational circle, with older adults caring for older adults. Leaders and assistants are commonly over age fifty. Adults under fifty in this area of specialized ministry are anomalies.

Other settings with older adults tend to outpace churches in their engagement and employment of late adolescents and young adults. It's common to see the young adults serving older ones in active retirement and assisted-living communities, nursing homes and other treatment facilities, in both paid and volunteer positions.

When we shut ourselves off from other generations who need us and connect almost exclusively with our peers, it's natural to feel isolated and abandoned. We're not behind prison bars, but closed circles almost inevitably lead to our grumbling like disgruntled inmates, unable to shake our victim mentality.

We're aware that ageism is alive and well in some American churches. But sometimes these are self-inflicted wounds. We have to move beyond ourselves—beyond our cozy peer group—and invest much more intentionally in younger generations.

And, of course, we are not talking about only financial investment, but that can be one quick way to build a bridge and get the attention of children and youth leaders.

Your youth leaders likely already know how vital it is for your church's young people to cultivate healthy Christian relationships beyond their peer group. "Sticky faith" research conducted by the Fuller Youth Institute points to how critical these older Christian relationships are for sustaining faith beyond high school. Genuine, ongoing relationships with five or more Christian adults can astronomically improve a younger person's chances for ongoing, vibrant, sustained faith.

We like to flip the five and ask adults over fifty, "Who are the *five* younger people you are investing in spiritually and relationally?" Relatives count, but don't stop there.

What do you do if leaders aren't receptive to your willingness to personally invest time in children's and youth ministry programs? Of course, you need to be completely willing to jump through whatever background-check hoops that are in place to protect kids. But let's assume for a moment that you're still not welcomed, even with a squeaky-clean background check.

Instead of starting a petition to get your children's or youth director fired, I'd suggest a biblically based remedy that you may not have yet considered. It relates back to the question of whom we might be excluding as we hang out in our fifty-plus-only ministry enclaves.

I heartily endorse broadening the age swath on your second-half adult-leadership team to include adults well under fifty. It can lead to better understanding and connection between generations. From personal experience, I can tell you that our YES! Young Enough to Serve board, when functioning best, has spanned five decades. Having adults in their twenties collaborating with seniors around a conference table can make a huge difference in coordinating ministry and bridging generational gaps!

Even though you may have a specialized focus on adults over fifty, you want the whole body to be concerned about each part, and each part concerned about the whole.

Just as Paul the elder asked Titus the younger to teach the older to reach the younger, we can benefit by inviting younger adults, even late teens, to help lead us into more collaborative relationships with younger generations. We need their help! We don't have to go at this alone.

Let's also look for opportunities to connect with younger people outside the walls and ministry of our churches, both faith-based and secular. Although some secular opportunities might place limits on openly sharing one's faith, you can demonstrate the love of Christ in many practical, life-changing ways. Your life will be positively affected too.

There is a plethora of nonprofit organizations that want to help adults connect in meaningful, helpful ways with young people. Check out www.generationtogeneration.org for a refreshing list of both local and national opportunities, mostly secular.

I pray that you will use these later years—gifts of longevity that prior generations did not necessarily possess—as opportunities to live fully for Christ. Pray, put your best foot forward, stay connected to younger generations, make disciples, and keep serving as God gives strength.

Yes, you are young enough to serve!

GET TO KNOW THE AUTHOR:

Wes Wick and his wife, Judy, are cofounders and directors of the interdenominational ministry of YES! Young Enough to Serve and are also US missionaries with the Assemblies of God, focused nationally on the serving and disciple-making potential of adults over age fifty. Before YES! started in 2008, Wes served in Christian higher education for a couple of decades and in vocational rehabilitation for more than a decade. He and Judy are the parents of four incredible adult children married to amazing spouses and are grandparents to four beautiful grandkids.

THINK OF IT AS YOUR HOME—THERE IS PLENTY FOR ALL OF US TO DO

— Kathy Addis —

Hi. My name is Kathy. I am a mom. Because I am a mom, I have a chore chart. There is always plenty to do around the house.

I have two children (both boys) and a husband. I learned quickly living on Testosterone Island that guys don't see housework the same way estrogen does. They are more than willing to help when the need is pointed out to them, but they don't seem to see it on their own.

Thus, the chore chart.

When the boys were tiny, I certainly did not expect them to help around the house. I figured the whole learning-how-to-walk-and-talk thing was plenty to expect. However, it was not long before I began to ask them to help with little things: "Put your toys away when you're finished," "Put your banana peel in the trash," "Find all the pieces to your game," and so on. Again, they were happy to help when directed to do so.

As they grew, the level of help expected also grew. Over time, I would ask them to do "harder" things: "Clean your room," "Take out the trash," "Wipe down the bathroom," "Vacuum." It was about this time that I realized that my children did not automatically know how to clean, replace a trash bag, properly wipe down a toilet, or even run a vacuum. They may have watched me do it, but that didn't mean they knew how. Consequently, none of these chores happened without some instruction first. As I've always heard, repetition is a work word; I had to show the boys over and over how I wanted something done before I could trust they would do it to my expectation. This was exhausting at times but eventually proved to be worth the effort.

When they are teenagers, my expectations are different but the same. I still expect them to do the basic chores they have always done, but now it is understood that when they clean, they "Mom" clean, not "do the minimum we can get away with" clean. It's understood that when they take out the trash, they are to also replace the liner. It's understood that when the chore chart says it's their turn to do the dishes, it's all the dishes, not just the ones in the sink.

We have recently entered into a new phase of household chores. Our oldest son is eighteen, has just started college, and has moved out, mostly. He is now residing in the apartment above our garage. Yes, he pays rent. Yes, he buys his own groceries. Yes, he does his own laundry. Yes, he still has his name on the chore chart. That may seem odd, but when he moved out, he chose to leave his cat in our home. Because this is his pet, taking care of the cat is still his responsibility. Therefore, changing the litter box is still his chore on the chart. Just because he relocated does not mean he is not still needed.

Don't worry, his brother was not left with all the remaining chores.

Because our house is "the house" where all the friends hang out, sometimes for days at a time, there are plenty of people to help. Yes, I have put their friends' names on the chore chart as well. There are no free rides in life, or in the Addis house. My thought is that if these boys hang out, eat, sleep, shower, and basically live in our home, they can help take care of it as well. Don't get me wrong. I didn't assign them chores the second time they came over. These friends have been unofficial residents for quite some time, thus earning their spot on the chart. I love them and welcome them into our home. I also expect them to help, as there is always plenty to be done.

I feel as though I should make one thing very clear. In all the years I taught my children how to clean, how to take care of the house, and how to help themselves and others, I have never once thought, *Oh good, they can do it all now!*

That would have been so nice so many times! Unfortunately, that is not how it goes. No matter how many chores I give the boys, there is always plenty for me to do as well. I am very grateful for their help, as I know I would have had to do it all (as when they were tiny) otherwise.

With that being said . . .

Hi. My name is Kathy. I am a pastor's wife. I have served in a local church for twenty-seven years. I have been married and in full-time ministry for twenty-three of those years. I have noticed that our home and the local church have a lot in common.

It occurs to me that many people in the local church are more than willing to serve/help if they are directed to do so.

Sometimes they are super eager to help but either don't know what to do or how to do it. They need someone to show them, instruct them, and encourage them.

Just as when the boys were tiny, we cannot expect new believers to jump right in and start teaching or filling the pulpit; however, they too should have a "chore," or ministry opportunity. We who have served for a while, walked with Jesus, and studied the Word should help them find what they are good at and help them develop those skills in the church.

As with teenagers doing housework, we can expect those who have been a part of our church for some time to help and serve regardless of their age. And, just as with my oldest, there is still the expectation of helping out, even if it doesn't look like it used to.

I have heard many times that you don't get to retire from church work; you just get to die. Although this can be a bit daunting to someone in full-time ministry, I do believe it.

We don't get out of helping/serving just because we have younger folks to help out. I never got to quit doing housework just because I had taught my boys how to do it. It's true that I did get to unload some of it on them, and it certainly made my burden lighter at times, but I still had/have my own responsibilities.

It's the same in the church. If those of you who have walked, taught, shared, cooked, witnessed, cleaned, encouraged, and prayed for all these years do not help those coming up behind you know how to do it, who will show them? How will they know how?

As a pastor's wife, I want to personally thank you for all the work you have done in, with, and for your church. I know the 10/90 statistic is true that 10 percent of the people do 90 percent of the work. That may not be scientific data, but I can assure you that it is real in most of our churches. I know that many of you have been a part of the 10 percent, and I cannot thank you enough. It's hard keeping the "house clean" when you feel as though you're doing it on your own.

This is all the more reason the youngers coming up after you need you to show them the way. Will they always like the lesson? Probably not. Will they always appreciate the hard work of ministering through service? More than likely no. Will they thank you for the time, effort, and energy you invest in them? Who knows. Is there still plenty to do? Of course.

Is it worth it? Always.

> Hold firmly to the word of life; then, on the day of Christ's return, I will be proud that I did not run the race in vain and that my work was not useless. (Philippians 2:16, NLT)

We will not hide these truths from our children;
　　we will tell the next generation
about the glorious deeds of the LORD,
　　about his power and his mighty wonders. (Psalm 78:4, NLT)

Only the living can praise you as I do today.
　　Each generation tells of your faithfulness to the next.
　　　　(Isaiah 38:19, NLT)

GET TO KNOW THE AUTHOR:

Kathy Addis is married to Andy, who is pastor of CrossPoint Church, and a mom of two boys, Noah and Nathan. Although her role as pastor's wife is important and demanding in the church, she believes that using her gift sets in the church is vital. She is a camera director for the tech team, a leader in the women's ministry, and a partner on the prayer team. Kathy has a degree in radio/TV/film from Fort Hays State University.

CHAPTER 17

YOUR ENTIRE LIFE HAS BEEN GETTING YOU READY FOR THIS

— Scott Haima —

The band is playing, the stadium is packed, and the players are slapping the sign "Play Like a Champion Today" before gathering inside the tunnel. The Notre Dame players are all standing there, glaring as their opponent runs down the tunnel first. As the camera pans down the line past the coaches and players, the team captain calls a name: "Rudy!" So short, Rudy isn't visible until he emerges behind several players. The captain grabs him by the face mask and asks him one question. "You ready, champ?" Rudy's response. "I've been ready for this my whole life."

This was an inspiring scene in a movie filled with them. In fact, the movie *Rudy* was ranked the fifty-fourth-most-inspiring film of all time by the American Film Institute.[1] To get to the point of being allowed to actually dress as a player for the team in his final game, Rudy had to overcome a lot—including himself. You see, he quit the team the week earlier after not seeing his name on the dress list. It was the stadium groundskeeper, who befriended Rudy

---

[1] "AFI's 100 . . . 100 Cheers," American Film Institute, http://www.afi.com/100Years/cheers.aspx.

as he worked to get accepted as a student to Notre Dame, who chastised him for giving up. He reminded Rudy he had nothing to prove to anyone but himself, and if he quit, he would regret it for the rest of his life. Rudy returned to the team and not only was allowed to suit up but he led the team out onto the field. His lifelong dream came true: the coach finally put him in the game.

Yes, Rudy had the lion's share of his life ahead of him. But this true story and movie can be an inspiration for all of us, even those with most of their life behind them. Looking back and reflecting, we see that each of our lives are not a series of unrelated episodes. Everything we do and have done affects all parts of us, so now at this point, your entire life has been getting you ready for what is about to happen next!

I had my own Rudy moment in late 2009. Indulge me for two minutes to share the path of my life. Let's go back to 1973, when I was eight years old. I vividly recall in our small church in Trenton, Michigan, my dad starting a group that was affiliated with a ministry called Royal Rangers. We earned achievement badges, went camping, and earned awards. I thrived in it. And loved that my dad was the leader. I stayed actively involved in it as a college freshman in the engineering program at the University at Buffalo. After two years and failing physics, my path led me to Fairbanks, Alaska, courtesy of the US Air Force. My military position afforded me time to be involved in Rangers at a local church as well as take evening classes. I enrolled at the University of Alaska Fairbanks and took Accounting 101. I aced every exam, which had me rethinking my career path. Doing well in additional evening classes after I transferred to Kentucky led me to shorten my military career, move my family back home to western New York, and pursue a business career. Upon graduating with my accounting degree, I accepted positions in accounts payable and collections and was the project accountant for the construction of the Buffalo Sabres hockey arena and then for an insurance company spanning nineteen years. I was still involved in Royal Rangers as a volunteer, and it was after switching churches that I became involved in a similar ministry, Christian Service Brigade (CSB). This happened between my time with the Buffalo Sabres and the insurance company. Then another pivotal event occurred: my wife of sixteen years left me and my four children. My resolve was stronger than ever to continue volunteering to serve my local church through CSB, and I became involved at the regional level and was asked to serve on the national board of directors. Not long after my very first board meeting, the full-time regional director in my area stepped down and I was asked by the CSB president if I would consider the position. I had a job and career I enjoyed, was well paid, and knew I would continue to volunteer in this ministry for a long time, so I was going to tell him no. This is where God led me on a discovery. I knew that my life had not necessarily panned out the way I had hoped or planned—my life's path was not straight at all! But now in this time of reflection, I realized that every twist and turn of the path (involvement with a similar ministry, career changes, the past hurts and failures) was preparing me and getting me ready to accept this position as a local missionary serving Christ through this ministry. I have never felt more blessed.

Passion is our fuel. I'm more blessed than ever because my career and lifelong passion are aligned. Now in my midfifties, I pray God allows me to do what I do for another twenty or more years! So many of you are thinking, *That sound nice, Scott, but I am retired and not thinking of another career!* My Rudy moment wasn't about a job; it was about pausing to reflect for a moment when asked to serve God in some capacity. Your life is a like a fingerprint: no one else has one just like yours. You have made thousands of decisions in your lifetime—some small and some very major—to lead to who and where you are today. Remember the old Uncle Sam "We Need You!" posters? Never before were they more relevant for our seniors than today! Scripture is clear regarding what God the Father commands of the older generation. This seems to be lost today in our culture, even in church. God Himself instructed Moses, who could not handle everything himself, to choose experienced men for the tribes. Paul wrote an instruction letter to Titus, who he left behind in Crete to appoint elders in every town because false teachings were infiltrating the churches they established. Often referred to as the Titus 2 mandate, Paul's instructions were clear: teach and appoint experienced men and women who in turn will instruct those younger. Churches need to be set up this way to not only survive but thrive in a culture dominated by the Enemy.

Many reading this might ask, "What if I'm not asked to serve?" My dad has been the single most influential person in my life. He has shown me the love of our heavenly Father through example after example. He led an exciting career of training others at water treatment plants across the country, still involved in Royal Rangers into his eighties. But he was the worst retired person ever! I think the count is up to three times he has retired and said, "This is it!" I think it was between number two and three that the national offices of Christian Service Brigade moved its headquarters, which were based in Chicago for seventy-five years, to Buffalo, New York. I was tasked with getting the new offices and warehouse up and running. Not long after my dad's retirement number two, he stopped by the offices. He said, "Scott, I'm now retired and need something to do. What do you have around here I can help with?" At times, it might take your being proactive in asking what you can do. It would be great if most church leadership sought out their seniors, but the reality is that most don't. Most church staffs are so overworked that they don't take the time, but it would be a rare instance a volunteer would be turned down. Some staff members might be shocked at your offer and at first can't think of something for you to do. Many times it takes a meeting, listening to the heart and passion of the volunteer, and asking questions to assess what a senior can do for the ministry.

What is next? Although you can have a large say in what that is, only God really knows. Even if you don't end up volunteering somewhere or switching careers, take some time to reflect. First, contemplate the value seniors truly have, not the perceived value. Think about a time when our culture wasn't so generationally separate. There may be some obstacles to overcome for the understanding of your wisdom and experience, but it is worth it! I seek out the counsel of older godly men often, and I know that many others do as well. We need you!

Second, reflect on your own life. I don't mean patting yourself on the back but rather thinking about how your whole life is a story and how each chapter is interconnected and related. Some chapters may have been out of your control, but they are parts of your story. And by pausing and reflecting now, you can take control of how the next chapter will play out!

Ephesian 2:10 sums it up well: "We are God's masterpiece. He has created us anew in Christ Jesus, so we can do the good things he planned for us long ago" (NLT). This is for *all* of us, not just those in full-time ministry. We have been getting ready for these next chapters our whole lives!

GET TO KNOW THE AUTHOR:

Scott Haima is president of Christian Service Brigade (CSB). After serving six years in the United States Air Force, he held various business-finance positions, most notably with the Buffalo Sabres hockey team and Merchants Insurance Group. He has three sons and one daughter and lives in Hamburg, New York.

For Personal Reflection or Group Discussion

- Where are you in relationship to your first, second, or third callings, as defined by the authors in an earlier chapter? What do you think could be your third calling?
- What would it take for God to get your attention and make you open to what He has for you to do?
- Have your attempts to serve your church been turned down? Rather than playing the victim role, how might you repackage yourself or re-navigate in your attempts to be more spiritually fruitful and available?
- If your church has specialized ministry for adults in life's second half, do you have leadership team members under age fifty? How might you more intentionally broaden the age swath of those leading this area of ministry? Or do you even think getting younger leaders involved seems worthwhile?
- In Western culture, the fear of aging keeps us from living full lives. There are some who, aging themselves, feel there is something wrong with them, and they are losing value. If we don't value ourselves first, others won't value us either. What are some ways we can, on our own and together, break down these barriers to regain the honor and respect so many other cultures embrace?
- After you've reflected on the twists and turns in your own life story, write out the many skills you have acquired through employment, hobbies, and other means. Then write down the character traits you have developed through the many pivotal events in your life, such as past mistakes, family celebrations, and tragedies. God is sovereign, so how can you use your history to bring glory to His story?

FIND YOUR "JASON STEVENS" AND CHANGE THE WORLD

PART 5

FIND YOUR "JASON STEVENS" AND CHANGE THE WORLD

What to Expect

In the 2007 movie *The Ultimate Gift*, based on the book by the same title by Jim Stovall, there is a primary theme, but there is also a secondary theme we should not miss. Ted (Theophilis) Hamilton plays the role of an attorney responsible for the estate of Red Stevens. Jason Stevens is the twentysomething grandson, and he's never been required to work a minute of his life. In the beginning, there is no respect between the two individuals. As the movie progresses, the relationship begins to develop.

Near the end of the movie, there is a scene in which Mr. Hamilton tells young Jason how very proud he is of him. As you watch this scene, it is difficult to remember the earlier times, when Mr. Hamilton saw no hope that Jason would ever amount to anything.

For me, the entire movie boils down to one scene. Mr. Hamilton is staring out the window of his office and his secretary walks into the room. She senses that something is about to happen when Mr. Hamilton asks her if she thought he was old. Trying to stay calm, she told him no.

He then tells her that he feels it is time for him to retire. Regaining her composure, she asks him what he was going to do if he retired.

His body language changed; he now had a smile on his face,

and his voice was different. His response was the movie for me. He stated, "Go to work with Jason Stevens. Change the world."[1]

As seniors, we must find our "Jason Stevens" and change the world.

Part 5 of this book is meant to challenge, encourage, and push you to invest in a younger person who is looking for a Mr. Hamilton who will work with him or her to change the world.

---

[1] *The Ultimate Gift*, http://www.imdb.com/title/tt0482629/quotes.

CHAPTER 18

YOUR CHARACTER REALLY DOES COUNT

— Rod Handley —

"Man of God" is a technical term used in 2 Timothy 3:17 (NASB) that means someone uniquely called to proclaim the Word of God. Verses 16–17 read, "All Scripture is inspired by God . . . so that the man of God may be adequate, equipped for every good work." Do you feel as though you are a "man of God" when faced with the reality of your sin, knowing you have numerous flaws and imperfections? Does your public life match up with your private world, or are you leading a double life filled with secrets? Are you a role model and an ambassador for Jesus Christ in all situations?

Sadly, there are some who publicly proclaim to love Christ, yet their personal and private moments reveal a totally different person. I believe that King David desired to be a man of character and integrity (see Psalm 26:1–2, 11). No hidden closets or secrets. It is total transparency with God, others, and self. Authenticity like this means you can live with a clear conscience. Great freedom is available to those who live this way.

I know firsthand that secrets have power. Secrets cause anxiety attacks. Secrets can literally paralyze a person. In my early years as a Christian, I had a secret. My secret was an addiction to pornography, which began when I was an early teen. I was able to hide my secret very well. No one, including my parents or other Christian friends, had a clue. I was able to hide my secret while leading Bible studies and sharing my faith with others. Ironically, I even helped mount a successful charge to rid my college campus of showing X-rated movies at our student union.

In my twenties, I joined the staff of the Fellowship of Christian Athletes (FCA) and also was part of the ministerial team for a large church on the University of Washington campus. In the late eighties, I was the co-chaplain for the Seattle SuperSonics basketball team before moving to Kansas City in 1989 as a vice president for FCA. I ministered to thousands of coaches and athletes (high school, college, and professionals) during those years, yet I kept my secret. As my responsibilities grew, my secret drove me to a place where I would wonder, *God, will today be the day people find out who I really am?* I prayed for authenticity but felt as if I was incapable of transparency and honesty.

My breakthrough happened when I got caught looking at pornography while in the Dallas airport by a dear friend from Seattle who just happened to be in the same gift shop as I was as I grabbed a *Playboy* magazine off the rack. He came up behind me, tapped me three times on the shoulder, and asked, "Rod, what are you doing here?" I scrambled for an answer and have never forgotten the look of disappointment in his eyes. Just about a month prior to this Dallas incident, I had entered into an accountability relationship with two other men. Upon my return home after this trip, I got in front of these two guys and told them, "I have been a phony, a fraud, and a hypocrite. I have a secret, and my problem is pornography." For the first time, I became real with someone about my struggle. It was an admission to God, others, and myself that I needed help to find victory. This disclosure began the process of healing and restoration for me. How about you? Do you have secrets, or are you living authentically? I can tell you firsthand that authenticity will bring freedom and a clear conscience. Be real. It will make you into a "man (or woman) of God."

As I've traveled the country the past thirty years, I've attentively listened to people speak on the importance of character. By reading only public-opinion polls, it's hard to determine if character truly matters anymore. Does character count? I propose that it does and that society will place a higher premium on character in the upcoming years. We see indicators of this as moral issues gain greater emphasis during political elections, in the media, from the pulpits, and on talk shows. There is even a resurgence of teaching character within the public and private school systems.

It has been said that ability might get you to the top, but character keeps you there. A person of character is marked by notable and conspicuous traits. Character cannot be purchased; it's a quality of life lived. Founder and editor of the *New-York Tribune* Horace Greeley said it this way: "Fame is a vapor. Popularity is an accident. Money takes wings. Those who cheer you today will curse you tomorrow. The only thing that endures is character."[1]

I'm greatly concerned that character is lacking in society, especially when it involves believers. There are numerous studies that indicate that Christians are as likely as non-Christians to falsify tax returns, plagiarize, bribe, shift blame, ignore construction specifications, illegally copy software, steal from the workplace, and selectively obey the laws of the land. Many believers have convinced themselves that their actions are justified even though they are questionable and inappropriate.

Character development prior to the sixties was learned early in life with a strong sense of right and wrong. Appropriate behavior was taught in the home, school, and church. Somewhere we lost it as we moved from developing internal character to teaching external appearances of charisma and personality techniques. Success models

[1] www.pbs.org/newshour/spc/character/quotes

were designed to help people achieve results without altering one's deep inner fiber. We exchanged truth for a lie, and today in America we're reaping what we've sown with the highest levels of immorality, drug and alcohol abuse, suicide, abortion, teenage pregnancy, murder, divorce, and pornography in our nation's history.

We must be reminded that good old-fashioned character is simply based on Jesus Christ. A desire to emulate our lives after Him should be the goal of every believer. When this takes place, true character begins to take root in our hearts and we become authentic. Unless we as Christians take this first step, we'll continue to see deterioration in our society. Man-made character will crumble when faced with adversity and failure, while character developed and molded through Christ will stand.

What is character? The word actually comes from the idea of an engraving. In the printing business, each letter is called a character. The idea is that each letter leaves a distinctive mark. Thus, your character is defined by the mark he or she leaves behind. Character is the sum of your values, actions, and attitudes. Your character is your spirit, which is a product of your heart. From the heart flow moral courage, conviction, compassion, and numerous other character qualities. Thus, your character can be either good or bad, based on the imprint you are leaving.

In terms of good character, I believe it is the will to do right no matter what the cost or consequences. True character development is established over time in multiple situations and environments, allowing the Holy Spirit to guide us with the Bible as our standard. Unfortunately, we have prioritized two things over character: achievement ("It is not important what you are, but what you do") and fulfillment ("It's not important what's inside, but what you produce outside"). When achievement and fulfillment take precedence over character, a new morality occurs and we can justify pretty much anything.

Many times *integrity* is substituted for the word *character*, yet they are indeed different. Character focuses on right actions and behaviors, and integrity pushes beyond actions and gets to our soul. *Integrity* comes from the Latin word *integritas*, which means wholeness, entireness, and completeness. The root word *integer* is used often in math to represent a whole number, meaning untouched, intact, and entire. Literally, *integrity* means having a complete soul. It's not synonymous with right behavior, though right behavior will often follow, but it's more related to the whole concept of being rather than doing. True integrity is not attained through a series of behaviors (doing) but by being internally transformed through a personal relationship with Jesus Christ.

God is into making integers; Satan is into making fractions. God desires to bring people to wholeness, putting all the pieces together, which will ultimately take place in heaven when we're united with Him; Satan, working through the vehicle of sin, tears things apart, dividing people and bringing confusion and conflict. Remember, God's plan will ultimately succeed, and His universe will one day become one glorious integer, whole and complete. But until that happens, we must live in a fractional world and experience the problems that come from fragmentation.

Integrity instilled on the heart is highly prized by God. In fact, it thrills Him when we demonstrate integrity as noted in Psalm 15. Look at the Lord's reply when the psalmist inquires as to what delights a holy God. The answer is "He who walks with integrity, and works righteousness, and speaks truth in his heart. He does not slander with his tongue, nor does evil to his neighbor. . . . He who does these things will never be shaken" (verses 2–3, 5, NASB).

I believe that the key to living authentically and being a person of character and integrity is making a commitment to accountability. Evangelical leader and author Ted Engstrom believed that "integrity is the greatest prize of accountability. Accountability starts with yours truly—with an honest appraisal of who we are, of what makes us tick." To understand the whys and hows of accountability, I would love to share my book *Character Counts: Who's Counting Yours?* with you.[2]

GET TO KNOW THE AUTHOR:

Rod Handley is the founder and president of Character That Counts, a ministry that was established in August 2000 and is committed to communicating life principles of character, integrity, and accountability. Previously, he served as the COO/CFO for the Fellowship of Christian Athletes. Rod has written more than twenty books, including the best seller *Character That Counts: Who's Counting Yours?* To contact Rod, you can e-mail him at rhandley@kc.rr.com or check out the website www.character thatcounts.org.

---

[2] Rod Handley, *Character Counts: Who's Counting Yours?* (Omaha, NE: Cross Training, 2002).

CHAPTER 19

A SHARED VISION TO CHANGE THE WORLD

— Pastor Jamey Bridges —

I know enough in my forty-one years to realize that people matter. Every relationship in your life right now, good or bad, is there for a reason. From our marriages, to mentors, to our pastor, to our friends we have known since we were young, relationships matter. What does that look like? Do I have relationships only with people I have things in common with? What about the next generation? The older generation? Over the past ten years, I have discovered that the people I do life with are there to play important roles in not only who I am but also who I am becoming. Relationships are a fulfillment of the call God has placed on our lives, and we can share in what He is doing through these relationships. I have realized as a son, husband, father, pastor, coach, and friend that there are key components to relationships, no matter who with or how different we might be. The most important (and difficult) step toward being authentic is purposefully developing a relationship with someone who knows all about us.

In March 2006, we left the comfort of home (St. Louis area) and moved to the cornfields of Omaha, Nebraska. We knew very little of our new town, much less any people, but welcomed this new season in our lives with anticipation and a hunger to be led. I instantly connected with my new pastor, Dobie Weasel, a strong leader and communicator, and gave him permission to be part of my life. I was vulnerable, hungry, and teachable and desired authenticity. The mistake we commonly make with being authentic is that we can be that *to* other people but we don't generally want that *from* other people. I was at a different place than I had ever been, as I wanted it *from* him. It did not take long for me to want to eat my words. This was no longer just a concept or motto to live by; it was happening. Our conversations over my first month of being in Omaha would change who I was as a leader for the rest of my life. One particular story happened after a Saturday night service, when I had spoken to the congregation for the first time. Keep in mind, I had many valid excuses for the way the service went: I had moved into our new house that day and I was traveling back and forth to St. Louis until my wife and three kids arrived. Again, all valid but not necessary to say. The first words that came from my pastor's mouth when we sat in his office after service were "That was the worst service I have ever been a part of." This would crush many people, myself included. However, what proceeded out of his mouth was life, health, comfort, and his desire to see me win. The mistake we often make in confrontation is pointing out the obvious with no correction, which is abuse. Truth must be married with love and kindness, or what is said has no validity and most of the time isn't heard anyway. In Paul's letter to Timothy in 2 Timothy 4:2, Paul told Timothy, "Preach the word of God. Be prepared, whether the time is favorable or not. Patiently *correct, rebuke, and encourage* your people with good teaching" (NLT). I was at a new place in my life, where I realized that someone was for me—that someone wanted to be part of what God was doing in me. This was about a leader who used this passage in 2 Timothy to pour into my life for my good and also for the good of the people. This was the first time in my life of ministry when I felt that I was part of a team—that when I win we all win and when I lose we all lose. This was about the kingdom of God advancing, and I was now part of a team with a shared vision. Ten years later, the fruit of the relationship with my pastor is still there. Even though we are hundreds of miles apart, he is still my pastor. He speaks into my life—some hard things, sometimes with correction and rebuke, but mostly with encouragement.

In 2011, my family embarked on a journey of planting a church in Columbia, Illinois. This was not something I wanted to enter into lightly, and as we sought the Lord, there was clear direction that He was sending us to partner with people. As I prayed, one of the things He spoke was that the people we would move forward with would be people we did not know, and the people we thought would be part of the plant would not be. This was both scary and exciting. I was having lunch with a friend, and he suggested I meet a guy in Bethalto, Illinois, by the name of Pastor Phil Schneider. He set up the meeting, and what happened that day will forever be one of the greatest conversations the Lord has allowed me to have. I discovered what true partnership was and what a shared vision looked like. This was not just from relationships of people I know but from relationships the Lord set up. The meeting started, and here was Pastor Phil's first question: "What is God doing in you?" As I explained the journey of where we had been, what God was calling us to in a community such as Columbia, I could tell something resonated with Pastor Phil. He proceeded to pull down a map from the wall behind him that had ten stars on the state of Illinois, with one on Columbia. He then said, "God told me ten years ago that I was going to help young men plant churches. One of those is in Columbia. We can do this together." The word I longed to hear: *together*. That was a sweet sound to my ears. It was confirmation that a shared vision is the only vision we need to be a part of.

I know that to some, relationships come easy, and for others, more difficult. However, we all have a desire for authenticity—to be intentional with who God has placed in front of us. Maybe that is a senior speaking words of wisdom into the next generation, or maybe it looks like a senior saying to the next generation how can I be a part of your vision? There are always two sides of the coin, two chairs at the table. If we make it one sided, we miss half of what God wants to accomplish by sharing in what He has called us to. Isn't that what it is all about? Doing life *together*? It can no longer be a motto or phrase we live by; it must be who we are. The generations are watching. What do they see?

GET TO KNOW THE AUTHOR:

Jamey Bridges is the founder and lead pastor of Life Community Church. He is also a high school soccer coach and Fellowship of Christian Athletes huddle coach at Columba High School. Before planting the church in 2011, Jamey served fifteen years in youth ministry in Granite City, Illinois; Omaha, Nebraska; and St. Louis, Missouri. He and his wife, Kelly, have four children and reside in Columbia, Illinois.

CHAPTER 20

GOOFY KIDS CAN BECOME WORLD CHANGERS

— Kip McCormick —

He was a young private first class (PFC) in the detachment I commanded in Special Forces. Intelligent, this young man had the potential to do great things in the military. The issue was that he had a drinking problem. That, matched with immaturity and a desire to be something he wasn't intended to be, led to a meeting in my office at 1700 hours (5 p.m.).

Meetings with the commander at 1700 hours were never fun. My right-hand man, the detachment sergeant, was there. Our young PFC had been involved, once again, in an incident that most likely would lead to his dismissal from the military with a bad-conduct discharge.

I had to make a decision. Should I go fight for this young man, throwing myself on my proverbial sword for just one more chance, risking the loss of reputation if he screwed up once again (and bad marks on the ever-important officer evaluation report, the number one thing reviewed for decisions about promotions)? Or should I let him pay the price for his mistake, causing him to be forced out of the military?

One word prompted me to go to my commander, a salty Special Forces colonel who ate nails for breakfast: *potential*.

This young man had potential. I could see it. In my conversations with him, I realized he lacked a mentor—someone who could encourage him, listen to him, and, if needed, put a stiff boot in a place where he would feel said boot placed.

I fell on my sword, and my commander was lenient and allowed this young man to stay in the military (with a heavy load of extra duty, classes, and other mandatory "fun" things). Over the next eighteen months, my detachment sergeant and I did our best to develop, mentor, coach, and encourage this young man.

The results were amazing.

All of a sudden, this soldier realized that he mattered—that he had worth. He realized that God gave him the gift of life and a passion for something bigger than himself. Through long conversations and a lot of listening on all our parts, we saw a huge, positive change in this young man.

Fast-forward twenty years.

This soldier—who should have been given a bad-conduct discharge, who should have left the service under dishonorable circumstances, who should have had any dreams of success shattered because of a character flaw—was promoted to command sergeant major, the highest enlisted rank in the army. He would then go on to lead within the Department of Homeland Security and become a recognized expert in terrorism studies and law enforcement.

He has become a world changer.

Recently, I read some of the social-media comments that followed him upon his announcing his retirement from the military. "You made such an impact on me, Sergeant Major." "What a legacy you've left, Sergeant Major!" "Thank you for all you've done for us!"

All of that because someone saw potential in a young man and decided to take a chance.

Which leads me to a question for you: Have you ever considered the impact you could have on one life by simply being an encourager for someone generations younger than you?

I know, you might have some legitimate excuses: "I can't relate to those younger kids. They're just, well, different," or "Kids these days don't have what it takes. They're soft. You can't pull them off their phones. They won't pay attention to me."

Legitimate excuses for sure. But in the end, they're simply excuses.

You see, God has called each of us to speak into the lives of others, especially those younger than we are. The psalter wrote in Psalm 71:18,

> Now that I am old and gray,
>   do not abandon me, O God.
> Let me proclaim your power to this new generation,
>   your mighty miracles to all who come after me. (NLT)

God has called you to affect change, to bring a little corner of His kingdom to reality, by proclaiming His power to this new generation.

If you look back on your life, undoubtedly you have had experiences that have grown you to be the person you are today. Those experiences, both good and bad, have had an impact on your life as well as the lives of those in your circle of influence. You've had spiritual, emotional, and physical challenges—wins and losses. You've most likely grieved those losses, yet you're still standing.

Read the last three words of that sentence again. Slowly. You're. Still. Standing. That fact in and of itself is enough to light a fire into the life of a younger man or woman.

So how do you do that?

First, it starts with prayer. Ask God to bring a younger person into your life with whom you can do life together on a habitual, frequent, periodic basis. Take time to discern who that person could be.

Next, set up a time to meet with that person to do one thing and one thing only: hear his or her story. Face it, each of us has stories. We all have pasts, we all have presents, and hopefully we'll all have futures. When you're listening to that story, stay focused on the individual, asking questions about him or her. The goal is to make him or her feel important.

Then, tell your story—the abbreviated version. No one wants to listen to someone for hours on end. Tell that young man or woman why you want to be a part of his or her life. Ask for a commitment to a once-a-week meeting over coffee. Put a boundary on it at first, maybe three or six months. Then meet with the person.

When you meet, consider asking open-ended questions (not yes-or-no questions but questions that require an explanation). For example, if the person is a Christ follower, ask questions such as:

- Where did you see God at work in your life this week?
- What was a cool "God thing" that happened to you this week?
- Tell me the toughest thing you had to go through this week.
- Tell me your greatest victory this week. (Showing up for the meeting may be the biggest victory.)

If the individual is not a Christ follower, those last two bullet points will work as a springboard for conversation. As he or she talks, look for places in which you can provide encouragement, and remember that only Christ can truly fix people. Last, ask what the one thing is that you can pray for them for the week.

After that, simply pray.

You'll be surprised at how just being there to listen and encourage will take a goofy young man or woman and give that person direction and hope.

In the book of Genesis, God gives us a calling to the younger generation. Although the calling given is specific to parents and grandparents of children, we can apply it to all of us within the family of Christ.

God speaks to Abraham and says these words in Genesis 18:19: "I have chosen him, so that he will direct his children and his household after him to keep the way of the LORD by doing what is right and just, so that the LORD will bring about for Abraham what he has promised him."

When we lovingly speak into the lives of younger generations, we have a chance to direct them into doing what is right and just. Each one of us can play a positive role in raising younger generations in our corner of the world.

My friend, you have a role in raising a younger generation who know Christ and follow Him; who see the need to live with and walk with character and integrity; who take responsibility for decisions, whether good or bad; and who want to make a difference in its corner of the world. It's a job that you as a senior saint must be part of in some way, shape, or form. It's an obligation that comes with honor and makes a difference in the lives of others and the future of our world.

Back to my story. It took courage I didn't have to fight for a young man who simply needed someone to stand in his corner and encourage him. God gave me the courage, and He'll do the same for you. He will use you to alter the spiritual landscape in ways unimaginable if you are available and obedient to His call in this stage of your life.

GET TO KNOW THE AUTHOR:

Kip McCormick is the creative arts ministry pastor for Cornwall Church in Bellingham, Washington. A retired army colonel, he combines his military experience as a senior officer, former US military academy (West Point) instructor, and intelligence professional with his desire to equip and encourage others in their walks with Christ. Kip and his wife, Linda, have three grown children.

CHAPTER 21

CREATE A COMMON GROUND

— Truman Abbott —

While raising my own children, I wanted to build a lasting relationship with them. So many fathers and grandfathers miss out on their children and their grandchildren growing up. They miss some valuable opportunities to create a common ground and form solid lifetime foundations. Being a coach, teacher, and administrator took up much of my schedule, so I made a commitment to spend quality time with my kids and grandkids every chance I got. That included attending their activities, whether sports, school, or church.

Although we are of meager means, we thought it was important to spend family time with our children and build common ground. We took some great vacations to Washington DC, Yellowstone National Park, Disney World, Disneyland, Rocky Mountain National Park, Mount Rushmore, and many other historical and fun places.

Doing things together doesn't have to cost a lot of money. We also took backpacking and camping trips, where I taught them how to enjoy nature, rappel down a mountainside, read a map, and other general outdoor survival tips. One of our favorite camping trips was to Great Sand Dunes National Park in southern Colorado.

One summer as our grandchildren were growing up, we set aside one day a week to do something special with them. These activities included picnics as well as trips to the Denver Museum of Nature and Science, the Colorado State Capitol, the Colorado Railroad Museum, Red Rocks Park, and many other places.

It was at the beginning of August 2010 when my daughter told me she had an appointment with an instructor at Exclusive Martial Arts to sign my grandsons Daniel and Sammy up for karate classes, but something had come up and she couldn't take them. She asked if I would be able to. "Sure," I said. Little did I know what lay ahead for me.

So off to Exclusive Martial Arts (EMA) we went for the appointment with Mr. Cisneros. He told us about the program and asked us a lot of questions: "What is your goal? Do you want to work toward your black belts?" He talked about the commitment that was required. We would meet two nights a week, either Monday and Wednesday or Tuesday and Thursday, for about one hour, and we would have a chance to participate in tournaments and special Friday night classes. I kept wondering what he meant by "we." He asked if we wanted to work toward our black belts. The boys said yes and that it sounded like a good goal. Then Mr. Cisneros said something that would change my life and my relationship with my grandsons. He asked me, "Are you planning on taking lessons too?" I told him I was almost seventy years old and that my daughter couldn't make the appointment and I was just filling in. He responded by saying that I should come take lessons with them, and the "hook" was "You can come for no additional cost—the family rate."

It really didn't take long for me to make a decision. I thought to myself that this would be a good way to stay in shape and bond with my grandsons, so I agreed. After the interview was over, we were given our white karate uniforms and our first assignment: learn the Black Belt Creed. On our first night of class, we would be required to say the Black Belt Creed before being given our white belts. We all received our white belts. Mr. Sal Cisneros, Mr. Matt Young, and Mr. Shawn Sager, the owners of EMA, would be our instructors.

On the wall of the studio were all the different levels as depicted by the various colored belts we would go through: basic levels 1, 2, and 3; conditional black belt; and finally first-degree black belt. It would be a total of thirteen belt colors to reach our black belts. It didn't cross my mind the time involvement that would be required to achieve each of the belts. It would require practice at home to be prepared for each class over a three-year period of time.

Sammy decided to drop out after his purple belt. Daniel and I were committed to getting our black belts together, grandson and grandpa.

The time Daniel and I spent together attending classes, going to tournaments, and talking about reaching our black belts was priceless. When we needed positive reinforcement, I was there for him and he for me. There were many nights that we didn't want to go to class, but we were always able to convince each other to make the effort. We would have great discussions as we rode to class together and spent time practicing together, getting our routines down. Karate had given us "common ground" that helped us grow close and bound us together.

The self-discipline needed to continue was hard, but it paid off. In November 2013, for our final requirement, we had to perform a routine of our choosing in front of the EMA members and their families. We had to pick out both the music and the weapons routine. We both graduated and received our black belts on the same night. We had reached our goal, together!

Karate was a tool that helped Daniel and I bond and grow close, but it was just a tool. There are many things you can do to establish common ground. Time spent together is so valuable. Watching my grandsons play soccer and be a part of school plays was so important.

I want to put in a plug for Exclusive Martial Arts in Denver, Colorado. Masters Cisneros, Young, and Sager are terrific instructors. They are personal and "kid" savvy and teach more than karate. They teach good character traits.

Another activity I have done with Daniel and Sam is have a movie night, where we watch old science-fiction movies and Westerns. There are so many activities available to share with your children and grandchildren. Don't let life go by without investing in them. Find that common ground. It will be worth more than any monetary gain you could imagine.

Thoughts from Daniel, my first grandson: "Getting to know my grandpa better—the discipline, exercises, perseverance, and fun we have had doing all kinds of activities together—has been a real enjoyment for me. Grandpa has given me support, and I love hanging out with him, sharing funny things and serious things, learning more about honor and respect from him to help me understand what is happening around me. We share and create a common ground as we walk down life's lane together. He is teaching me, by example, how to stay humble and levelheaded in the face of adversity, both externally and internally. We have a bond that will not be broken."

My brother Tony has shared that he and his oldest son, Andy (who's fifty-five years old), have grown really close over the past few years by taking drives down through the Texas Hill Country. They go at least once a month, sometimes staying a night or two or sometimes going just for the day. The stories of their adventures and the times they have shared together have become their common ground.

He is just now getting ready to take the first of many trips with his younger son, Danny. It's never too late to establish common ground!

There is a song from the movie *The King and I* that goes "Getting to know you. Getting to know all about you. Getting to like you. Getting to hope you like me."

Are you ready to make a commitment to take the journey of a lifetime? To take a mysterious journey? A fun journey?

Are you ready to establish common ground?

GET TO KNOW THE AUTHOR:

Truman Abbott served in the United Air Force Academy from 1962 to 1966, with a year in Vietnam. He is a retired educator, and has been a coach, teacher, K–12 Christian-school administrator, and Bible-college president. After retiring from education in 2008, he became a fund-raising consultant with The Champion Group and recently retired from that role. Truman and his wife of fifty-two years, Loretta, live in Littleton, Colorado, and have two children, one unofficial adopted child, and five grandchildren.

CHAPTER 22

COMMUNITY. IT'S WHAT WE ARE. IT'S WHERE WE ARE.

— Molly Ramirez —

Community. It's what we are. It's where we are.

There is a lot of hurt in this world, and no matter the age you find yourself, that hurt and pain becomes more and more evident.

For most people, the pain and hurt starts at a young age, specifically those who suffer trauma or neglect. Others experience hurt as they go through life. The pain helps them grow and become stronger and eventually turn into people they are meant to be. Going through the journey of life and all the events that come with it should never be experienced alone. Children learning how to navigate life need the guidance of someone who has been through the tough times as well.

My name is Molly Ramirez, and I am the clinical and community services director at a nonprofit organization named Shiloh House. We work with youth of all ages who have been affected by abuse, trauma, or neglect. We work with youth who have been pushed to the edges of society and might be looked at as inconveniences, similar to maybe how the older generation currently feels they are looked upon. Also similar to the older generation, these young individuals have unique and special talents that they oftentimes forget they have until they get a necessary reminder from those around them. This is the reason that it is imperative that we blend these two generations better than they have ever been blended before.

We are all familiar with the current go-to complaints about our younger generations: "Those millennials have ruined . . . [blank]" or "Kids these days have no idea what it was like to . . . [blank]" or "The younger generation has no idea what hard work is or respect or commitment." Everyone has an opinion on whose job it is to teach our new generations these traits. We expect parents or teachers to take on this responsibility, and sometimes they do take it on and do a fantastic job at molding the minds of the future. And sometimes no one picks up the baton to help these youth learn how to be the type of people we hope and expect for them to be. All too often, these children fall through the cracks of society, passed from one relative or foster home to another.

As a therapist, I have seen many different kids come through the doors of Shiloh House with similar stories. Typically, through no fault of their own, they have been abandoned or mistreated by those who were responsible for them at some point in their lives. These youths have differed in their behavior, mental-health diagnoses, family backgrounds, and trauma histories, but they all come to us in desperate need of healing. There was one youth that I worked with for a year and a half, and I will never forget him. Brian was eleven years old when he came to Shiloh House to live in one of our residential homes because he had not been successful in foster placements or other residential placements. Brian didn't have any biological family in his life other than his grandmother. Both his parents had their parental rights terminated when he was a young boy, and he had experienced trauma in his biological home as well as his adoptive home. Brian had experienced physical, sexual, and emotional abuse as well as severe neglect for the first eight years of his life. It was too much for Brian's little eleven-year-old brain to process. He was diagnosed with post-traumatic stress disorder.

He didn't know what it meant to be safe or how to tell whether someone was going to hurt him. He was constantly anxious and waiting for the other shoe to drop. He was familiar with chaotic environments, and so they were the only type of situations that made him feel a level of comfort. Brian would therefore create unsafe and chaotic environments multiple times a day. These days would be filled with aggressive behavior, cursing, threatening others, destroying property, and statements about wanting to hurt himself. Brian struggled in his interactions with other children and adults. However, there was one specific group of people Brian always flourished around: men and women over age fifty who were kind and had a heart for him. Brian struggled with following directions and misbehaving with most people he spent time with, but as soon as he was around someone who was from this older generation, he no longer strived for a chaotic environment. Very quickly, we began having Brian spend time with as many mentors over age fifty as we could and saw the benefits immediately. Brian would spend time with his grandmother, a retired veterinarian, and a retired art teacher on a consistent basis. During those times, none of his typical behavior was ever observed. Brian's love for art and animals came alive during the time he spent with his mentors. We were able to see his childlike characteristics. What was previously covered up by pain, anger, and aggression was replaced with sweetness, helpfulness, and innocent curiosity. Brian once told a residential staff person who was an older woman, "I feel safe with you because I have never been hurt by someone like you."

I don't think Brian's story is that much different from most other youths in our society. Brian will require therapeutic services for many years to come to combat the traumatic experiences he has had in his life. However, something that can be just as transforming as therapy is the opportunity for him to spend time with people who make him feel safe—people who have successfully navigated their own obstacles in life and are willing to share their love and lessons with those who do not have anyone to guide their way. We ask children from difficult circumstances to not give up. I ask the same from our older generations. It isn't time to give up. There is still so much to give, and there is still a need for your wisdom and guidance.

It is clear that we live in a divided nation and an even further divided world. God calls us to live in community with one another, and that includes living in community with those who fall outside our comfort zones. That can be especially hard when you have spent more than fifty years developing your safe space. Hebrews 10:24–25 states, "Let us consider how we may spur one another on toward love and good deeds, not giving up meeting together, as some are in the habit of doing, but encouraging one another—and all the more as you see the Day approaching." As followers of Christ, we are called to feed into those around us, especially those in need.

We need to move from being a culture of sympathy to a culture of empathy. We can no longer stand on the sidelines and feel sad for youths affected by trauma or poor life circumstances. We need to feel the pain these children are going through and climb down into the trenches with them. That means you might hear some really heartbreaking stories. You might feel uncomfortable. You might sometimes feel inconvenienced. But the most important thing is that you feel something—something that keeps you fighting alongside those youths rather than continuing to walk by and shaking your head about how sad it is. It's not time to pass the baton and get out of the race quite yet. There are still many thousands of kids in our country who need to learn from people like you how to even enter the race.

GET TO KNOW THE AUTHOR:

Molly Ramirez is the clinical and community services director at Shiloh House. She is a licensed clinical social worker who received her MSW from University of Denver and her BA in sociology from Azusa Pacific University in California. Molly comes from a family of five girls, of which she is the youngest. She resides in Littleton, Colorado.

CHAPTER 23

THE CRY FOR SPIRITUAL FATHERS AND GRANDFATHERS

— Dan Schaffer —

Almost from the moment men are born, we seek to establish our value and prove our significance. Our accomplishments, careers, sports, conquests, and addictions are some of the things we use to evoke self-worth and demonstrate our value to others. We tend to search for significance by focusing on ourselves and hope to create something that will last, while at the same time we fear getting to the end of our lives only to discover that our time here has been insignificant.

From childhood through adolescence and into adulthood, our desire for significance influences our decisions and actions, even though we may not be aware of it. As we approach middle age, the quest for significance becomes a conscious motivation. Many men in midlife find themselves at one of two points: either they have accomplished their goal and find themselves asking, "Is that all there is?" or they realize they will never reach the goals they have set for themselves (their means of gaining significance). The first will predictably lead to a midlife crisis; the second leads to despair. Is there any other alternative?

I believe that the goal God has set before us is attainable and has eternal significance. He has called His men to mature in their relationships to Him and become spiritual reproducers who are spiritual fathers and grandfathers. This is the spiritual legacy that we as Christian men can and must leave.

In 2001, I was in Germany speaking on the impact of the "father vacuum" in the lives of people in modern society. While I was there, God began working in a very unusual way. As I ministered to men and women, they began to view me as a spiritual father.

When I was at the airport leaving Germany, I was speaking with one of the men I had been ministering to on this trip. I referred to him as "brother" and he stopped me. He told me that I was more of a spiritual father than a brother. This made me a little uncomfortable, and as our conversation continued, I called him "brother." He stopped me again and said, "You are more of a father to me."

During the flight back to the United States, I began to hear God speak to me about the opportunities I had missed to be a spiritual father. I had not even seen the possibility and the privilege of being a spiritual father. I had been so focused on establishing my value through "doing ministry" that I had failed to see the greater opportunity to build a spiritual legacy. In the months following my return home, God opened my eyes as I saw men and women becoming whole and growing as they experienced the blessing and affirmation of a spiritual father.

Do you feel this need for significance? Do you desire to leave a legacy that will last for eternity? It is only through an intimate relationship with Christ that we can leave an eternal legacy.

This is your destiny. This journey of becoming a spiritual father is described in 1 John 2:12–14 and summarized below:

THE MAN'S PATH TO SPIRITUAL MATURITY
Spiritual Child
1. Sin has been forgiven
2. Beginning to know God the Father

Spiritual Young Man
1. Know the Word of God
2. The Word is in him
3. He is overcoming evil

Spiritual Father
1. Knows God intimately
2. Beginning to know God fully
3. Reproducer, life giver, reproducing spiritual children who mature into spiritual mothers and fathers

A spiritual father or grandfather is one who:
1. Is driven to know God
2. Is a servant leader
3. Loves God and has a spiritual passion to reproduce that love into others so they can become reproducers themselves

The responsibilities of a biological father to his children are:
1. Protecting
2. Providing
3. Correcting
4. Affirming value through the spoken word and physical touch

Above, I listed four attributes of a spiritual father, but he also has parallel responsibilities to God's children that are similar to those of a biological father. Based on years of "fathering" others, I find that "spiritual children" mature at different levels, depending upon their unique makeup and physical and spiritual maturity. This especially affects the first three responsibilities: protecting, providing, and correcting. It is the fourth responsibility, to provide the affirmation of value, that gives a spiritual father the greatest opportunity for influence, growth, and healing. I want to focus on this vital responsibility to clarify a man's potential impact as a spiritual father.

I have yet to meet a man who hasn't spent a major part of his life trying to prove his value and significance. We put everything into accomplishing goals and accumulating possessions that will prove we are valuable. But almost all of us have a nagging feeling of insecurity that says that if people really saw us for who we are, they would see through the charade. Out of fear of exposure, we hide ourselves in complex mechanisms that we are sure will demonstrate how really valuable we are, but the nagging feeling of worthlessness is like a shadow that haunts our every move. I've observed many men who get to this point and take one of two separate self-protection paths: move toward arrogance and control or move toward total disengagement. Have you ever felt this? Have you caught yourself responding defensively as you attempted to protected your fragile sense of self-worth?

We must ask what makes us truly valuable. Is it our accomplishments or maybe the position we obtain through them? Is it our abilities or money? Could it be the fact that we are loved and needed by others? Any of these can bring a sense of value, but it's fleeting. In Philippians 3:5–8, the apostle Paul lists his many accomplishments and credentials and then describes their value as garbage or dog dung. In verse 10, he clearly states that he wants to know Christ (the word *know* used here is the same one used in other passages to describe sexual intercourse). It is through knowing God intimately that one is transformed and can participate with God in the Father's role of confirming value. It is through knowing God that spiritual fathering gives us the power to affirm value, and that leads to eternal significance.

I believe that the church is at a crossroads. In 1 Corinthians 4:15, the apostle Paul said, "Even if you had ten thousand others to teach you about Christ, you have only one spiritual father. For

I became your father in Christ Jesus when I preached the Good News to you" (NLT). We have many "teachers" but far too few fathers! The church's crying need is for spiritual fathers.

Fathers affirm the value of God's children. Confirming others' worth releases God's children to serve Him and His church and restore their world. The benefit of fathers who affirm is immeasurable. Every man speaks something—will you speak death or life? Will you commit to becoming a father who passionately follows Christ and reproduces generations of fathers who will begin to meet the crisis in the church, culture, and family and in men?

GET TO KNOW THE AUTHOR:

Dan Schaffer is the founder and president of Building Brothers. He has a deep, spiritual passion to strengthen men and has been a spiritual father to men for more than thirty years. Dan was one of the four men who founded Promise Keepers. His love for the outdoors often finds him hunting and fishing in the Colorado Rockies. He and his wife, Jan, live in Littleton, Colorado, and have two grown children.

CHAPTER 24

THE CRY FOR SPIRITUAL MOTHERS AND GRANDMOTHERS

— Julie Thomas —

She was missing, and my six-year-old wondering self went looking.

As I inched down the hallway and turned that left corner, I saw her. Once again, on her knees by the side of her bed. My mother, knelt in prayer, for what felt like forever to my young impatient heart.

Mom, I need something. Mom, let's eat. Mom, a question. But she was undeterred for this moment because she knew this to be true: on her knees was the best place to be as a mother.

What a gift, to have the earliest memories of my mom in prayer at her bedside. My mother was, and still is, a prayer warrior and a God seeker, and my life has been forever influenced by her love of Jesus.

What are your earliest memories of your mother? When you think back on your childhood, what pictures come to mind? Are they moments of warmth and deep love, or are they difficult scenes to step back into?

I think the older we get, the more we recognize that deep-seated need to have that mother figure (or grandmother-figure) to bring a love that only they can bring. Because there is something about a mom, isn't there? Fathers are vital, fathers are necessary, and fathers are instrumental in speaking into our lives. But the role of a mother is irreplaceable. Moms bring a warmth to our lives that can be found nowhere else, through their feminine strength, their natural nurturing, and a fully instinctual mama-bear-ness. #donotjackwithmychild.

Moms are not perfect, and shockingly neither was mine. Maybe perfection was the furthest thing from your home, and your early years hold painful memories of awful words. Maybe you are a child of divorce or experienced horrific trauma or abuse. Maybe you were raised by someone else—a grandmother or father or other relatives. However, we all have a knowing that we need women in our lives who possess those qualities that only a mother can bring. We need women in our lives who provide godly leadership, true compassion, and moral compasses for our paths forward.

I can point to five women who have provided that for me throughout my life. Now, most of them are not old enough to be my mother; however, they are women further down the road. They are women who have shown me, through their example, how to be a woman of God, an intentional wife, and a determined mother. These five have been my mentors and have constantly encouraged me to wrangle and fight and stand strong in this one and only life:

My mom. My mom has taught me the power of God's Word and my desperate need for prayer. As I was growing up, my mother attended prayer meetings. Held prayer meetings. Prayed with me, prayed for me. When my teenage questions came, her question was always "Have you prayed about it?" As a husband and babies arrived for me, with each one she would announce that she had a blessing she prayed over them and had written it out and wanted to give it to them. Psalm 91 is her daily prayer passage of choice, praying we all would dwell in the shelter of the Most High and rest in the shadow of the Almighty (see verse 1). Prayers prayed. Every single day. All of my days. *What does an example like that do for my life?*

Kathy. Kathy taught me the beauty of hospitality and the power of opening up one's home and welcoming everyone to the table. Kathy and her husband, Ray, were my adopted family when I was single and living in a town without my own family. Kathy invited me in—to family dinners, to holidays, to ping-pong, to vacations and football games. I had a front-row seat as she created life in her home with joy and taught me that it was okay to laugh hysterically at the dinner table. She showed me how to open the front door and be fully present with whoever walked in. And that a good Dr Pepper always helps make a good meal. Hospitality, plain and simple. *What does an example like that do for my life?*

René. René taught me the power of an intentional marriage. René has been married to James for thirty-four years and still completely adores him. René and I met every week for a year when I was a new mama, and she spoke directly into my life on what it means to continue to love my husband fiercely and pray for him fervently. To not just make time for date nights but to fight for them. To speak highly of my man when he's with me, and even when he's not. And to be intentional in my thoughts, actions, and partnership with him. To love and to cherish, 'til death do us part. *What does an example like that do for my life?*

Brenda. Brenda taught me how to pray hard and lean hard on Jesus in the middle of raising my four strong-willed children. Brenda has four kids of her own, and I was first introduced to her while hearing her speak at a moms' group. All I could think was, *This woman is living my life, just a few years down the road. I have to know her.* So of course I stalked her and finally got brave enough to ask her to mentor me. Through the years, Brenda has shown me what it looks like to be a valiant warrior for one's family.

She has taught me how to pray intentionally and specifically for my children. She has also taught me what it looks like to laugh easily, give myself a break, and keep my house fully stocked with stuff to make great nachos for my forever-hungry boys. Faithful endurance in raising children. *What does an example like that do for my life?*

Paula. Paula has taught me the unexplainable gift of receiving God's love in a real and experiential way. Growing up in a pretty fundamental denomination, I had a hard time taking the theory of Jesus's love and making it a reality in my life. To me, obedience equaled good performance, and good performance warranted Jesus's love. Paula's words of receiving God's love contradicted my works-based agenda. She recommended books for me to read. She met with me and listened to my hard questions. She asked even better questions that went beyond the issues I had. She encouraged and challenged me to simply be still and know that He is God and that if I did nothing else, He completely loves me, so very much. Through her kindness, beauty, and snarky humor, she taught me about God's incredible grace, forgiveness, redemption, and great love. Over and over again. Lessons in receiving God's love. *What does an example like that do for my life?*

We need women like that in our lives, don't we? Women who will pour into us no matter where we're at in life. You might read this and feel pain because you wish you had someone like this in your world. But let me ask you something: What if this is your time to be that in someone else's life? What if you could be that encourager and mentor to a woman who just needs what you have to offer?

Ladies, no matter where you're at, no matter what life has dealt you, *we need you*. We need you like never before. We need women who have gone before us, who are just a little further down the road. Women who know what it's like to have "been there, done that, and bought every last T-shirt."

We need women like you to speak into those places of our lives that need a mother's insight—to speak in ways that are unique to a mother's role, words of strength, femininity, warmth, character, and fight.

We need women like you who intentionally seek out God's purposes and are not afraid to hold tight to Jesus in this distraction-filled world. Women who will stand strong in the middle of a storm and fully claim Joshua 1:9.

We need your wit, your grit, your audacity, and your courage. And we surely need your recipes, because you know you have some good ones.

We need your stories. Those stories—the ones that make up the whole of a life. The good ones that make you laugh until you cry. The tough ones that make you cry until you laugh. The stories about how God was faithful and true, and the stories of how you questioned every last thing. We want to hear how you endured, how your faith was tested, and how God provided a way when there seemed to be absolutely no way. Testimonies of the beauty in your life, the heartbreak you've witnessed, and the goodness of your amazing God.

Ladies, we need you.

But so often there is a lie that we believe: I have nothing to offer. Even as I am writing this, I am shaking my head because nothing could be further from the truth. God is in the business of redemption, and His job is to use *all* things for our good and His glory. And whatever you may have, whatever you may possess, small as it may seem, God can grow it out into all its fullness and all its beauty, beyond what we could ever hope or imagine.

What are you good at? As you read the examples of the five women in my life, who did you seem to connect to? Do you find yourself praying often for others? Do you love to entertain? Do you laugh easily? Do you have some amazing stories that have God-sized endings? Do you love teaching His Word? Do you find yourself encouraging others? Do you know how to make great nachos? Then you have something to offer.

My life has been forever changed for the kingdom of God because of the examples of other women in my life. What if *you* are meant to play a role in the story of someone's life—how she became a better woman, wife, and mother as a result of your influence?

Make no mistake, if you are reading this book and you have breath in your lungs, we need you.

GET TO KNOW THE AUTHOR:

Julie Thomas is the founder of Women Who Believe, a writer, a real estate agent, and a really faithful friend of strong coffee. She's a pastor's wife and has been married to Joel for seventeen years. They have four children and live with much gratitude in Arvada, Colorado.

For Personal Reflection or Group Discussion

- What pain have you experienced that you could use to help someone else? Perhaps a divorce, the loss of a career, setbacks or failures in your personal or professional life, or just the sheer grit of waking up, doing your duty to earn a paycheck, pay the bills, and care for your family for multiple decades. God never wastes our pain if we are willing to be vulnerable with others and talk about our past failures, losses, and pain.
- When you think of meeting an hour each week with a younger man or woman, who immediately comes to mind? If no one comes to mind, that's okay. God will bring someone into your life if only you ask, seek, and knock.
- Discuss Psalm 26:1–2, 11. What insights do you have from these verses?
- Can you identify with the "secrets" story? What went through your mind as you read it?
- Why is it hard for most people to be authentic? Which of these three relationships is the most difficult: with God, with others, or with self? Why?
- What happens to people who lead secret lives—whose public lives don't match their private ones? What are the consequences associated with the differences between public and private lives?
- How are you influencing a generation different from yours?
- Who do you share a vision with?
- What is your comfort zone? What populations of people do you feel fall outside your comfort zone?
- What God-given talents and skills do you have that you feel you could benefit others with, and what is stopping you from finding someone to mentor?

PART 6
FOR GENERATIONS YET TO BE BORN

FOR GENERATIONS
YET TO BE BORN

What to Expect

You will leave your legend by what you do, and you will leave a legacy by who you are. Legacy is comprised of the fiber and fabric of who you are and what is invested in the next generation. Depending on the translation, Psalm 78:6 speaks of children to be born or generations yet to be born.

The chapters in this part speak not just of leaving a legacy but of the need to help the younger generation begin to understand and establish theirs.

We are hoping these chapters will stir you to ask yourself if you are living this season of your life to cause younger generations to remember what you have done or or if you're investing in the generations behind you because of who you are.

CHAPTER 25

YOUR LEGACY FOUNDATION: THE FAMILY BLESSING

— Rolf Garborg —

My father, Trygve Garborg, was the youngest of ten children born and raised on a farm in Norway. He and his next oldest brother came to America in 1926 when my father was nineteen years old. Here these two brothers met and fell in love with two sisters, the second and fifth of fourteen children born to another Norwegian couple. My father came to America to study to become a minister, but ultimately he never became one. However, he and my mother, Blanche, loved the Lord passionately and committed their lives to walking in obedience to Him and raising their three sons to know and love Him too.

My father wanted each of his boys to serve the Lord as missionaries. He often said to me, "Rolf, if God calls you to be a missionary, don't stoop to be a king." We all got that message, and each of us attended Bible college with the goal of becoming missionaries.

After I graduated as a twenty-two-year-old single man fresh out of Bible college, I went to Puerto Rico and began selling

Christian books door to door while sharing my faith with anyone who would listen. I was full of passion and knowledge of what I had learned in class and couldn't wait to share those things with others. During the next nearly three years of visiting as many as seventy thousand homes, I shared my faith and offered books that would help introduce the occupants to Christ or help them grow in their faith in Him. Amazingly, God blessed this work with many coming to faith in Christ and countless thousands of Bibles and Christian books sold.

After nearly two years, I returned to Minnesota and married "Sweet Mary." Upon our return to Puerto Rico, our mission work grew rapidly with bookstores throughout the Caribbean and Mexico and a Spanish publishing house. During this time, I began to think about what it would be like to be a father. How would I be able to pass on to my children the heritage I had received from my own parents. Not long after our son, Carlton, was born, I was asked to teach an adult Sunday school class at our church from a book by Larry Christenson called *The Christian Family*. As I studied his book, I was particularly intrigued by one act that Larry mentioned he did every night as he put his four children to bed. Each night he would place his hand on the head of each child and pronounce a blessing on them, usually the Aaronic blessing from Numbers 6:24–26.

I wanted to learn more about this practice, so I published *The Christian Family* in Spanish. When the book was ready to be released, I invited Larry to come to Puerto Rico and speak in several churches, sharing about being a parent who wanted his kids to follow Christ. One evening, Mary and I had about ninety minutes of alone time with Larry and I asked him to tell me everything he could about his practice of blessing his kids at bedtime. When he left us that evening, I turned to Mary and said, "This is for us!" I didn't know where it would lead or what the results would be, but I knew I needed to start that very night.

It was late and our son, Carlton, age two and a half, was sound asleep in his room. When I sat down on the edge of his bed, I prayed, "Lord, I don't know what You have in mind or where this will lead, but I know it is Your will for me to speak blessing on my son every night." Then I placed my hand gently on his head as he slept and said, "Carlton, the Lord bless you and keep you, the Lord make His face shine upon you and be gracious unto you, the Lord lift up His countenance upon you and give you His peace. In the name of the Father and of the Son and of the Holy Spirit. Amen."

And then I wept!

I knew that something special had just happened. They weren't just words. I was a vessel through which the eternal God of the universe had just imparted His peace and favor. I rushed back to our bedroom, where Mary, six months pregnant with our second child, was already in bed. I told her what had happened and said, "I can't wait until we have another child so I can bless that one too." She said, "We already have a second child. We just don't know if it's a boy or a girl. Let's start now blessing this child too." I could hardly wait. I placed my hand on Mary's tummy and prayed, "Lord, I don't know what You have inside Mary, a boy or a girl, or even how many, but I want to set this child apart for Your glory and want to begin blessing now." And then I repeated what I had just done moments earlier to Carlton and once again was overwhelmed by what had just happened and wept in awe.

Three months later, our daughter, Lisa, was born "sunny side up." Both children received daily blessings from Mary and me throughout their childhood, and when they left for college, we did it over the phone and when we saw them. They are now in their late forties with children of their own, and we still bless them when we can.

I know that God is a generational God—a God of lineage. I once read that inside every acorn is an entire forest! That blew my circuits. I had thought of an acorn only as either squirrel food or at best the seed of an oak tree. But an entire forest! That would take, well, generations! And then I realized that the same is true when we bless our children. If we faithfully and with love exercise the practice of blessing our children, they will in all likelihood continue the same practice with their children, and that is exactly what has happened in our family.

A friend of mine who is the pastor of family and parenting at a large church in Minneapolis shared a story with me. He has two girls who are now grown. Throughout their lives, he and his wife would speak blessing over their girls every day. One day he said he had a vision of a father kneeling beside the bed of his son with his hand on the son's head, giving him a blessing. My friend thought this wasn't strange because he did that with his own girls. But then he realized that the vision he saw was of his great-great-great-great-grandson blessing his great-great-great-great-great-grandson and how God is truly a generational God.

Many years ago, I was asked by a publisher if I would consider writing a book on blessing from the perspective of God's Word and our own experiences. I reluctantly agreed, and in 1990, *The Family Blessing* was published by Word Publishing. In writing the book, I learned much about what it means to bless. I learned that there are two primary words used in Scripture for blessing and they are very different. The Hebrew word used in the Old Testament is *berakah*, meaning to impart God's favor and the power of His goodness into another person. This was usually done by a father to the oldest son or by a priest while laying their hands on that son.

The Greek word used in the New Testament is *eulogeo*, which means to speak well of or express praise. We get the word *eulogy* from this Greek word. Clearly, a eulogy was intended to be delivered to an individual while he or she was alive and could benefit from its words. Unfortunately, in our culture we wait until a person has died before we give the individual a eulogy, saying all those nice things. I am sure that when Jesus gathered the children in his arms and blessed them, He gathered both boys and girls, and I like to think that when He did, He gave both forms of blessing. I can picture Him putting His hands on each child's head and imparting His father's favor and the power of His goodness on them. But I can also imagine that He found something in each child to compliment or encourage—some way to speak well of him or her.

My book, *The Family Blessing*, is still in print and is available directly from me. It has been published in ten languages, and more than 350,000 copies have been sold. I am deeply heartened that this powerful and important message has been read and embraced by so many people in so many countries. If you wish to contact me personally, you may e-mail me at familyblessingrg@integra.net and I will happily reply. The book is filled with teaching on blessing and many personal stories of how it has been used. Some churches even use my book as a gift to parents of newborns as they present them to the Lord in dedication or baptism. I love this idea.

As I enter the last quarter of my life (I do expect to live to at least a hundred!), I reflect on what I believe God has made real to me that I want to pass on to my children and grandchildren and following generations. Clearly, imparting God's favor and the power of His goodness and the practice of speaking well of them and expressing praise to them is a key part of that.

But wait, there's more!

I believe there are four things God wants us to know—four things He wants us to receive from Him—and each of these four things has two parts. The first part is God's part. All four of these are gifts from God that He gives without qualification by us. The second part is ours. Each of these four things must be received by us and passed on by us to others in order for them to accomplish what God intends them to.

Not long ago, I was privileged to visit Israel and Jordan. It was heart stirring, to say the least, to see all these places where Christ lived and died. But there was one visual image that struck me, and it was the difference between the Sea of Galilee and the Dead Sea.

The first was vibrant and full of boats, with people fishing, cruising, and enjoying the beauty of it. The second was, well, dead! It was much larger, but there was not one boat on it. There were no people enjoying it, and it had no life in it. Then it hit me: the Sea of Galilee receives fresh water from the Jordan River, which flows freely into it and benefits all that's around it and then releases it so that more can come in. The Dead Sea had no outlet. Everything it receives "freely" from the Jordan River it keeps to itself, and consequently it dies and destroys everything in it. I want to be a Sea of Galilee and not a Dead Sea.

So here are the four things that I believe God wants us all to know:

1. He loves us unconditionally. There is nothing we can do to make Him love us more or less. He is love! His love for us is not based on our behavior or actions; it is based solely on His nature. It is who He is!

2. He forgives us unilaterally. Before we even realize we have sinned against God, He made provision for our forgiveness through the gift of His son. Jesus exhibited this from the cross. The first words from Jesus's mouth while He was being crucified were "Father, forgive them, for they know not what they do" (Luke 23:34, ESV). Before He said, "My God, why have you forsaken me" (Matthew 27:46), He said "Father forgive them." Before He said, "I thirst" (John 19:28, ESV), He said, "Father forgive them."

3. He invites us into His presence. We are His disciples. Think about what that meant in Jesus's time. They walked with Him, sat at His feet, were taught by Him, and observed Him. They asked Him questions. They saw how He resolved conflicts among them. They learned from Him.

4. He wants to bless us. He knew that without Him in their presence, His followers would be afraid and powerless

to stand against what was coming and promised to send them a comforter. He knew what they were capable of when He was with them and knew that they needed the Holy Spirit to withstand what was coming.

Think about it. The God of the universe loves us, forgives us, welcomes us into His presence, and wants to bless us! As the song says, "How can we say thanks?" We thank God by receiving His gifts with open arms and then sharing them with all we meet, beginning in our own homes and families.

Get to Know the Author:

It has been Rolf Garborg's joy and privilege over the past fifty years to travel the world, loving people, sharing his faith in Christ, selling tens of millions of Christian books, and training other believers in the same. He has been to more than one hundred countries on all seven continents, and one thing he has seen is that all people everywhere respond to the love of God shown to them. Rolf's desire is to walk in the light and then let that light shine through him. He wants to learn to love unconditionally, forgive unilaterally, invite people to know Christ, and bless them.

CHAPTER 26

TAKING THE "BLUR" OUT OF YOUR LEGACY

— Clarence Shuler —

What kind of legacy do you intend to pass on? Some legacies are chains of pains and others are blessings. There is no in-between. The good news is that as long as we're living, we can and will influence our legacies. So it is not too late to make an eternal difference no matter what we've done in our past!

What exactly is a legacy? A legacy is not how many grandchildren you have (if you have grandchildren). Rather, it is the relationships you have with your grandchildren. You may say, "I don't have children, so I don't have grandchildren." But you still have a legacy. You aren't less than if you don't have children or grandchildren. You'll discover a biblical answer to what a legacy is as you read this chapter.

My most recent influencer was the late Robert E. Cook. Bob was ninety-one years old when he went to be with the Lord in February of 2017. We met in 1994 at a committee meeting to sponsor a new Fellowship of Christian Athletes chapter in Springfield, Illinois. Bob as a person and his prayers drew me to him. I asked him to mentor me. He graciously agreed. Speaking of legacy, I actually met Bob in 1974 through his son, Robin. Robin and I played for Sports Ambassadors, a Christian basketball team that traveled the world sharing the gospel through the medium of basketball. Once you've met Robin, you'll never forget him. Robin was greatly influenced by his father. Robin affected me.

For years, Bob and I met weekly. He would share his love for Christ and wisdom with me. Bob told me that he felt that God called him to serve me. By example, he modeled to me how to more effectively love Brenda, my wife, by the way he loved Jean, his wife.

Our relationship qualifies as a legacy for him. What I do the remainder of my life on earth adds to his legacy. Bob was white and I am not. Legacies can't be limited by differences.

Dr. Gary Chapman has been the most consistently influential person in my life. He introduced me to a personal relationship with Jesus Christ many years ago when I was a youth. Gary began discipling me when I was seventeen years old. He still is discipling me. Years later, he did the premarital counseling for Brenda and me and then was my best man in our wedding. Gary is my human spiritual dad. He is a grandfather to my children. He helped them with college. His children are like a younger brother and sister to me.

Gary modeled to me courage. His wife shared some of the consequences he experienced because of our friendship, as Gary is white and I'm not.

He is teaching me humility by asking me to write a book with him.

When African Americans hear about our relationship, it endears him even more to them. Dr. Gary Chapman's legacy is obviously his book *The Five Love Languages*,[1] but it is so much more! His legacy crosses racial barriers and languages.

My other mentors who continue to influence me are Dr. Don

---

[1] Gary Chapman, *The Five Love Languages: The Secret to Love That Lasts* (Chicago: Northfield, 2015).

Sharp, pastor of Faith Tabernacle Baptist Church in Chicago; Dr. William Pannell, retired from Fuller Theological Seminary; Gordon Loux, former CEO/president of Prison Fellowship; and Brian Teel, businessman. Some of these gentlemen are in their eighties.

Several of my spiritual mentors were and are women. One was the late Rushella Latimer. With her prayers and godly wisdom, she provided insights into life and kept me out of some trouble! Two of my favorite preachers are women: Karolyn Chapman and the late Jerra January. The late Viola Daniels daily shared her wisdom with me before I got married when I lived in Tulsa, Oklahoma.

For me, my primary legacy will be with Brenda, my wife of more than thirty-two years, and my three adult daughters, Christina and Michelle (twins) and Andrea. In them, I see both of my positive and negative effects. I'm constantly working on being a better husband and learning how to parent adult children. And it ain't over!

Also part of my legacy are those young and old men and women I've discipled since 1972. They are all over the United States. There are also those few men who honor me by calling me Dad.

Additionally, there are those individuals and couples who God empowered me to help overcome pornography and affairs. It is so rewarding when someone thanks you for saving their marriage and their family. Of course, I know that God did the work; He just let me go along for the ride. I just love them with His love.

My mother's mom comes to mind in terms of legacy because she powerfully mentored my mom in how to mother me. Mom said that as a toddler, I'd often bite her on her legs. My grandmother told her to bite me back. My mother did. I'm told that I stopped biting her. According to my mom, my grandmother said, "Jerl [short for Jerleane], your son is going to be special." Mom constantly told me this. This was so encouraging to a young black boy in America (this was before we became African Americans) in the late fifties, sixties, and seventies.

My parents also tremendously influence my legacy. We weren't poor; we were "po." Poverty had its riches. Frequently, my parents couldn't afford to hire a babysitter, so they took my sister, Jean, and me with them to work. Mom sold Stanley Home Products, which required a lot of traveling by car, so family time was precious, special, and normal.

One of the greatest gifts my parents gave my sister and me was telling us that we could be anything we wanted to be. That resonated with me and motivated me. They taught me that neither my lack of height nor my skin color could stop me. Slow me down, yes, but definitely not stop me.

So how does all this pertain to you? You're not too old to influence someone who will then influence the next three to four generations. Remember, one of my mentors was ninety-one years old!

Middle and high school students have asked their church leaders to have me speak with them about friendships with the opposite sex, dating, biblical sex, pornography, and sexting. Christian colleges and universities such as Moody Bible Institute have also requested my interactive presentation. Initially, this was shocking to me because I'm in my sixties. But younger people really desire to interact with senior citizens because they know we have lived life. They also believe we'll be honest and transparent about controversial issues.

Your legacy can extend far beyond your family. Your influence can cross cultures, generations, and economic lines. I have yet to meet a young man who does not want to be mentored or spend time with older men. I can't speak for young women, but I imagine they have the same desire and need. Many of all cultures and races are looking for godly father and mother figures.

Your legacy is not about perfection or else I'd be disqualified. God turned my sin and misery of pornography into one of my most life-changing ministries that positively affect family generations. Once we ask for God's forgiveness, He can turn our mistakes and sins into something He can use to build and strengthen His kingdom.

Older people have always intrigued me. Maybe it is because my grandparents on my father's side were in their nineties when I was ten or eleven years old. I regularly ask older people who have certain traits I lacked to mentor me. But I'm told that is unusual.

You are needed to make a difference in the lives of many. Consider asking God to guide you to a younger person who you see has potential or needs help. Ask God for someone to mentor who will mentor others. Please don't feel that you failed or are disqualified from creating a godly legacy because of your past, no matter what your past was. Legacies bring clarity to life. Godly legacies are about biblical relationships in marriage and parenting and being a godly child to your parents and more. Legacies are about discipleship. Chuck Stecker and I say, "Legacy is not an event, but legacy is an opportunity to honor God through a relationship."

Creating a godly legacy is about being. No one has all the answers. Mentoring isn't about always being right or smarter than the person you are mentoring. It is about being there for someone. It is about loving others the same way Christ loves us: through and in spite of our imperfections. Mentoring is about the older serving the younger.

Take a step of faith and get to work on your legacy. Don't wait. Start now!

GET TO KNOW THE AUTHOR:

Dr. Clarence Shuler is president/CEO and founder of Building Lasting Relationships (BLR). After twenty-eight years of serving as a minister, a church planter, a pastor, and often the first African American to work for some Christian organizations, he has been running BLR for nearly twenty years. Clarence and his wife, Brenda, have three adult children and live in Colorado Springs, Colorado.

CHAPTER 27

CAN YOU HELP ME THINK ABOUT MY LEGACY?

— Maddison Hardin —

Everyone has a legacy in this life. Your legacy is the only thing of real value that you get to leave behind for your children, loved ones, and others. Travel back in time to when you were in your twenties and think about your mind-set. Maybe you were single and working hard and enjoying life with your friends, or maybe you were newly married to your sweetheart and enjoying each other, or maybe you were married with young kids and just trying to figure out parenting. Wherever you picture yourself back in those days, you probably didn't give your legacy much thought. There's hardly time to think about tomorrow, much less years from now. You probably did not see yourself where you are today in this world with iPhones, robotic vacuums, and Donald Trump as president. But here we are. Did you imagine that your kids and grandkids would be living in this kind of world? If you could tell yourself anything back when you were a new parent, what would you say?

Do you remember the days when you were up all night with a newborn or teething baby? My days are filled with baby cuddles, diaper changes, feedings, cleaning up messes, cooking dinner, and lots of love. It's the most exhausting but rewarding time I've ever experienced. My son has changed my world in the best way possible. I am overwhelmed with joy and love. The whole world seems to slow down when I'm with him, solely focused on taking care of him and my husband, but the world keeps turning. Conflict, political discourse, and prejudice surround me as laundry has to be done, the house cleaned, and appointments met. Most days, I hardly have time to think about the next day, so I rarely think about my what my legacy will be for my little boy. But when I do think about my legacy, I picture it being a lighthouse guiding my baby and reminding him of who God is and, more important, who he is in God. Fifty years from now, will I trust my legacy to guide my children in trying times?

A baby will change your whole world and affect your identity. In fact, your identity evolves many times. You begin life totally reliant on your parents, and then your identity shifts to being an independent teenager. You then add to your identity your education and career. You now are not only someone's son or daughter but also an alumnus of a certain college, a teacher, a doctor, a pastor, and so on. Those who get married become a spouse. Then kids enter the picture and you become a parent. You get involved with the church and become a volunteer or choir director. And eventually your identity might be one of a grandparent and a retiree. This only scratches the surface of the many identities you might have in life, and each identity adds to your legacy. It's like tossing a stone into a pool of water. Each identity shift has a ripple effect. Although your identity shifts and changes throughout life, your most important identity is being a child of God.

Your identity and your legacy go hand in hand. What do I mean by this? How you live your life and where you find your identity is how you will be remembered. My son is the fifth generation of living relatives today, so I see my great-grandma's legacy as well as my grandparents' and parents' legacies all unfolding before me. My great-grandmother now lives with a relative and spends most of her days in front of the television. However, before this, she spent her time mentoring and speaking into young women's lives. She found her identity in being a mother figure for many young ladies. I know that she touched the lives of many of her friends at church and in her town as well as her family. She will be remembered as a friend and confidante, but she seems to have lost sight of her identity and purpose now. Her sphere of relationships seems to have narrowed to only a few. If you are breathing and able to communicate on some level, God has a purpose for you on this earth.

One of my grandfathers recently passed away, but up until his final breath, he was using his identity to minister to others. He left a great legacy for all my family to remember even in his final moments. I'll never forget after he passed, my dad (who was with him in his final days at the hospital) said, "I never realized how many people he impacted." My grandfather left an impression on my dad even at the end. In his final days in the hospital, numerous friends and family members called, video chatted, and visited to say their final goodbyes. My grandfather found his identity in Christ above everything, and this directly affected his legacy. Although he appeared to be finished growing his legacy toward the end of his life (as he lived with diabetes and used a powered wheelchair to get around), he took the opportunities that God provided to encourage and love others.

My grandfather was not perfect. He stumbled and had his hang-ups, but he loved people. I'm not talking about just his family and close friends; he loved people who were sometimes hard to love. He participated in prison ministry and was always so kind regardless of someone's social or economic status. The love and encouragement he showed people comes only from the Lord, and he made sure everyone around him knew that. This is his legacy and what everyone who encountered him will remember. I want to encourage you to always remember your identity in Christ. You are a child of the Most High. You have access to the Creator of the universe, and He loves you beyond measure. Find your identity in Christ, and your legacy will be the richest it can be.

Don't lose sight of your identity and your legacy because of your age, social status, shortcomings, or circumstances. I'm reminded of 1 Timothy 4:12, "Let no one despise you for your youth, but set the believers an example in speech, in conduct, in love, in faith, in purity" (ESV). Although the apostle Paul is talking about youth being overlooked because of age, we can also think the same way about being a senior. We spend our lives building futures and legacies for our children. Whether that is leaving them money or something more important such as prayers and words of wisdom, we all work toward this. Why should we reach a point where we stop building, growing, and trying and hope that what we've done is enough? The apostle Paul says in Hebrews 12:1 to run the race with endurance. I have not run a race in quite some time, but I know that when you get close to the finish line, you don't slow down or coast. You run your hardest and fastest at the very end because that one last push propels you to the goal.

Maybe today you find yourself lacking an identity or purpose. You've run the race but feel as though you are just coasting now. Let me encourage you. You are not finished building your legacy yet. You can still influence the people and the world around you. You can continue to grow your identity and enrich your legacy, or you can hope that what you've already done is good enough to carry your loved ones through. Your legacy is all you get to leave your children, church, and friends. I know that you want to leave the very best for your kids. As a new mom, I have discovered a deep love for my son and want the very best for him. I try every day to give him the best, and I hope I can leave him with wisdom and an example of God's love that will show him the way to God despite this troubled world.

More than ever, this world needs godly men and women to be beacons of light in the darkness. God has a reason for your being here for such a time as this. Today's youths need your wisdom, experience, and life lessons. They need you to step in and be a voice of God's love, compassion, and reason. You have words of wisdom and knowledge that can change the world, so don't think you can or should slow down. Your legacy will affect many more people than you will ever realize. This world and these young children need you. Keep growing your identity, learning new things, and speaking the truth to those around you. People are listening and are thirsty for the truth and love you have within you, so share it. And when you get to the finish line, you might be exhausted, but you can be confident that your legacy will continue to influence people through your children. You will know that your seed, one of the most important legacies you can nurture, will join you in paradise having followed your example and run the race boldly and strong to the finish.

GET TO KNOW THE AUTHOR:

Maddison Hardin began writing at an early age and continues to enjoy it. She became a published author at age seventeen and also enjoys photography. Having worked in the retail and insurance industry, she loves to help others. As part of five living generations, Maddison has a unique perspective on legacy and longevity. She currently lives in Nashville with her husband and young son. Maddison can be reached by e-mail at maddisonhardin@gmail.com.

CHAPTER 28

THEY ARE LISTENING

— Chuck Stecker —

We have all heard the saying "Actions speak louder than words." I believe that the younger generations are listening and there is a hunger to hear from those older.

Part of the confusion stems from the idea that others must listen in the same manner as we listen. As I write this chapter, I am sitting at our kitchen table and there is not a sound in the house. It is very early in the morning, and the stillness is conducive to writing and thinking. At this same table, our granddaughter Hannah often comes by for some of Grandma Billie's comfort food and to do some of her homework. When she works at this table, she plays music from her playlist and puts in her earbuds. I did not know what a playlist and earbuds were until a few years ago. I feel younger by using those words!

Now another scene with the same granddaughter. A few weeks ago, Hannah returned from a month of serving at a Young Life camp in Oregon. She had researched the opportunity and raised her support. For more than an hour, she gave her report to six of us regarding her experiences, lessons learned, and what she had done with her life for a month.

Her report was filled with the phrase "And then I remembered what _____ told me." Most of the sentences were filled in with *Grandma*. Often the person whose name was mentioned did not remember making the statement, but Hannah had been listening and remembered.

They are listening.

I often find it humorous when we seniors talk about how tough things were back in our day. We often wear our stories like badges of honor. "I had to walk to school in the snow every day, and it was uphill both ways." "We did not have any fancy phones with music and games." The list goes on and on. The problem is that the world has become a much more complicated place to live for the younger generations.

If we of the older generation want to be heard, we must take advantage of opportunities to communicate. My wife, Billie, always told me there was a short window of opportunity to hear from our kids. It was normally immediately after school, and we had to capitalize on the moment or it was lost. This certainly applies to the lives of the young men and women I know and want to bond with. Their lives are busy, so I must take advantage of the moments and opportunities.

I do not mean to insinuate that we older folks just sit around doing nothing, waiting for younger men and women to call. Most of us are busy as well, yet we must make time to invest in others.

If we want to be heard and have relevance in others' lives, **we must be available!**

The younger generations hunger for people they are able to trust. The younger generation lives in the social-media world, where they may have hundreds of friends on Facebook, Instagram, or the latest app and have very few they can truly trust.

If we want to be heard and have relevance in others' lives, **we must be trustworthy!**

While attending a Christian Association of Senior Adult Ministries (CASA 50+ Network) conference for seniors age fifty and older, I listened to Stuart and Jill Briscoe as they participated in a discussion. Jill shared the story of a young lady she'd mentored and encouraged. The young lady was in her teens and Jill in her seventies. After their relationship developed, the young lady told Jill, "Because you listened to me, I knew you loved me. And because you loved me, I listened to you."

In any relationship, we earn the right to be heard by first listening. We are never too old to work on our listening skills.

If we want to be heard and have relevance in others' lives, **we must listen!**

I truly believe that one of the keys in developing meaningful relationships with younger men and women is to become a master of the question. To be clear, it is important to remember there is a significant difference between asking good questions and interrogating someone. Good questions are intended to help someone focus on his or her issue, and interrogation is designed to focus on our issues. The purpose of good questions is to help others grow and improve their situations. Interrogation is used to obtain information we want for our purposes. The person who guides the conversation is the one who asks the best questions, not the one with the best answers.

One of the men in my life is a "spiritual son" of mine. We have done life together for many years. Our relationship began when he was a student at Denver Seminary and has continued as he met and married the love of his life, tried farming, became a manager in a significant business, and started a family. We have many years invested in our relationship. During one of our recent meetings, I asked him a question. After answering the question, he paused and then stated, "Chuck, this is why I need to meet with you. No one else asks me these tough questions." After breakfast, I sat in my car for a moment and realized that I do not recall ever telling him what to do; instead, I remember some of the questions I asked him.

If we want to be heard and have relevance in others' lives, **we must ask good questions!**

After speaking at a seminar, I had dinner with a man I had met that day. He was there to observe, and I wanted his assessment. One of his statements that has stuck with me was "The speaker cannot be the hero of every story." This is very important in our conversations with anyone, particularly with younger men and women. They need our success stories, but they also need us to be honest and talk about our mistakes and what we have learned that will help them. There must be a willingness on our parts to be honest and vulnerable with our successes and failures.

I remember telling a young man, "I have been in a similar situation in the past, and I did not handle it very well." In that moment, the conversation changed. He leaned forward and wanted me to explain. It is one thing to say I understand or have been there too, but it was important for the young man to know details, and revealing them indicated I trusted him.

If we want to be heard and have relevance in others' lives, **we must be honest and vulnerable!**

They are listening.

But in addition to listening, they are watching.

This next memory remains vivid for me. I had stopped by a local business to renew our membership. (And yes, I know how to use a computer and realize I could have renewed online.)

The person assisting me was new to the job. This might have been her first day. As we progressed through the renewal and my payment, she needed help from another worker and was very apologetic. I laughed with her and told her to take her time, as the only way to learn was to do something. It would have been very easy to become frustrated with the amount of time a simple transaction was requiring. I have had many occasions in my life dealing with people in which I have been, you could say, less than perfect.

In this situation, it was a good day. As we finished the

transaction, a woman had approached the counter. She was another employee and she waited patiently. When the transaction was complete, the woman who was standing at the counter said, "Excuse me, but are you Chuck Stecker?" I laughed and told her that if what she remembered was good, then yes. But if it was bad, it was my evil twin. She then told me in front of several other customers and employees that she had heard me preach on several occasions. We discussed where and when. But then came the big statement. She said she was certain it was me when I came in but just waited to see how I acted. She said, "I just hoped you were not a stinker in real life."

Young men and women want to be with people who do not preach one thing and then are totally different in real life.

Again, it bears repeating: I have had several occasions in my life dealing with people in which I have been less than perfect.

If we want to be heard and have relevance in others' lives, **our lives must match our words!**

As seniors, we are not irrelevant. Younger men and women are listening. We live in a season of incredible opportunity. Whether you realize it or not, the truth is that younger people are looking for answers. They are in search of truth and trustworthy men and women to follow.

One of my favorite Scriptures regarding leadership and life is found in the book of Judges. In this instance, Gideon is leading three hundred unarmed men against what is believed by many historians to be between 150,000 and 175,000 Midianites.[1] Gideon's order to his men is written is verse 7:17, where he tells his men, "Watch me. . . . Follow my lead. When I get to the edge of the camp, do exactly as I do."

Consider the incredible impact of living in such a manner as to have this Scripture speak for your life without your saying a word.

---

[1] www.enduringword.com/bible-commentary/judges-7

If we are willing to seize the moment, our older years should be the greatest season of ministry and significance of our entire lives.

GET TO KNOW THE AUTHOR:

Dr. Chuck Stecker is executive director and founder of A Chosen Generation, which he and his wife, Billie, launched in 1997. After twenty-three years in the US Army, he served on staff of Promise Keepers as regional director in field ministry division for south-central region. Chuck and Billie have three children and nine grandchildren.

CHAPTER 29

FILLING THE LEGACY VOID

— Greg Bourgond —

Mother Teresa, Bill Clinton, Billy Graham, Ronald Reagan, Bono of U2, Tiger Woods, Charlie Sheen, Bill Cosby, Bishop Desmond Tutu, Joseph, King David, C. S. Lewis. How will these people be remembered? What legacy have they left? If those who are alive today keep doing what they are doing, what legacy will they leave?

Some time ago, I met with businesspeople who were responsible as benefactors in the renewal of a run-down area of their city. As they settled in, I told them that what they accomplished was remarkable. However admirable their achievement, chances are that few would remember their financial sacrifice over time. I told them, "If they erect a statue in your honor, it will primarily serve as a perch for pigeons within the first two weeks of its construction. If they name a building after you, people passing by will wonder how much money you had to give for such a distinction. Few will take the time to learn about the substance of the person's life." I continued to say, "I'm not against philanthropy. However, from a biblical perspective, the only legacy worth living and leaving in the lives of others is a godly one."

Everyone leaves a legacy. Legacy is the aroma left in the

nostrils of those we leave behind, those who God brought within our sphere of influence, long after we are gone. For some of us, it is a stench; for others, it is a pleasant fragrance that recalls who we were and how we lived.

What legacy will you leave? What will remain long after you are gone? What artifacts will bear testimony to your life and how you led it? How will you finish the journey? At some point in time, we ask ourselves, *Why am I here? Where am I going? What is the significance of my life?*

Personal questions of purpose, progress, and permanence haunt us throughout our lives, compelling us to repeatedly ask ourselves, *Is there more to life than I am experiencing?* We cannot claim originality in pondering these issues. God placed a spark of the eternal in our souls that beckons us to contemplate the purpose of our being (see Ecclesiastes 3:11). Not only were you on the heart of God before you ever came to be, but God has prepared, in advance, a unique purpose for your life (see Psalm 139:13–18; Ephesians 2:10). Finding your niche and meaning can be attained only when you tune your heart to God's heart.

After an encounter with Ahab and Jezebel, Elijah sought God's voice. He wasn't in the wind, the earthquake, or the fire. His voice was heard as a "gentle whisper" (1 Kings 19:12). In the chaos of life, we too often succumb to the tyranny of the urgent. The business of our lives creates so much noise that we can't hear God's voice. I believe that God speaks so profoundly in a gentle whisper because it forces us to lean forward to hear it.

At the turn of the century, small communities would erect icehouses to preserve their food. These buildings were generally made of thick walls, no windows, and a door at the front and back. When the weather turned cold and rivers and lakes began to freeze, the men in the community would cut large chunks of ice and transport them to the icehouse by horse and sled. They would cover the ice with straw or sawdust. People would bring their perishable foods into the icehouse. Because of the house's construction, the ice would often last into the summer before the icehouse needed to be cleaned of rotten food and debris. On one such occasion, a small boy was witnessing the men going in and out of the icehouse as they cleaned it. One man came out frantically declaring that he'd lost a family heirloom, his watch, in the rubble. The boy quickly ran into the icehouse and emerged ten minutes later holding the watch. The men were astonished and asked how he'd found it. He said, "It was simple. I lay down in the straw until I heard ticking." When is the last time you lay down in the "straw" to hear the "ticking" of God's voice?

Erik Erikson and social scientists after him identified a stage of adult psychological development that happens during middle adulthood between the ages of approximately forty and sixty-five called generativity. It elicits a growing concern and need "to nurture and guide young people and contribute to the next generation," to pass on a legacy to others, something that matters to them.[1] This finding correlates with the Bible saying that we are to entrust to others what we have learned (see 2 Timothy 2:2; 1 Chronicles 28:8).

There are four possible legacies you could leave. One is no legacy whatsoever, which is a legacy itself; some people are born, live, and die with few people, if any, remembering they existed at all. The second legacy is a bad legacy that leaves scars and damage in its wake. We have plenty of examples past and present of this type of legacy. The third is a perishable legacy—such as a company, a business, a medical breakthrough, or some other tangible manifestation—that reminds others of the contributions we have made.

The fourth legacy—the only one that will echo in eternity—is the godly legacy we leave in and on the lives of others. It is never

---

[1] Erik H. Erikson and Joan M. Erikson, *The Life Cycle Completed* (New York: Norton, 1998). "Generativity." Merriam-Webster Medical Dictionary, August 7, 2017, https://www.merriam-webster.com/medical/generativity

too early or too late to begin living a legacy worth leaving for others, especially those closest to you. It doesn't matter how you start the journey; what matters is how you finish it. Each of us has been given something of value by God to give to someone He values.

Early on I gave values to each of my grandchildren. My hope is that the decisions they make in life will be filtered through these values.[2] At first they were terms of endearment. I would greet them with their values. "Strength and honor, Braedan. Goodness and integrity, Gaelan." They would return the greeting by stating their values. "Strength and honor, Papa. Goodness and integrity, Papa." I would look for teachable moments to illustrate the importance of their values. I embedded them in blessings I wrote for each of them, realizing that the world wouldn't be so kind. I wanted them to know what I saw in them, that they were valued and esteemed, that they mattered—my legacy for them.

My mentor, Dr. J. Robert Clinton, identified several possible legacies one could live and leave. He called them ultimate contributions, lasting legacies of Christians for which they are remembered and that further the cause of Christianity by one or more of the following means:

- Setting standards for life and ministry
- Influencing lives by enfolding them in God's kingdom or developing them once they're in God's kingdom
- Serving as a stimulus for change that betters the world
- Leaving behind an organization, institution, or movement that will continue channeling God's work
- Discovering ideas, communicating them, and promoting them so that they further God's work

---

[2] Derrick: peace and justice; Braedan: strength and honor; Talisa: love and joy; Kieran: courage and valor; Gaelan: goodness and integrity; Lochlan: truth and wisdom.

Here are other examples of legacies you can strive for by visualizing a preferable future and making present-day decisions that will guarantee that outcome:

- *Rekindle* broken or strained relationships by forgiving and asking forgiveness and acting in the best interest of others.
- *Live* out your faith by winning, enfolding, equipping, and deploying faithful followers of Christ.
- *Find* someone to mentor in spiritual or personal matters.
- *Invest* in others by becoming actively involved in a ministry area.
- *Serve* as a stimulus for change that betters the world.
- *Be* a loving, godly husband or wife, father or mother, son or daughter, sister or brother, grandfather or grandmother to those who should mean the most to you.
- *Live* your life for an audience of One!

GET TO KNOW THE AUTHOR:

Greg Bourgond is president and founder of Heart of a Warrior Ministries. He has served twenty-nine years in the US Navy and has been an executive pastor in large churches and a vice president of operations and strategic initiatives for Bethel Seminary. He also has held numerous leadership positions in corporate and defense businesses. Greg and his wife, Debby, live in Shoreview, Minnesota, and have one daughter and six grandchildren.

For Personal Reflection or Group Discussion

- What fragrance will linger when God calls you home?
- Are you investing the treasure God has given you in the lives of your loved ones, in the lives of your friends, and in the other lives God has given you an opportunity to influence on His behalf?
- When you meet the Lord face to face, will He honor you for wisely investing your talents in the lives of others, or will He chastise you as He did the servant who buried his talent in the ground (see Matthew 25:14–30)?
- How do you want to be remembered?
- What can you do to continue to build your legacy? Think small daily, weekly, or monthly goals.
- Listen to the song "Dear Younger Me," by MercyMe, and think about what you would say to your younger self.
- How would you rate your listening skills? Now ask someone who cares about you (but will be honest) how he or she would rate your listening skills.
- If you were to listen to yourself, does your life match your words?

FINISHING STRONG

PART 7

FINISHING STRONG

What to Expect

Over the years, there have been many articles and books written on the importance of finishing well. Several studies and surveys have been done on the number of men in the Bible who finished well, and the numbers are sad at best. Without citing specific references, most studies I have read put the number of those finishing well at between 25 and 40 percent. I am yet to find anything to indicate the number to be more than 50 percent.

To say the figures are sad would be a great understatement. The word coming to my mind is *tragic*.

If that is the case for individuals in the Bible, are we, as seniors, doing any better?

In this part of the book, our hope is that you are going to be challenged to take a good look in the mirror and ask yourself if you are becoming positioned for success in this season of your life.

In addition to chapters on the issues of spiritual, mental, physical, and emotional fitness, there are two chapters on dealing with personal loss and helping family members recover from it.

CHAPTER 30

RESILIENCE: THE KEY TO FINISHING STRONG

— Bob Dees —

What does finishing strong look like? I know. I know because I just spent time with Dr. John George. This man, a longtime professional and spiritual mentor to me and so many others, has humanly incurable cancer and is just beginning hospice care. When my wife, Kathleen, and I entered John's room, we found him seated in a chair with the familiar hospital table extending across his lap, praying over the worn lists of family and friends accumulated over many years of service to others. He showed us our names on that day's list. We shed a tear, certainly not the last on that meaningful visit to this godly man.

The once strong, athletic, and active military officer, ministry leader, college professor, father, and grandfather was now inhabiting a body ravaged by cancer and other ailments of age. Nevertheless, he radiated joy and peace that were greater than ever before. He spoke matter-of-factly about his preparations to die and with great enthusiasm about what God continued to reveal to him from the pages of his treasured Bible. In line with his life mission, John obviously continues to "set his heart to study the law of the LORD and to practice it, and to teach His statutes and ordinances in Israel [at Liberty University in his most recent venue of service]" (Ezra 7:10, NASB). Although I could add much more to this account, I think you get the point. Through the many inevitable storms of life, John has shown himself to be a resilient warrior, with his equally resilient wife, Judy, at his side. This is what finishing strong looks like!

For another example, consider God's servant Job. Soon after Satan smote Job with boils, Job's wife said to him, "Do you still hold fast your integrity? Curse God and die!" (Job 2:9, NASB).

Gratefully, Job chose the better of the two options; he held fast to his integrity throughout his ordeal, at one point declaring, "Though He slay me, I will hope in Him" (13:15, NASB).

This is the choice for each of us as we navigate the realities of growing older, diminishing vigor and health, and finite time left on earth. Will we hold fast to our integrity ("seamless integration of faith, family, and profession into a God-honoring life message"[1]) and finish strong? Or, will we become angry and bitter old men and women, eventually cursing God when we die? In 1916, Archibald Signorelli astutely observed, "We fall the way we lean."[2] May each of us ensure we are leaning in the right direction so that when we fall, we fall into the loving arms of family, friends, and Jesus.

In this vein, let me discuss some resilience principles that allow each of us to continue to grow through every adversity, run our race with endurance, and press through to the finish line of earthly life, leaning forward with optimism and anticipation to our very last breath.

---

[1] Robert F. Dees, *Resilient Leaders* (San Diego, CA: Creative Team Publishing, 2013), 107.

[2] Archibald Signorelli, *Plan of Creation, or Sword of Truth* (Chicago, IL: Charles H. Kerr & Company, 1916), 220.

FIRST THINGS FIRST

Willie Mays, the great all-star baseball player of yesteryear, was once asked by a sportswriter, "Why are you a great baseball player?" He simply replied something like, "When they throw it to me, I hit it. When they hit it to me, I catch it." Mays attributed his baseball prowess to the foundational basics of hitting and catching. So what are the resilience foundational basics that will allow each of us to finish strong? Let's start with Jesus.

> One of the scribes . . . asked Him, "What commandment is the foremost of all?" Jesus answered, "The foremost is, 'HEAR, O ISRAEL! THE LORD OUR GOD IS ONE LORD; AND YOU SHALL LOVE THE LORD YOUR GOD WITH ALL YOUR HEART [emotional], AND WITH ALL YOUR SOUL [spiritual], AND WITH ALL YOUR MIND [mental], AND WITH ALL YOUR STRENGTH [physical].' The second is this, 'YOU SHALL LOVE YOUR NEIGHBOR AS YOURSELF [relational].'" (Mark 12:28–31, NASB)

This Great Commandment is the foundation on which true resilience rests. In my book *Resilient Warriors*, I term this Comprehensive Personal Fitness (CPF)™, specifically referring to fitness in each domain identified in the Great Commandment: physical, mental, spiritual, emotional, and relational. Each of these elements, all critical factors in the resilience equation, will be addressed in subsequent chapters of this book.

BUILDING ON OUR RESILIENCE FOUNDATION

Although Comprehensive Personal Fitness™ is the essential foundation for personal resilience, there is another paradigm that helps us weather the storms of life, particularly as we grow older. This is called the Resilience Life Cycle©, pictured here.

RESILIENCE LIFE CYCLE©

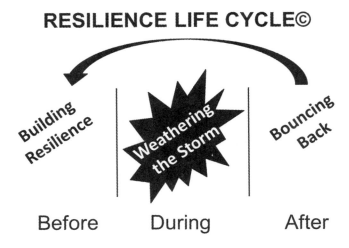

Before   During   After

I refer readers to the pages of *Resilient Warriors* for in-depth explanations and applications of this Resilience Life Cycle©, but a summary will be useful for our purposes here. It goes like this: Jesus said, "In the world you will have tribulation" (John 16:33, ESV). This is so true! We all get body-slammed by the many storms of life, whatever form they may take. Hence, it makes sense to do all we can to (1) prepare for these storms, including aging and our eventual death; (2) weather the storm, hiding under the shelter of God's wings until the destruction passes by (see Psalm 57:1); (3) bounce back from the storm without getting stuck in the toxic emotions of guilt, false guilt, anger, and bitterness; and (4) learn and grow through the adversity, recognizing that hurricane season comes around again and again. This process is represented by the before, during, after, and learn and adapt phases you see in the diagram above.

How does this model apply to aging? How does it help us live resiliently? How does it help us finish strong? Here are a few ideas you may not have considered:

1. **Continue to grow spiritually.** During the time I commanded the "Fighting Eagles" (First Battalion, Eighth

Infantry) at Fort Carson, Colorado, Dr. Jerry White, former Air Force major general and president emeritus of The Navigators, taught our Sunday school class at Pulpit Rock Church in Colorado Springs. After class one Sunday, we learned that his young adult son had been tragically murdered. Appearing back in class a few weeks later, he relayed his primary takeaway from the traumatic experience. He stated, "As we grow older, if we are growing spiritually, we grow in hope. If we do not continue to grow spiritually, we grow in bitterness."

I have found this to be very true. As the physical maladies of aging become more obvious and painful, it is easy to become cantankerous, critical, and bitter and even sink to despair. The spiritual "secret sauce" of personal relationship with Jesus is even more important in our later years as we fight to maintain our "vital optimism" and increase our knowledge and application of God's Word. Instead of the typical "organ recital" (continuous talk about the latest aches and pains) that becomes the fixation for many aging people, we must instead play a continuous organ of praise to God for His everlasting mercy and goodness. Such worship is the best possible medicine for the physical, mental, spiritual, emotional, and relational challenges we all face as we age. Continued spiritual growth is critical for being ready for the increasing challenges of aging, for maintaining hope, and for finishing strong!

2. **Understand your limits, and work within your gifts.** Following His resurrection, Christ told followers, "You will receive power when the Holy Spirit has come upon you; and you shall be My witnesses both in Jerusalem, and in all Judea and Samaria, and even to the remotest part of the earth" (Acts 1:8, NASB). Analogously, at the height of personal vigor, professional competence, and

ministry engagement, most men and women operate with a broad radius of action, frequently multitasking and operating well beyond their core gifts, even to the ends of the earth. As we grow older, we eventually start to lose a step or two, unable to operate competently with the same tempo, complexity, and radius of action. We have all encountered those who are not aging gracefully, who lose all their filters, who have increasing difficulty navigating personal relationships, or who experience "embarrassing moments" when attempting highly visible tasks (such as public speaking) that were easy in younger years. A key goal in this scenario is to not be the last to know, meaning to have sufficient self-awareness to understand your increasing limitations and begin to shrink your perimeter wisely around the core gifts God built into you for eternity. I have been greatly inspired by older folks in their eighties and nineties who operate with gracious and confident ease, knowing they are operating within their God-ordained limits and God-given gifts and purpose for their twilight seasons of life. This is also what finishing strong looks like!

3. **Recognize that your story is a link in the long legacy of God's story in you and others.** Sometimes getting older is accompanied by regret and disappointment for what was not accomplished. We must remember, however, that finishing strong does not mean we will get closure on all our life goals. Christian recording artist Michael O'Brien has a powerful song titled "And the Story Goes On," which includes the line "There's always a soldier to carry a cross." Most of the time, finishing strong means handing the baton, entrusting our life's legacy, to others who will "carry the cross." Mark Batterson, an inspiring author and pastor of the National Community Church, often reminds

us that our story is a part of God's divine story, a "story within a story." In biblical context, David aspired to build the temple in Jerusalem, yet it was Solomon who completed the task. Finishing strong includes the principle of legacy, "run[ning] with endurance the race that is *set before us*" (Hebrews 12:1, NASB), confident that many other God-honoring races and life stories will blossom from ours.

Let me conclude in prayer for each of us with the words of David from Psalm 71:

> Do not cast me off in the time of old age;
> Do not forsake me when my strength fails. . . .
> O God, You have taught me from my youth,
> And I still declare Your wondrous deeds.
> And even when I am old and gray, O God, do not forsake me,
> Until I declare Your strength to this generation,
> Your power to all who are to come. . . .
> You who have shown me many troubles and distresses
> Will revive me again. (verses 9, 17–18, 20, NASB)

May these truths be reality for each of us. May we be resilient warriors. May we finish strong!

GET TO KNOW THE AUTHOR:

Bob Dees is president of Resilience Consulting, following careers in the military, business, military ministry, academia, and most recently politics as Dr. Ben Carson's presidential campaign chairman. Bob and his wife, Kathleen, have two children and seven grandchildren. They are grateful for the privilege of serving God, our nation, and others during these critical times. www.ResilienceGodStyle.com.

CHAPTER 31

FAITH: THE PATH TO FINISHING STRONG

— Peggy Fulghum —

Faith is the assurance of things hoped for, the conviction of things not seen. (Hebrews 11:1, ESV)

My name is Peggy Fulghum. If you could hear me talk, you would probably pick up on the fact that I am a Southern girl—Atlanta, Georgia, to be exact. My mama and daddy moved here before I was born. Being from Minnesota and South Dakota, they spent one winter without snow and never went back. But we all thank the Lord for air conditioning every summer.

I am going to talk about faith as the path to finishing strong. I mean the kind of faith that Hebrews leader Joshua had when the Lord told him to cross the flooded Jordan River carrying the national treasure, the ark of the covenant, as the waters stood high above their heads—the kind of faith that Joshua had when the Lord told him to march his men and the ark of the covenant around the walls of Jericho in order to capture an impregnable walled city. How strong is your faith when you are confronted with a larger-than-life problem? How strong is your faith when it seems doors have closed?

"[I hope] that your faith might not rest on human wisdom, but on God's power" (1 Corinthians 2:5).

My dad was born in a house made of sod in the plains of South Dakota in 1918. His dad died a few months later in the 1919 flu epidemic. My grandmother gave up the homestead, left her baby with neighbors, and went to Minneapolis for a teaching job to financially support the baby. It was the Depression and people had to make many tough decisions, but one dream she never relinquished. She wanted her boy to go to college. She wanted him to be a self-made man. It was in college that he met my highly intellectual and beautiful mother and gave up a career in Hollywood to marry and start a family. My dad *was* a self-made man. Eventually, they moved their family of five to Atlanta, where he became an entrepreneur. They enlarged their family with two more girls. It was during this period that my parents changed from their Christian heritage to join the Unitarian fellowship.

> Don't let anyone look down on you because you are young, but set an example for the believers in speech, in conduct, in love, in faith and in purity. (1 Timothy 4:12)

At age seven, I visited church with a friend and knew immediately that I would reject Unitarian beliefs and belong to Christ. Because the family went to the Unitarian church every Sunday, I attended Christian camps and meetings at other times. I waited until I was married to be baptized and officially join a church. I began praying for my parents' salvation, but they remained entrenched in their Unitarian fellowship.

Faith can move mountains (see Matthew 17:20).

At the age of ninety, Mother died. After sixty-seven years of marriage, my dad was lonely. I was leading a mission trip to Bulgaria in two days and wanted to reassure him I would go to see him as soon as I returned. He told me, "Mom and I traveled the world, but we never went to Bulgaria. I would love to see Bulgaria." I heard a voice saying, "Take him." Frankly, I resisted. After all, he was ninety, our travel arrangements had been made months ago, and I was responsible for leading a group of ten older people. Really! The team was made up of people aged sixty to eighty-three. Nine people in my group had never been on a mission trip and were going to need a lot of hand holding. We were going to work in an orphanage of severely handicapped children. I couldn't possibly take my ninety-year-old Unitarian father, could I? "Please don't ask me to do this, Lord!" The prompting grew stronger, so I made a deal with God: "I will take him if the arrangements can be made and if my siblings agreed." Within thirty minutes, arrangements were made, my siblings thought it was a wonderful plan, and I was still in shock.

"Very truly I tell you, whoever believes in me will do the works I have been doing, and they will do even greater things than these, because I am going to the Father" (John 14:12).

But here is the thing. My dad was quite moved by the way our group loved and cared for these deformed babies and the physically and mentally handicapped children. Moreover, the way these precious, vulnerable children openly responded and embraced us completely overwhelmed him. Dad went out to rest on a bench in the yard and was joined by a couple of our teammates. Although these teammates were there to love the children, they were not experienced in evangelism. Instead of any formal presentation, they simply shared their faith from their hearts. It was there, sitting on a bench outside a Bulgarian orphanage, that my ninety-year-old father finally accepted Jesus Christ as his Savior!

> The righteous will flourish like a palm tree,
>> they will grow like a cedar of Lebanon;
> planted in the house of the LORD,
>> they will flourish in the courts of our God.

They will still bear fruit in old age,
    they will stay fresh and green. (Psalm 92:12–14)

Growing older is not an option, but *how* we age is. Perhaps the reason so many people dread growing older is the fear of the unknown. After all, we have experienced being younger, but the future and aging is scary. As the massive tsunami wave of baby boomers enters the next phase of life, there are lots of bold statements: "I will never retire. I will stay young and not become old like my grandparents! I will play golf every day. I am going to travel." I say, "Good for you!" Go boldly into this phase of life with hope and purpose. You should anticipate the myriad ways God will use you for His kingdom. Be as intentional in your faith as the priests who carried the holy ark of the covenant, the mobile throne of God, into the flooded Jordan River. Think how confident their faith was as they dipped their toes in and found the riverbed dry. Take your step of faith and grow strong like a tree planted in the court of God.

"We remember before our God and Father your work produced by faith, your labor prompted by love, and your endurance inspired by hope in our Lord Jesus Christ" (1 Thessalonians 1:3).

So what's next? Your faith is strong but you don't know what to do? First Thessalonians tell us that your labor is prompted by love. Think about what you love. Could your priorities be your children and grandchildren? Do you love to travel and see the world? Are you happiest on the golf course? Are you happiest when you use your spiritual gifts or the skills you acquired during your career? These are not bad things to love, as long as it is work produced by faith in Jesus Christ as Lord. When you do what you love, you are not doing it out of guilt or pressure. You endure because of the hope and love of Christ.

Assuming you follow the Great Commandment of loving the Lord with all your heart, soul, and mind, then you fulfill the second Great Commandment of loving your neighbor as you love yourself. That means you will love others even if they are not Christ followers. You love the unloved and even the unlovable because Jesus loved us all the way to the cross. Because you love the Lord with all your heart, soul, and mind, you will put aside your comfort zone and take a step of faith to follow the Great Commission sharing the good news. Will you fulfill the Great Commission next door, across town, across your state, across your nation, or to the uttermost parts of the earth?

You love golf? Fulfill the Great Commandment and Great Commission by organizing golf games between believers and unbelievers for the intentional purpose of sharing the love of Jesus. You love to travel? Take a group of believers to do missional work such as building houses in Nicaragua while you proclaim the gospel, assist with providing medical care for refugees from persecution, or take school supplies to an impoverished school in your own town. The list of missional opportunities is endless.

"As for me and my house, we will serve the LORD" (Joshua 24:15, ESV).

You love your family? Then make sure they know your God stories. Be intentional as you tell them how He has worked in your life. Follow the example of Joshua and build a monument of what God has done so your children and children's children will ask about it. It is your family legacy for nephews, nieces, cousins, those yet to be born, and future and unknown spouses of your children and children's children. Pray for them and let them know that you have prayed over them. Make a video or write letters to each member of your family and those to come. The list of ideas is endless to ensure that the legacy of faith lives on.

"Faith comes from hearing the message, and the message is heard through the word about Christ" (Romans 10:17).

Look, we will age differently. Some will age through frail bodies, but they can still pray. Some may grow old socially and be totally baffled by modern technology, but they can still write. Others may age through loss of memory but trust their loved ones to remember for them. Consider these words: "The testing of your faith produces perseverance" (James 1:3) and "Who is it that overcomes the world? Only the one who believes that Jesus is the Son of God" (1 John 5:5). You can share your faith at any age and bring honor to the Lord your God. Following God's Great Commandment and Great Commission is finishing well in God's eyes. That is my prayer for you.

GET TO KNOW THE AUTHOR:

Peggy Fulghum, minister to baby boomers to building generations at Johnson Ferry Baptist Church in Marietta, Georgia. She began her ministry career after being a stay-at-home mom and being involved in numerous community services. After ten years of ministry, Peggy earned her master of divinity degree from New Orleans Baptist Theological Seminary. At the age of sixty-six, she is completing her doctoral dissertation and plans to graduate in spring of 2018. Her future plans are to "finish well."

CHAPTER 32

INTELLECTUALLY: YOU ARE NEVER TOO OLD TO LEARN

-- Russ Counts --

Is learning fun? That is exactly what we all want it to be. I can remember back in school, there were classes that made learning fun. What made it fun? Some would say it was the teacher. Others would say it was the environment. Still others say it was a relationship with like-minded people or instructors. What I do remember is that I had to like what I was learning for it to be fun. Then there were the other classes, the ones that were not so fun. However, even though they were not as fun, they were important for my life. Learning comes in many forms. Sometimes it is fun. Sometimes it is a struggle. At times it can be forced on us, and other times we get to choose what we want to learn. As we get older, we begin to glean from our learning and begin to call it wisdom. However, through the years, one thing will always remain: learning is a part of life.

There is a phrase in the professional world that holds many professions in line. It is called continuing education. In career professions such as dentistry, finance, health care, insurance, and law, just to mention a few, education is part of a yearly routine. It is this ongoing learning that helps these people remain on the cutting edge of their fields. Continuing education ensures they stay relevant and current.

As a pastor and head football coach, I look to learn new things that will help me be a better pastor and coach. I do this by reading, going to conferences, collaborating with other people, watching videos, and listening to audio teaching. We all live in a world that is in many ways powered by learning. Therefore, I want to get a more hands-on view of learning from the perspective of those I learn from and glean from their knowledge and wisdom.

To do this, I pulled together a group of influencers. They range from all walks of life: a pastor, a college math professor, an independent business owner, a schoolteacher, a stay-at-home mother now grandmother, and an active leader in a retirement community. My goal was to hear their stories and ask them what learning at their stage of life is really like. Also, I want find out what motivates these amazing people to learn new things. In the following pages, you will experience the candid authenticity of real-life learning at any age.

I sat down with Sue. She lived her life as a stay-at-home mom and now is in her late sixties. Within the past year, she and her husband bought Fitbits. These modern pieces of technology would make many nervous, but not Sue. I asked her for her reasoning for the Fitbits. Sue provided me with a great answer. She said she knew that she and her husband had been slowing down over the years. The Fitbits provided a great way to get a benchmark. This way they could learn to use technology to find out where they stood physically and where they needed to get to so they could enjoy one of their true passions, which was traveling.

Sue went on to explain that at times, learning is very hard, even painful at times. She said, "I don't go out looking for new things to learn, but I do look for ways to increase what I already know." I asked Sue to go a little deeper with that statement. Here is what she said. "At my age, I am forgetting what I once knew. I am learning to stay focused on what I enjoy in my life, and I work to stay relevant in those areas and make them better."

Several years ago, I walked into a college classroom and met my math professor, Gene. He is a driven man who starts and finishes strong. A few years back, he retired from teaching and became involved in a club of people who played the card game bridge. Gene had played the game years ago when he was in college, and he wanted to rekindle that enjoyment. He could have just started back up, but he didn't. He sought out a teacher to show him how to play the game and play it in a very competitive way. Gene thrives on competition. He wanted to learn the game at a deeper level, and I asked Gene why that was important to him. He said, "If I'm going to play these guys in club tournaments, I need to learn from the best to beat the best." He is an amazing teacher. He told me that the best way he learns is when he gets the opportunity to teach someone. Three years ago, Gene took me out to a gun club. He had become a member of this gun club for shooting skeet. He began teaching me all he had learned. He did a great job, because I fell in love with skeet and still love to go shoot when I get a chance. Gene said to me, "I learn from books and collaborating with other people because whatever I do, I want to do it to the best of my ability." For Gene, learning is about bettering himself and honing his skills.

This next couple I am introducing to you are Rob and Peggy. They have been very involved in many lives for years as marriage counselors. Rob has run an independent business in food safety, and Peggy has served on several different statewide boards. When Rob decided it was time to slow down his business, they packed up and moved to a retirement city in Phoenix, Arizona. Although he was slowing down his business, as a couple, they were not slowing down at all. Rob and Peggy are difference makers. They are incredible at learning about an environment and finding where their gifts and talents can be used. Rob is now serving in the government side of his new city. I asked him what that transition is like. He answered, "It is an ongoing learning event." Rob now works in a very high level of government within his city and continues to learn more about the departments a city has, including police, buildings, personnel, and collaboration with the neighboring cities. It is challenging for him, but he thrives on making a difference. Peggy jumped right in and is now holding a prominent position with all the clubs and recreation centers. This is a huge responsibility for Peggy due to the massive area this city occupies. I asked Rob and Peggy why they were so eager to jump right into their new community. Why didn't they wait a while and feel their way through things and then start helping? They both agreed that learning should be an experience much like on-the-job training. Rob said, "At my age, I get to pick what I want to do and what I want to learn about." Peggy is a social butterfly, and her learning comes from being around people—lots of people and as often as possible. People stimulate her and increase her learning power. Rob loves the challenge; it's what spurs him on. He summed it up by saying that he wanted to make sure that where he lived would be where he wanted to live as he aged. He also made it clear that learning all they could and being involved helped them feel safer for their future.

The final couple I will introduce to you, and I am very honored to do so, is my mom and dad. Bob and Kaye Counts are the most influential lifelong learners I know. We have all heard people say the phrase "They have great work ethic." Well, my parents have that too. However, what I want you to hear from them is their desire to continue to learn throughout their lives. My parents are both in their seventies. My dad is a pastor and has been for more than fifty years. He loves to read. He reads to learn and for fun. He reads deep theological books and also books about birds and wildlife. I asked my dad why it is so important for him to continue to push himself to learn new things. His answer was a bit blunt: "If I stop learning, I will start dying." My father lives by the motto that active learning strengthens the brain as a muscle. Just as he works out his body by walking, he must also work out his mind. As my dad told me, "I want to finish strong." I then asked him what his most exciting and most challenging things are to learn at his age. His answer was the same to both parts of my question. His answer was technology. He said he loves learning about technology but that it can be very frustrating for him. A few years ago, he got a smartphone. One night I received a text from my dad wishing us good night. It shocked me. I really didn't know he knew how to text. Since that night, there have been only a few times that the nightly text has not come through, and it's been three years now. My dad desired to learn how to text to stay in communication with his family. Family is very important to him, and he is using the very thing that frustrates him the most to learn how to stay connected with all of us no matter where we are.

My mom is also a lifelong learner. Ever since I can remember, she has been a student of vitamins and natural health. I asked her what motivates her to constantly learn about vitamins. She told me that she enjoys learning about ways to enhance her life physically because keeping her body healthy helps her minister to people. My mom recently started a ministry to widows. It came to her from a verse in Proverbs 15:25, "The LORD will tear down the house of the proud, but He will establish the boundary of the widow" (NASB). My mom thought back to her mom. When her mom would plant a vegetable garden, she always planted a border around the garden with flowers. My mom learned from her mom and now uses this same idea this to help border widows. My mom and the widows meet once a month at a restaurant, at a home, or at the church. They are learning from each other. My mom began to give some examples of things that are very frightening for some widows. The reason they are frightening is that the widows are forced to learn things they have known nothing of. Some of them had to learn how to put gas in their cars. Some had never used an ATM. Some found it scary to seek help for things that needed to be fixed around the home. This forced learning curve happens because their spouses had always been there and taken care of these things and now they are gone. The ministry my mom is doing is helping these widows learn from each other and stick together.

I asked my mom if becoming a grandmother has caused her to learn some new things. She said that, yes, it had. It had taught her to be more loving, active, and understanding. She left me with this golden nugget that I will share with you. She said, "When I raised you, I was focused on putting you and keeping you on the right track. As a grandma, I am focused on adding to my grandkids' lives as they move down their tracks." She said that the transition to grandmother is a learning curve but one she is committed to overcoming each day.

"Walk worthy of the Lord, fully pleasing Him, being fruitful in every good work and increasing in the knowledge of God" (Colossians 1:10, NKJV). As a pastor, I believe that learning the Word of God helps rejuvenate the mind and that learning about the grace, mercy, love, and power of God will enhance our lives. "The things which you learned and received and heard and saw in me, these do, and the God of peace will be with you" (Philippians 4:9, NKJV). The Word also tells us to learn from others and be active in our learning, which keeps us sharp.

The amazing mentors in my life continue to be lifelong learners at any age. I need these people because they teach me. I desire to be like these mentors in the coming years. Keep on learning. Learn things to enhance what you do and what you know. Learn to be active. Learn to strengthen your mind. Learn to finish strong.

GET TO KNOW THE AUTHOR:

Russ Counts is the senior pastor of Foundation Baptist Church in Clovis, California, and the head football coach at Fresno Christian School in Fresno, California. He has been married to Angie for twenty-eight years and they have two children, Celeste and Annabelle. Russ's passion is to inspire people to live their lives to the fullest, invest in others, serve the Lord, and give Him praise.

CHAPTER 33

PHYSICALLY: GOD MADE IT, YOU MAINTAIN IT!

— Toby Quirk —

Hi guys, I'm Toby Quirk, and I'm here to tell you to get your big butt off that La-Z-Boy recliner and get your marvelous machine into shape.

Sometimes you Christian guys amaze me. Not in a good way either. I'm talking about the slick excuses you come up with that keep you from enjoying the deeper call of our Lord. I've talked with hundreds of sincere disciples who dance all around God's clear instructions about the importance of keeping their bodies in good working order. I wondered how they could have missed all God's very pointed commands about body maintenance, but then I looked back at myself when I retired from twenty-three years in the infantry. I had slipped into the lazy lifestyle of the typical middle-aged American male. So I totally understand where those chubby couch potatoes are at.

You all know, without a doubt, that God wants you to be strong and healthy, and you know darn well how to get that way. So why don't you step up? You guessed right. You lack motivation.

Look at me. I'm genetically predisposed toward plumpness. I'm five foot seven, wide bodied, and addicted to stuff like brownies and ice cream. My two nicknames as a West Point plebe were "The Rotund One" and "Stuff Gut." The severe discipline at the Academy, the physical demands of Airborne School, and the rigors of Ranger School reprogrammed my brain from chunky high school teenybopper to hard-bodied infantryman. I stayed pretty much in that warrior mode until I retired in 1993 at the ripe young age of forty-five, all systems still operating at a pretty high level.

When I retired, my wife, Linda, and I followed God's call into pastoral ministry in New England. Gradually, without all the external stimuli from Uncle Sammy, I let my body bloat up from a lean 175 pounds to a portly 220. I had to get bigger jeans and T-shirts. I made countless unsuccessful starts to regain some modicum of self-control, but they all were dead-end roads.

Then something powerful happened to me, and this powerful experience is what you need to energize your motivation. God has a way of changing your "want-to." My powerful, supernatural encounter with His truth not only caused me to start working out again but also reprogrammed my heart and caused me to *want to* get in shape. Today I love exercising and can't wait to challenge my body with a good high-intensity workout.

Here's what happened. In my hypersensitive spiritual state, the love of Jesus washed over me, beckoning me to respond with the best of my love. "'Love the Lord your God with all your heart and with all your soul and with all your strength and with all your mind'; and, 'Love your neighbor as yourself'" (Luke 10:27). I realized that I may have been responding to Jesus with my heart, soul, and mind, but I wasn't loving Him with all my strength. I had neglected to maintain His marvelous creation: my body.

So this fifty-three-year-old butterball intensified his love for our amazing Savior, and He reenergized my heart, soul, strength, and mind. Gradually and consistently, Coach Jesus encouraged me to enjoy His physical training regimen. Within a few years, I was doing 10K runs and finishing sprint triathlons. Today, sixteen years later, I'm still working out, feeling great, and loving my Lord with all my strength as well as my heart, soul, and mind.

God has invited me to speak at men's conferences and meetings. I tell guys about the inextricable bond between physical training and spiritual training. They've been responding with excitement and enthusiasm. I tell them, "If you're over thirty-eight years old, welcome to the second half. This is no time to slow down. That soft flab hanging over your belt is not a sign of maturity or wisdom. It's a sign that you have forgotten all the good stuff in Psalm 139:

> You created my inmost being;
>> you knit me together in my mother's womb.
> I praise you because I am fearfully and wonderfully made;
>> your works are wonderful,
>> I know that full well.
> My frame was not hidden from you
>> when I was made in the secret place,
>> when I was woven together in the depths of the earth.
> Your eyes saw my unformed body;
>> all the days ordained for me were written in your book
>> before one of them came to be. (verses 13–16)

"Step outside your body for a minute. Check it out. Your Father formed that amazing machine with love in His hands. When He designed your physical frame, He did it right. God is thrilled with that creation called 'You.' You are the product of God's love, so doesn't it make sense that you would respond to your Father's love with all your love?"

See where I'm coming from? I'm talking about motivation,

guys. It's not about how great you want to look with those rock-hard abs you see on the covers of men's fitness magazines. It's not about being able to bench-press three hundred pounds and run ten miles. It's not even about getting really healthy. The deepest level of your motivation for becoming physically fit is your loving response to your Father's unfailing love for you. "Love the Lord with all your strength."

There are a bucketful of benefits for improving your fitness. Your energy level ramps up. You can move better: bending, lifting, walking, climbing stairs, pretty much all the everyday activities get much easier. Your heart and lungs get stronger, so every cell in your marvelous machine gets more oxygen and nutrition, which is what cells crave. Even your brain cells get more good stuff, so you can think better. Your confidence improves because you know you have more strength and look better.

Now, here's the big one: when you're maintaining your body at a healthy level, God can use you the way He wants to. You are more valuable to your family. Your kids and grandkids get to enjoy the dad and granddad they love. Your strong, active body is capable of loving the Lord and your neighbors, thereby building up the kingdom and accomplishing His divine mission. When you let yourself get out of shape, you limit how God can use you. When you reach a high level of fitness, you remove the limits.

Okay, I'll finish up this little epistle with a quick picture of how my new-and-improved model is serving the kingdom. The grace of God has imbued me with the desire to get in shape and stay in shape. As a result, I'm able to be a fire chaplain and chaplain to the Soldiers' Home in Massachusetts, represent Jesus Christ. Both ministries require some level of physical fitness. My wife, my two grown children, and my grandchildren aren't burdened with worry about me; rather, they are having fun with me in all kinds of activities, like swimming, sailing, canoeing, and outdoor games.

Yesterday I hauled a bunch of groceries up the stairs to my

neighbor's apartment. I'm helping another neighbor with his move to Florida. When I speak in front of a group, my body is a testament to God's power to heal and sustain a man who's nearing seventy years old. All those benefits of being fit are great, but more than that, I know that I'm responding to my Father's abounding love for me by loving Him with all my heart, soul, strength, and mind. The only reason I am able to maintain this strong healthy body is by God's amazing grace. All the credit, all the honor, all the glory belongs to God in Jesus Christ.

GET TO KNOW THE AUTHOR:

Reverend Toby Quirk is the chaplain at the Soldiers' Home in Chelsea, Massachusetts, and fire chaplain for the city of Saugus. He is an adjunct professor at Wentworth Institute of Technology in Boston. After twenty-three years in the US Army, he received his ordination in the Assemblies of God and served as senior pastor of two churches in western Massachusetts. He and his wife, Linda, live in Nahant, Massachusetts and have two grown children and two grandsons.

CHAPTER 34

OVERCOMING OUR LOSS

— Cathy Erickson —

According to the dictionary, *loss* means "the fact or process of losing something or someone" and the feeling of grief after losing someone or something of value."[1] When you lose something of value, there is a process of recovery. I would like to use some of my experiences to prepare you to deal with future losses and, if you are walking through a loss, help guide you to the light at the end of the tunnel.

There are all kinds of loss. You might lose your keys or your car in the Walmart parking lot. Maybe you have lost a treasured memento. All of these are legitimate losses that can bring sadness. In this chapter, I would like to explore loss and specifically loss of a valuable person in your life. Have you ever had a loss so deep down and gut wrenching that you felt as if you couldn't breathe?

My gut-wrenching experience began in July 2016, when Dan, my husband of forty-five years, was diagnosed with ALS or Lou Gehrig's disease. He and I had spent our lives in ministry helping people find hope. This diagnosis was quite a shock to both of us. I reacted with tears when the doctor gave us the news. Dan, on the

---

[1] *English Oxford Dictionary Online*, s.v. "loss," https://en.oxforddictionaries.com/definition/loss.

other hand, said to the doctor, "My hope is built on nothing less than Jesus Christ." Amazingly, he carried this attitude every day.

At first there were small changes in Dan's life, beginning with the loss of use of his right hand, which made it hard to write, eat, and do a lot of things we don't realize we need our hands for. Eventually, the losses became more profound. It was the loss of his ability to drive that was a huge transition for both of us. I became the driver and he always wanted to help me! He had some loss of memory and couldn't share memories of our past life together. One day he shared that he didn't feel he could continue to do the thing God had given him to do: speak to men about their relationships with God, family, and friends. I remember falling on the floor crying when I was alone. Dan began to drift away every day, as he was unable to communicate in the way he normally did. Before these losses, his personality was always like a bright light shining wherever he went. Let's just say, if he was in a room, you knew it.

On March 13, 2017, Dan graduated to heaven, and his light went out here on earth. I lost a huge piece of myself. When we were married, we became one, and when Dan took his last breath, I felt that half of me was gone.

If you have experienced this, you realize the days are lonely and the nights unbearable. Waking up first thing in the morning, you once more face your loss and have to deal with it all over again. Some days, memories flood your mind like that old Kodak commercial, "Times of your Life" when Paul Anka sang, "The memories are time that you borrow to spend when you get to tomorrow." Your brain has taken pictures of your life, and a song, a place, or even a scent brings you right back to those moments.

I spent the first days of loss in a fog of shock. I was alone at my house, and it was quiet and unpleasant. After a time of solitude, I chose to see old friends. It was hard, but it helped to just talk about normal things.

After a few months, a light came on and I repeated something my husband had often said: "Good morning, God. What are You doing? Can I join You?" Basically, I was asking if I could do something for Him, even just a little thing for someone else. If you are experiencing a loss or know someone who is, it would help so much to get involved in your church or community or send a card to someone to encourage him or her. When you go out, just say hello to someone and smile. You will be surprised how doing this will make you feel.

I am definitely not saying I am over the loss of the love of my life, but I can get out of bed and complete tasks I need to do. Although it seems I move slower and tasks that could be completed in a day now take a week or more, I keep doing the thing in front of me.

When dealing with loss and grief, you must realize that it is a journey, not just a onetime event. Read that again. It is a journey. It's not over after the memorial service or when you pass through the first month they are gone or the first holidays without them. My mom and dad died years ago, and I am still sad when I think of them, wishing I could talk to them. It is at times like that when we must remember the journey.

Sometimes you might feel that your situation is unfair and you wish it would just be done and over so you can go on with your life, but we must be patient with ourselves. Some days you might feel as though you can't even pray, but God knows your heart.

I heard someone say, "Grief is like a child. Sometimes you might not even hear your child as they play in his room. Then all of a sudden, he is right beside you crying and wanting attention." Your loss can go hours without affecting you, and then it's in your face, calling to be noticed. Sometimes you may have to tuck feelings away for a short time, but when you can, let them out. A friend said that when those feelings overcame her, she gave herself a certain amount of time and then went on. Stuffing feelings is unhealthy and can cause problems later in life. Even Jesus wept when He went to see his dear friend Lazarus, who was dead (see John 11:35).

Always remember, "The Lord is close to the brokenhearted and saves those who are crushed in spirit" (Psalm 34:18).

What advice can I give on experiencing a loss?

1. Know God, and more than just His name. Lean into Him. Fall in love with Him. If I didn't have this, I would probably be an angry, self-absorbed person. He wakes me up in the morning, and though I try to avoid doing so, I get out of bed.
2. Have a family, and not just relatives, but people who know you and who you love deeply. You will need them on your journey of loss. If you have bridges that need to be mended with people, repair them now!
3. Be thankful as often as possible. I am so thankful for all the people in my life, where I live, my church, and especially my family. It is hard to be thankful and angry at the same time.
4. Be part of a fellowship with people who can encourage you, not criticize you. Don't just drop in when you feel like it; get involved. When you are ready, use the gifts God has given you. Join a small group or a Bible study. Don't retire; refire!

I've always heard that I should lean into the Lord, and I often wondered what that really meant. Now I know it's Him being your everything, realizing that He understands better than any person here on earth. He knows and cares exactly where you are. In the night or in the morning, He is there. In a crowd, when you feel totally alone, He is there. He is there if you don't feel you can take another step. He knows that life will go on even though you don't know what it is going to look like. He is there! "My flesh and my heart may fail, but God is the strength of my heart and my portion forever" (Psalm 73:26).

God wants us to walk alongside those with losses, and sometimes that is very hard because grieving people often don't know what they need or want. Don't expect them to call and request help. Ask them if they would like to have coffee or go for a walk. Let them talk freely, and encourage them in their small strides, even though it might be repetitious sometimes. Give a piece of yourself to them, but give advice only if it is asked for.

If you don't know them well, send cards or e-mails. When they come to your mind, send your message right then because life is busy and you will forget to do it later.

Pray for them. It is the best thing you can do. Anyone can do this!

GET TO KNOW THE AUTHOR:

Cathy Erickson's greatest passion is her relationships with her two children and seven grandchildren. She loves to mentor and encourage others. She is a mentor for Real Moms of Preschoolers, started a ministry to single mother families, and is a chief servant leader of People Matter Ministries. For the next chapter of her life, she plans to write, travel, spend time with her grandchildren, and encourage others to find hope.

CHAPTER 35

HELPING OUR FAMILY OVERCOME OUR LOSS

— Ross Holtz —

"It's bad. It isn't pneumonia, it's cancer, and it's in a late stage." How does a Christian husband of forty-nine years respond to hearing those words about his wife? Indeed, how does he, who has shepherded so many other families through this, now shepherd *his* family?

Many times while doing premarital counseling, I thought about the fact that if these young people do it right, if the marriage goes the distance, one of them is going to say goodbye to the other. Now I and my family were faced with this reality. I have walked this pain-filled path hundreds of times with friends and parishioners, but this was different. I was no longer a spectator. This was up close and personal.

We were starting to plan our fiftieth anniversary. We were going to go to Europe, her lifelong dream. But now, according to the oncologist, this was all coming to an end, quickly. We did all we knew to do to postpone the inevitable, and 126 days later, she stepped into Jesus's arms.

If You Passed Your Baton . . . Take It Back

I have heard pastor and radio preacher Chuck Swindoll say that life happens while we are making plans. After more than forty years of shepherding, I know that most of it is done without a blueprint, no plan. Often, it is a matter of responding to crisis situations the best we can. It's like in the case of David in the Bible. He talks about having to defend the flock from wild animals. He didn't know when it was going to happen, but he knew the potential and prepared for that possibility. When it happened, he reacted instinctively to protect his sheep.

We have scriptural instructions and examples for dealing with grief and loss, but applying them is often a seat-of-the-pants kind of thing. Of course, I knew the possibility of one of us becoming sick as we were getting older. But when it came, I didn't have a set of steps to follow. I had to rely on what God had taught me over the years about dealing with loss in the lives of people I cared for.

I can't give you steps to take. I can tell you what I did, what we did, and offer that as a help. Maybe you will remember some of this if and when you are faced with such loss.

I PRAYED.

While Cathy was sick, I prayed for her healing. I don't think my prayer life was ever as active before this. I believe in healing, and I believe we can ask for it. But God doesn't always heal physically. I prayed believing He could. I prayed hoping He would. After Cathy passed, I prayed about what God was going to do in and among us as a family. I prayed that her gain, being given access to heaven itself, would become our praise. I prayed that the pain would not leave wounds that wouldn't heal or scars that would become stumbling blocks.

I LISTENED.

As a pastor and counselor, I have been taught to listen, and as an introvert, it comes somewhat naturally. I know the steps of grief:

248

denial, anger, bargaining, depression, and acceptance. It was not intentional but instinctive for me to watch for these steps in myself and in my family members. In the months after Cathy's passing, my home became a gathering place for the family. The conversations would often start down a mundane path and then become about Cathy or some situation she was in. I listened. When there were several members there, the stories were generally about some funny thing that was said or done. Often a humorous anecdote would remind someone of a serious or sad story, and there would be tears.

At times, one of the grief stages would appear. There was little denying at this point, and the time for bargaining had passed, but anger and depression would show in some of the recollections. I listened. There were times when I felt angry and depressed and others in the family heard. They were listening too. Although I was the paterfamilias, I was suffering too.

Listening and hearing became an integral part of the family-shepherding process. If I was not paying attention—and that did happen once or twice—important information about someone's feelings would be missed, and opportunities for ministering to people important to me would be missed. The experts say that listening is the most important part of communication, and most of us know this from hard lessons. And in dealing with grief and loss, it is critical that we hear the other person accurately before we speak. The Bible concurs: "My dear brothers and sisters, take note of this: Everyone should be quick to listen, slow to speak and slow to become angry" (James 1:19).

I TALKED.

My family is rather large. I have three sons, one daughter, three daughters-in-law, three grandsons, and three granddaughters. I am blessed to have a family who like each other and live close to me. During Cathy's brief illness, we were together often. Although I am a preacher by calling and vocation, I have seldom felt it necessary to "preach" to my family. A time of crisis, tragedy, and loss is really not the time to preach. Talk, yes; preach, no. Talk to, not talk at. I found that my words during this time could be highly charged and that those I was talking with had highly charged hearing. After a couple of instances of poorly chosen words and phrases that caused unintended reactions, I chose to be very careful in my choices of topics and opinions. My words needed to be pain and stress relieving; they needed to be encouraging and healing.

One episode comes to mind. One of my sons asked, "Why would God take Mom when there are so many bad people He allows to live?" In the moment, I took it to be a real question and gave him the answers that I know. I said, "Isaiah says that sometimes good people are taken to spare them evil that is to come" (see Isaiah 57:1). And I added, "We live in a fallen world where, from the time of the fall of man, bad things happen to good people." Well, when I came to my right mind, I realized that my son's question was rhetorical. He was expressing his anger toward God, a natural part of grief. Again, in the moment, I missed that and tried to use reason and logic to address his pain. Wrong. He knew all the answers, but he was mad about what God was doing. He needed to work that out with God as he healed. It was not my place to remediate his pain. My place was to listen and guide him back to God, who is the only one who heals pain.

When I used scriptural passages or pastoral injunctions, if they weren't lived out solidly in my own life, the reaction could be swift and direct. My family are all believers, but there were strong feelings about God's love with some of the members. They were not at all open to clichés and pat phrases.

WE SHARED.

After Cathy died, we were together even more. I didn't have to initiate conversations about the struggles we were all feeling; they just happened. Sometimes we could talk about the pain in groups, like group therapy. Sometimes the deeper feelings of anger and depression were left for me to speak to in more intimate settings. But we talked and talked and talked. Everything was on the table. There were even times when we talked about conflicts each of us had with Cathy, pain-filled memories that needed to surface and be talked about to heal. Things that could have, or should have, been resolved when she was alive needed to be addressed for inner peace.

But mostly, we talked about our love for her and our sorrow at her passing. The family wanted to hear, or re-hear, old stories of her past and our past. Now they wanted to hear about her youth and her likes and dislikes that up until then were sort of ignored. I talked. I told them all that I knew about her and about untold parts of her life. Sometimes we laughed and sometimes we cried, but we were celebrating her and, in our way, praising God for being a part of her life.

WE GREW STRONGER.

I would be remiss if I didn't add that often throughout the healing process, it was not I who led but one of the other family members. As my family matures, I find myself more a player coach than pastor, or maybe that is the best description of a pastor. I felt blessed to see others take up the leadership and shepherd the clan. And there were times that the group took up the mantle and ministered to me. Our loss was communal. I lost a wife; they lost a mother and grandmother. The feelings of our loss were different but shared. It's been said that facing adversity together produces a bond. The together part is integral. From the day the diagnosis was made, I knew that my most important task would be to keep us together, praying, listening, and sharing our sorrow. It has now been four years. We are still healing. We are still together, maybe tighter than ever. God is good.

GET TO KNOW THE AUTHOR:

Ross Holtz—founding and senior pastor of The Summit Church (EFCA) in Enumclaw, Washington—was named "Pastor of The Year" in 2014 by the National Coalition of Ministries to Men. He is the author of *Are You in the Game or in the Way? A Question for Pastors and Men's Ministry Leaders* and wrote a chapter in the NCMM's new anthology *How To Disciple Men*. Ross and his wife, Athena, have a blended family of eight adult children and seventeen grandchildren.

FOR PERSONAL REFLECTION OR GROUP DISCUSSION

- What will it look like to shrink your perimeter? When do you think that will make sense for you?
- When did you demonstrate resilience in the face of adversity? What did you learn from the experience? How are you getting ready for the next storm of life?
- Have you ever walked with other people through their loss? What did you learn?
- Have you lost a family member to death? What did God teach you through it?
- Why is it important for a disciple of Jesus Christ to maintain a consistent regimen of physical fitness?
- What can you do to improve your level of physical fitness?

WHERE DO WE GO FROM HERE?

PART 8

WHERE DO WE GO FROM HERE?

What to Expect

Each chapter in part 8 is meant to help you come to a place of action. This book was never meant to be merely *informational* or even *inspirational*. It is designed to be transformational.

If what we have presented is nothing more than "good reading," we have failed.

The chapters in this part are to encourage you to get started. Although that is clearly a theme throughout this entire book, this part is meant to push you over the line and get going.

Each of the authors will encourage you from a different perspective. Pull key points from their chapters to get you to your starting line.

CHAPTER 36

THE STARTING LINE IS TODAY

— Jeff Baxter —

None of us knows when our time on earth is coming to a close, but you are in a unique position of knowing you have less time on earth to make the greatest kingdom impact. Why not make it count for eternity? The starting line of your life is today! You might be tempted to cash in your chips, throw in the towel, or say your goodbyes, allowing the coming generations to take over. Do not give in to this temptation. The Bible does not talk about a retirement plan; it talks of planning wisely and making your days count. God never had in mind for us to coast into heaven. Today you might have some limitations, but this does not give any of us permission to stop advancing the kingdom for God's glory.

Stay in the game. We need you!

Your life is God's good gift to you. No matter how difficult your circumstances, your life has far more potential even today than you have ever realized. As long as you have breath, your life has only begun. In front of you is a great opportunity. It is yours to spend. No matter what your age, now is the time to plan and expand. You might be up in age (depending on who is asking), but your daily choices still have eternal consequences. You must choose wisely how you are going to spend your time. Jesus still came to give you abundant life today (see John 10:10). God still has plans for you to prosper with a hope and a future (see Jeremiah 29:11). God is still measuring your life, words, thoughts, secrets, motives, tears, hopes and dreams.[1]

I have a friend named Dan who is ninety-one years old. He has lived a full life building his successful business and enjoying his family and hobbies. Dan could be tempted to check out of this life, looking to the next life, especially because his wife of many decades passed away last year, but he has chosen to stay engaged. His physical health is failing, but he is choosing not to let that distract him. His time is not up yet. He attends our church every week, making his way up the ramp through the door with his walking cane guiding his every step. He arrives with a smile on his face, a cheerful greeting, and determination to figure out what Jesus has for him that day. Dan has decided to stay in the game.

My friend Barbara is seventy-eight years old. She lives in a retirement community across the street from our church. With enthusiasm and plenty of questions, she arrives at our Bible study each week. She has loved Jesus for many years and has not stopped learning. She loves to explore what it means to live for Jesus daily. Barbara starts conversations with the residents each week around coffee, at the dinner table, or at a social event. She loves to turn the communication to spiritual things, helping anyone think about becoming a follower of Jesus. Barbara has decided to stay in the game.

I pray that you decide to stay in the game too.

There are a few things I'd like to encourage you to do in order to keep growing to love God and love people as you advance His kingdom in these mature years. Would you consider proactively going for it today?

---

[1] All of the areas mentioned are measured by God (see Psalm 19:14; 94:11; 139:2; Proverbs 15:26; Ecclesiastes 12:14; Isaiah 55:7; Malachi 3:16; Matthew 12:36–37; Romans 2:16; 14:10–12; 1 Corinthians 3:11–15; 2 Corinthians 5:10; 1 Peter 4:5; Revelation 5:8; 8:3–4).

LIVE JOYFULLY.

First, live joyfully! Possibly the most attractive attribute about a person who is getting up in years is their joy. The second fruit of the Spirit is joy (see Galatians 5:22). Joy is the most evident and most powerful witness to the Holy Spirit's fullness in others' lives. You can see it in their eyes. Next to love, joy is contagious. New Testament Christianity is life-transforming joy. A person pursuing holy living is a rejoicing person. Heaven will be full of joy as we worship Jesus forever. Why not take it on during this season of your life? It would be tempting to be bitter, angry, or regretful looking back, but don't give in to this temptation. Look forward today with joy.

Happiness is a fleeting feeling, but joy can be permanent. Happiness tends to be dependent on circumstances. This is part of our character. A habit of grumbling and complaining tells us something about our spiritual lives in Christ. Look at the Spirit's work in your life by the deep abiding joy regardless of life's circumstances.

When Jesus was sent to earth by his Father in heaven, He had a mission. It was clear! Jesus was to seek and save the lost, but that was not all. Not only was Jesus to preach good news to the poor and freedom to the captives and bring light to the darkness, He was also "to bestow on them a crown of beauty . . . the oil of joy . . . and a garment of praise" (Isaiah 61:3). That is a mouthful. Jesus was full of gladness and came to fill our hearts with joy that runs over onto everyone else. Take a look at your life. Does the joy of the Holy Spirit fill you up to the point of worship?

The joy of the Lord makes it easy for your light to shine before those around you (see Matthew 5:16). As you climb in age, don't let your joyful light go out. Keep it lit! Measure your life by your joy. Is it normal for you to smile? Do you give an encouraging word to those around you? Are you blessing the next generation with your joyful outlook on life?

Now, don't misunderstand. The joy-filled person is a realist, too. We are used to fighting spiritual battles that start in our minds, but these battles do not rob us from our eternal joy in the Lord. When physical pain comes and circumstances are difficult, we are still joyful in our souls, and it leaks out through our words and actions. There is great joy in fellowship with God and others, sharing in worship, and serving others.

A Christian evangelist from London, George Müller was taught and passed on to others that the most important daily spiritual priority was to be blessed to the point of joy in the Lord. When your life is bubbling over in joy, others are attracted to you. It is a powerful example of Christ's grace and makes a lasting impact on those around you.

I pray that you would know and pass on God's "inexpressible and glorious joy" (1 Peter 1:8). It is the joy of the Lord that is your strength today (see Nehemiah 8:10). Do not stop living joyfully.

INVEST GENEROUSLY.

All of life is an investment. This was God's idea. For every hour we sow in this lifetime, there will be millions of years of reaping during eternity. There is no greater time in your life to invest generously than today! Once we are conceived in our mother's womb, we will never cease to exist. Think about it. Death does not end existence. Why wouldn't you invest strategically?

All of life is an opportunity to sow on earth. And in the end, you are sowing two kinds of seeds. You should make sure you are sowing the right seed, especially as the days on this earth come to a close. First, we can sow "righteousness" and the result is "reward" (Proverbs 11:18), "unfailing love" (Hosea 10:12), and "eternal life" (Galatians 6:8). The second option is we can sow "sin" (see Proverbs 22:8, MSG), and the result is trouble, sadness (see Galatians 6:8), and everlasting destruction separated from God forever (see 2 Thessalonians 1:9). We have some choices to make. There are only two roads. One leads to wise investments and the other to devastating ones. Which road are you headed down?

The good news is that in this life, we begin to reap investments. If we invest kindness, love, helpfulness, and service, we often begin now to see the fruit of a good reputation, respect, appreciation, joy, and God's blessings. A follower of Jesus makes double investments and reaps double blessings, both here on earth and for all of eternity. You have a wonderful opportunity to not check out of the game and to put yourself on God's playing field by making wise investments with your time, talent, and treasure.

The Bible teaches us that we will reap what we sow. "Do not be deceived: God cannot be mocked. A man reaps what he sows. . . . Let us not become weary in doing good, for at the proper time will reap a harvest if we do not give up. Therefore, as we have the opportunity, let us do good to all people" (Galatians 6:7, 9–10). You have many opportunities in front of you to invest. You will see the harvest now if you do not give up on doing good.

Financial investments are good, but the opportunities for nonfinancial investment are endless. God's kingdom is waiting to be advanced through your words and deeds. You might be limited in your resources, or maybe God has given you more than you can imagine. Either way, invest with your life. Measure your investment by how much you love. How much love do you invest in others and in your local church? Are you rejoicing when someone comes to know Jesus as their Savior or turns to Him with more of their life?

Don't become stingy and tight in your investments. Invest yourself for God so that you become one of His own "special treasures" (Malachi 3:17, NLT). When you invest your whole life, devotion, time, love, and possessions in God, you are a delight to Him (see Deuteronomy 7:6; Psalm 147:11; 149:4). Life is given to you by God for investment. He continues to have great plans ahead for you. Measure your life not by how man measures but by how God measures. Measure your life by your eternal investments today. Invest generously!

PRAY DEEPLY.

If there was ever a time in your life when you could pray deep prayers, today is the day. Your earnest prayer can expand your life beyond any limits that you can reach. You might be slowing down physically, but do not slow down prayerfully. When stories are told in heaven, how many will rise to thank God for your prayers? You have a tremendous opportunity to pray with width, depth, height, and length. Keep a journal of your ever-expanding prayers and praises.

Do your prayers run wide? Let your intercession reach your whole community. Pray for your local officials by name. Pray for the influence of churches in your city. Pray for the pastors and leadership of those churches. Take your prayers to schools, children, youth, and families in your community. This is an opportunity to be a spiritual watchman or watchwoman for your church and your city.

> I have posted watchmen on your walls, Jerusalem;
> they will never be silent day or night.
> You who call on the LORD,
> give yourselves no rest,
> and give him no rest till he establishes Jerusalem
> and makes her the praise of the earth. (Isaiah 62:6–7)

This is God's call on your life. Be an intercessor staying spiritually awake for those around you. Do your prayers extend wide enough to include the state, governor, senators? Do you intercede for the nation and president? "I urge, then, first of all, that petitions, prayers, intercession and thanksgiving be made for all people—for kings and all those in authority" (1 Timothy 2:1–2).

They need your prayers. Next, head to the world. Stretch your prayers for the nations and world leaders and bring God's purposes on earth as it is in heaven.

Do your prayers have depth? Most people live superficially. They talk about the weather and athletic teams. Are you going deeper? Are you burdened for people far away from God? Do you shed tears for those who do not know Jesus? King David felt great spiritual responsibility for his nation. Enemies surrounded him and wanted to wipe him from the earth. As David prayed for his people, he said, "My tears have been my food day and night. . . . I pour out my soul" (Psalm 42:3–4). He knew that God measured his prayer tears. "List my tears on your scroll—are they not in your record" (56:8). When is the last time you prayed heart-wrenching prayers going below the surface? Now is the time.

Do your prayers reach the heavens? As you head toward the end of your life, why not take your prayers all the way to heaven? Why not go higher in intercession? Daniel's prayers touched heaven. In a series of amazing encounters, the angel Gabriel assured him that his prayers were going to the throne of heaven (see Daniel 8:15–18; 9:20–23; 10:10–14, 18–19). It is precious when you know that your prayers are touching God's heart. Do the angels know you are the one coming before the Father on behalf of your family, friends, church, community, nation, and world?

Do your prayers have length? This is the time of life when your prayers will outlive you. We are still reaping the results of prayers of David, Isaiah, Jeremiah, Paul, Peter, and Jesus. The prayers of Luther, Wesley, Finney, Calvin, and Bounds are still being answered in our time. When we pray prayers after God's heart, they last for generations. The answers are like the river in Ezekiel 47, which flows wider and deeper over the years. God partners with his people to do exceedingly and abundantly more than we could even ask or imagine (see Ephesians 3:20–21). Please pray deep prayers for those around you. Your prevailing prayer will transform generations. It has been said that you can do more to move the world for God on your knees than in any other way. Please pray deeply.

Live joyfully. Invest generously. Pray deeply. We need the older generations to show off the glory of God to the younger ones. We need you to come alongside us. Give your joy, investment, and prayer away. Stay involved. Serve your local church. Love and encourage your pastor. Pass on your stories of God's faithfulness to those following you. Don't lose your moments, hours, days, and years. Don't lose your life's greatest opportunities. From this day forward, love God and those around you with all your heart. Make your remaining days count for all eternity. Start now!

GET TO KNOW THE AUTHOR:

Jeff Baxter is the lead pastor of River Church in Lakewood, Colorado. He is a creative and passionate Bible teacher. Being a lifelong learner, leader, and author has led him to receive his advanced theological degrees from Columbia International University and Fuller Theological Seminary. He has traveled and trained extensively oversees as well as at Christian Universities, camps, churches, and conferences. He has written a few books, his latest being *From Broken to Beautiful: What Repairing Streams Has Taught Me About Healing the Church* (fmcusa.org/bookstore). You will often find Jeff in coffee shops for community, conversation, and study. He is married to beautiful Laurie and they have three wonderful kids.

CHAPTER 37

GOD RESTED, BUT HE DIDN'T RETIRE

— Marni Mrazik —

True confessions! After Chuck Stecker, the general editor of this book, called to ask me to write a chapter for this book and we said our goodbyes, I cried. I thought, *Me? Why me? What can I contribute from my little corner of the world?* I felt overwhelmed at being chosen, and at the same time honored to be asked. It's not that I don't think I'm special in the eyes of my Savior, and I don't have an inferiority complex, but this seemed so much bigger than my regular sphere of ministry. I live in Edmonton, Alberta, Canada, with my wonderful husband and two amazing teenage daughters. I was a children's pastor for seven years and am now the director of community life at our church. I love Jesus with all my heart, soul, mind, and strength, and my desire is for others to do the same. Really, nothing out of the ordinary, nothing that would set me apart, but God chose me for this task. After I wiped away my tears, I praised Him, thanked Him for His goodness, and decided to wait to see how the Lord would lead me to write. And I prayed—a lot.

Maybe you have moments in your life like that. Perhaps you have questions about what God is calling you to do or if He's still calling at all. Maybe you've wondered if He still has deeds for you to accomplish and you're asking, "Then where do I go from here?" First, I want to establish that God absolutely has more in store for you. Let's look into His Word:

"You saw me before I was born. Every day of my life was recorded in your book. Every moment was laid out before a single day had passed" (Psalm 139:16, NLT). Hmmm, so it says that God has all our moments accounted for, not just the ones until we hit the age of sixty-five or otherwise retire. So there must be a plan for the later moments God gives us.

"We are God's handiwork, created in Christ Jesus to do good works, which God prepared in advance for us to do" (Ephesians 2:10). Ah, God has prepared jobs for us to do, and it doesn't say they stop once we become seniors.

"Therefore, go and make disciples of all the nations, baptizing them in the name of the Father and the Son and the Holy Spirit. Teach these new disciples to obey all the commands I have given you. And be sure of this: I am with you always, even to the end of the age" (Matthew 28:19–20, NLT). So God will be with us until the end of the age, again not just until we reach a certain age. Here's the thing: the Bible says that God rested (see Genesis 2:2); He didn't retire. And neither should you from making an impact for His kingdom.

Recently, I had the opportunity to meet with a senior who said, "I used to be a single mom and I know it can be hard. I want to reach out to single moms." She is now leading the charge and starting a group specifically for single moms. One of the many benefits of age is experience. Perhaps your life's journey includes experiences you could turn into God-glorifying, life-changing moments or ministries.

There is another "retired" gentleman I know, who, in the words of his wife, "loves to feed people." Guess what he does? He feeds people. He heads up the brunch ministry at the church and once a week supplies a meal to one of the shelters in Edmonton. If other ministries require meals, guess who's cooking? Perhaps you love to do something that you could continue to do so that it ministers to someone or to a group. Even better, you could invite someone to join you. Show the person what you're doing, or find out who else is doing what you love and join them.

My dad is always on the go. He's still working in the classical sense as he continues to run his business, but his real passion is to see men rise up and be leaders of their homes and families and in the church. But he doesn't just think about it; he does something about it. He mentors, he teaches, he advocates, he meets, he prays, and he encourages. The scope of his influence is grand because he chooses to engage. Maybe you have a passion you could mobilize to make a difference. Maybe you could partner with someone who has the same passion.

For the past eight years, our church has run a summer soccer camp, and when you run a soccer camp, you need coaches. One of our most influential coaches is a woman with fourteen grandchildren, and she is on the field. She can't run as fast as the children or the teenage coaches, but she creates relationships with the campers and camp staff, and her presence adds to the discussions and group talks a depth that would otherwise be missing. Her eyes see things that others may miss. She is not intimidated by the youth around her but rather embraces them. If there is something that intimidates you or you just don't see how you could get involved, ask the question "How?" and overcome.

I have read many books on parenting, and something I always remember from one of those books is the importance of teaching and modeling to children the principle of "See a need, meet a need." That principle doesn't just apply to children; it applies to all of us. Look at your city, your community, your church—what are the needs? God has given you gifts and talents that can be used to meet needs around you. There is definitely a place for you to serve. When I used to be in charge of scheduling workers for the nursery, there were many unsurprising names on the list; they were, after all, the mothers of the children in the nursery. The more surprising names belonged to the women who had long since watched their own children grow up and leave home. They knew something that some seniors have forgotten: there's always space to serve in children's ministries, and the love, wisdom, and experience of seniors is most welcome. Really, that's true for any ministry, both in and outside the church.

Instead of sitting back and waiting for the next seniors' brunch, look for opportunities to enter into relationship with those around you, and not just those who share your life stage. There is nothing wrong with a seniors' brunch, but it's time to take stock to have a wider impact. Take an inventory of your experiences, gifts, talents, possessions, and passions. It's time to see how they match the needs in your neck of the woods, and it's time to engage to bring glory to God and grow relationships between all generations. Serving together is a great way to accomplish that.

I just finished reading a book that recounted a *Reader's Digest* story from February 1998 that told about a couple who took early retirement. They moved to Florida, cruised, played baseball, and collected shells. The author goes on to say, "Picture them before Christ at the great day of judgment: "Look, Lord, see my shells."[1] That is a tragedy. Don't buy into the lie that retirement is about taking it easy until Christ's return. Stay in the game!

So where do you go from here? First, start at the place where you absolutely believe, beyond a shadow of a doubt, that God continues to have a call on your life and something for you to do. After that, I can't tell you specifically where to go, but I can tell you to "go." Remember, you won't be going alone; God will be with you each step of the way. Those alongside of you as both

---

[1] John Piper, *Don't Waste Your Life* (Wheaton, IL: Crossway, 2003), 46.

coworkers and recipients of your ministry will span many ages, and your lives will all be enriched because of it.

I pray that you feel empowered, encouraged, and inspired by the Holy Spirit, because you have so much to offer and more to do. Remember the tears I told you about at the beginning of this chapter? I don't know, maybe some of them were in response to answered prayer. In my confession at the beginning of this chapter, what I didn't tell you was that I have been praying more fervently than ever that God would use me—that He would open up doors and opportunities and allow me to share His love and grace more and more. Maybe this is one very unexpected way He is answering my prayer, and maybe, just maybe, He has more unexpected assignments for you, too. I believe He does!

GET TO KNOW THE AUTHOR:

Marni Mrazik is the director of community life at Terwillegar Community Church in Edmonton, Alberta, Canada. She taught high school, finished graduate school, stayed home to take care of her young daughters, and pastored children for seven years. She and her husband, Martin, have two beautiful teenage daughters.

CHAPTER 38

IT'S "WITH," NOT "FOR"

— Joel Thomas —

Please do not think highly of me. Don't make the mistake of thinking that because my name is on this page, somehow that means I have deeper and more profound things to say than you do. In truth, I am on this journey with you. We are sojourners together through a sea of different yet often interconnected stories—stories of loss, confusion, joy, redemption, and discovery. These stories are not written by us any more than *A Christmas Carol* is written by Ebenezer Scrooge. The God of the universe, this Jesus who pitched His tent in the midst of our cluttered and dysfunctional camp, chose us as His instrument to communicate His great good news. Though seemingly disparate, the power of our stories, when viewed through the lens of God's providential plan, begin to form an overarching narrative of intentional generational legacy.

I was raised the youngest of three in northeastern Indiana in a small rural town. There were two institutions that governed our weekly schedule: school (my mom was an elementary teacher and my dad was a high school teacher) and our local church. It was a toss-up as to which was more important. Growing up, I wasn't entirely sure where one stopped and the other began. It always seemed a little odd when I would hear of someone attending a "Christian school." *Wasn't every school Christian?* Though I lived geographically north of the traditional Bible Belt, it felt like I was coming of age square on the buckle.

Upon reflection, it is no surprise that traditional educational principles and theological concepts commingled in my head and heart to form what I believed to be best practices for healthy ministry. Ideas such as teacher-centric instruction and the accumulation of information all translated into how I led and developed ministry tools. I was to collect all the information necessary to produce a disciple of Jesus, condense it into palatable portions, contextualize it for optimum receptivity, and develop programs tailored for specific life seasons. Basically, I was to do ministry for whatever age group I was focused on.

I set upon my task with determination, passion, and a not entirely healthy dose of pride. Programs, curriculum, and to-do lists flowed out of me. I was writing weekly Bible study curriculum for teenagers that I handed off to our volunteers. I was producing weekly original messages for Sunday youth group. I was scheduling volunteer-leader trainings. I was handing out actual checklists of "How to maximize your gospel," "Being the leader God has called you to be," and "Seven Habits of an effective witness." I had accumulated the necessary information and, in good teacher-centric theory, was busy shoveling that information out to those I led.

Can you guess the result? Can you shake your Magic 8 Ball and project the impact of such a philosophy of ministry?

Each ministry I led saw immediate and significant numerical growth. We were adding people, volunteers, resources, and programs on almost a monthly basis. It was intense and riotous, but above all it was exhausting. And ultimately it was unsustainable.

I was consumed with what I needed to do for my volunteers, for the students, for the parents, and for our local partners. It was a roller coaster that was high on thrills and speed but offered little in the way of lifelong transformation. Eventually, even the external numerical success was leaving me drained, unsatisfied, and wholly unfulfilled. As if that weren't enough to trigger some intentional soul searching, I was also beginning to identify more and more with Macbeth's evaluation of his situation from act 5, scene 5:

Tomorrow, and tomorrow, and tomorrow,
Creeps in this petty pace from day to day,
To the last syllable of recorded time;
And all our yesterdays have lighted fools
The way to dusty death. Out, out, brief candle!
Life's but a walking shadow, a poor player,
That struts and frets his hour upon the stage,
And then is heard no more. It is a tale
Told by an idiot, full of sound and fury,
Signifying nothing.[1]

All my well-intentioned efforts for others on behalf of God were not resulting in generational transformation. There was much "sound and fury," but I suspected that it signified nothing (or not much) that would leave a legacy for eternity. This painful but priceless lesson sent me on a journey with Jesus that continues to this day.

Jesus said to them, "Come with me. I'll make a new kind of fisherman out of you. I'll show you how to catch men and women instead of perch and bass." (Mark 1:17, MSG)

"With me." That phrase has been transformational in my understanding and implementation of ministry. The way of Jesus

---

[1] William Shakespeare, *Macbeth*, act 5, scene 5, lines 19–28, https://www.owleyes.org/text/macbeth/read/act-v-scene-v#root-71686-9/81080.

always involves doing life with others. The early disciples did not leave everything of their former lives because of what Jesus did for them. Their lives—and ultimate deaths—laid the foundation of a legacy of faith that continues through us today because they spent time with Jesus.

Matthew left a lucrative business collecting taxes and skimming off the top, and he did it not because of a program designed specifically for him or a sermon preached for him but rather because of a Savior who said, "Come along with me" (Mark 2:14, MSG). "With" has the power to transform for generations to come:

- "With" invites the next generation to come alongside you as you serve.
- "With" welcomes those who are different into the journey of faith Jesus has laid before you.
- "With" doesn't limit our involvement because of age, season of life, or current circumstances.
- "With" says yes to new relationships, new learnings, and new ideas together.
- "With" builds bridges across denominations and political affiliations.
- "With" is sustainable.
- "With" is a pool of faith filling everyone's cup.
- "With" is the "how" of the Great Commission.

I recently returned from spending a week in Chiang Rai, Thailand, and a week in Yokosuka, Japan. These two weeks were the highlight of my summer. Not because I love to travel. Not because I love new experiences. Not because I rode an elephant through the mountains of northern Thailand or because I drove a go-kart through downtown Tokyo while wearing a Spider-Man onesie (seriously!).

Those two weeks were the best because I spent them with two younger men who were both living out their callings for Jesus

Christ. For several years, I met one on one with each of them, listening, praying, mentoring, crying, and laughing together. I invited them to serve with me as we led men's retreats, small groups, and mission trips. Both these men (and their families) are heroes of mine. We have done life together for years, and it is so very humbling to sit with them as they share with me the highs and lows of following Jesus as full-time missionaries.

Whoever you are, at whatever season of life you find yourself, if Jesus has allowed you to continue pulling oxygen into your lungs, there is someone you can come alongside and do life with. "With" transforms you both and creates a bridge that leaves a legacy for generations.

GET TO KNOW THE AUTHOR:

Joel Thomas is the lead pastor of Harbor Church. With more than twenty years of ministry experience, he has served as a men's ministry pastor, teaching pastor, and youth pastor and has been a board member for local and international organizations. He and his wife, Julie, live in Arvada, Colorado, and have four children.

CHAPTER 39

OVERCOMING THE ROADBLOCKS

— Amy Hanson —

Everyone knows what it is like to run into a roadblock. Whether driving across town or on a long road trip, no one likes to see the orange and white barriers that tell us, "You can't go this way!"

Initially a barricade makes us think, *Well, I'm no longer going to be able to get where I want to go,* or, *I might as well turn around because this will be too hard and take too long.* The destination we deemed valuable moments before becomes less important because we don't want to take the extra time or effort to get there.

There is no question that the time, experience, and resources of older adults is valuable and that there is tremendous potential for those who are in the second half of life to make a tremendous impact for the kingdom of God. Marc Freedman, founder and CEO of Encore.org, says that older adults are the country's only increasing natural resource.[1] But what do we do when we come up against barriers that keep us from "taking back the baton," plowing ahead, and making an eternal difference with our lives?

---

[1] Marc Freedman, "Encore," YouTube video, 2:32, posted by "Citizen Film," February 21, 2014, https://www.youtube.com/watch?v=QSS8mX1lJ3U.

I'll tell you what we do. We recognize those barriers, call them out, and keep fighting to live the abundant life God has called us to. Let's take a look at some of the big barricades that can trip us up and ways to work around them.

AGEISM

Ageism is a term coined in the late sixties by physician and psychiatrist Robert Neil Butler. It was initially used to describe the negative biases people have about older people, but now it is descriptive of any discrimination of people because of their age. So both young people and older people can experience ageism. In fact, when the apostle Paul was speaking to Timothy in 1 Timothy 4:12, he was referencing ageism:

> Don't let anyone look down on you because you are young, but set an example for the believers in speech, in conduct, in love, in faith and in purity.

I believe that to the millions of older adults alive today, Paul would say, "Don't let anyone look down on you because you are *old* [including how you look at yourself], but set an example for the believers." And he goes on to say in verse 14, "Do not neglect your gift." In other words, don't let age keep you from doing the work God has called you to do.

To break down the barrier of ageism, we have to recognize the myths of aging and counter them with truth. Take a look at these and see how many you might subtly believe.

Myth: Older people can't learn new things. Sometimes we don't serve in a particular area because we don't believe we can learn what is required to do the task, but research shows that in the absence of disease, we are all capable of learning new things and making new connections in the brain. As we age, it does take us longer to learn something new, but we are able to do it!

Myth: Older people can't change. Sure, we all know folks who appear to be stuck in their ways, but the ability to change has more to do with temperament than with age. If change was hard for you when you were young, it might be hard for you in these later years. But remember, God is in the business of change.

Myth: Chronological age is the best determinant of what we're capable of. Chronological age is merely what our birth certificate says. Social security, discounted movie tickets, and inexpensive coffee might all be based on chronological age, but that doesn't mean it is a good basis for choosing where we will or will not serve. Socrates wrote one of his greatest philosophies at age seventy,[2] and Noah Webster published his dictionary around age seventy and continued making revisions into his eighties.[3] Also, consider Moses, who led the Israelites out of Egypt in his eighties, and the apostle John, who was writing Revelation in his nineties.[4] Age is just a number and has no bearing on what God can do in and through our lives.

RETIREMENT

A second barrier to overcome is our view of retirement. Many of us have bought into the world's view of retirement and see this as a time to focus primarily on ourselves, but God's Word paints a much different picture. Numbers 8:23–26 is the only passage in Scripture in which we read about retirement. The Levites were instructed to begin working at the tabernacle at the age of twenty-five and then retire at age fifty. But then it goes on to say that they were to assist their fellow Levites, suggesting a mentoring role of coming alongside the younger priests.

No one will deny that certain roles and responsibilities change as we age. We might no longer go to an eight-to-five job every day, and our responsibility for raising children diminishes as our kids become

[2] www.wikipedias.org/wiki/Socrates
[3] www.wikipedia.org/wiki/Websters_Dictionary
[4] www.bibleprobe.com/revelation

adults and have children of their own. But we can be sure God has new avenues for ministry and service in which to use our gifts and talents.

Not Knowing Where

The third barrier is simply not knowing where to serve. There are so many needs and opportunities that we can get paralyzed trying to discern what to do. A few things can help us find where to invest ourselves.

Of utmost importance is to be connected to God so that He can lead. He is the one who gives us our ministries. Author and evangelical pastor Henry Blackaby, in his best-selling study, *Experiencing God*, said that we are to watch to see where God is working and join Him.[5]

Several years ago, I met a man named Hal who was serving in the Houston prison system. When I asked him how he got involved, he told me that twenty years earlier, he had been sitting in church one Sunday, listening to a sermon the pastor was preaching from Matthew 25:36, and heard these words: "I was sick and you looked after me[;] I was in prison and you came to visit me." Hal told me that for months he had thought about becoming involved in a prison ministry, so he decided to be trained as a volunteer for one. He then began spending at least one night a week visiting men, helping their families, and doing what he could to support and encourage. When I met Hal, he was almost eighty years old, so I teased him by asking how long he was going to keep this up. He quickly and passionately replied by telling me all the statistics about incarcerated men and how much of a need there was for people to minister to them. Lives were transformed all because one retired man was connected to God and His Word and responded in obedience.

Another way to find your sweet spot is to simply serve where you have always had an interest but haven't yet had an opportunity.

---

5 Henry Blackaby and Claude King, *Experiencing God* (Nashville: LifeWay, 1990), 15.

Bobbie was an eighty-year-old woman who had always wanted to go on a mission trip. When her church planned to go to Nicaragua, she didn't hesitate to sign up. Thankfully, her church did not discourage her, and actually she complained less than the young people about the heat and uncomfortable conditions. She was also a great blessing to the people they served.

If you are not sure where to serve, consider how you can use your hobbies for ministry. If you like to fish, invite the young neighbor boy who doesn't have a father figure in his life to go with you. Maybe you and your spouse enjoy traveling in your RV. There are many ministries in which you can enjoy camping and also serve.

Finally, think about how you can use your past experience in a ministry capacity. My dad was an accountant and manager for a major oil company. Upon his retirement, he planned to volunteer with Habitat for Humanity, swinging a hammer, but when the local Habitat chapter learned of his financial background, they asked him to be the volunteer financial director. He still gets out and swings a hammer from time to time, but he is using his work experience to make a difference.

WHERE WILL YOU LEAVE YOUR HEART?

In her book *The Second-Half Adventure*, author and speaker Kay Marshall Strom recounts hearing a speaker tell about the missionary David Livingstone, who opened up Africa to the gospel and spent much of his life caring for the people who lived there. When he died, the natives knew he had to be buried in England, but according to Livingstone's wishes, his heart was removed and buried under one of the native trees. His body was then carried to an awaiting ship and buried in Westminster Abbey, but his heart remained in Africa.[6]

There is nothing wrong with golf, fishing, and travel, but we must consider where we are going to leave our hearts. Are we going

---

[6] Kay Marshall Strom, *The Second-Half Adventure: Don't Just Retire—Use Your Time, Skills, and Resources to Change the World* (Chicago: Moody, 2009), 126–127.

to invest in something that will make a mark for eternity? Without a doubt, there will be barriers and challenges that will discourage us. As we age, there will be difficulties to press through, but when all is said and done, will we have lived our lives such that we have made eternal differences? I believe there is no greater investment than doing so—and no better place to leave our hearts than on God's field.

GET TO KNOW THE AUTHOR:

Amy Hanson, PhD, is a speaker, writer, and consultant who equips the church for ministry with the new old. She speaks throughout the US with pastors, church leaders, health-care professionals, and older adults about the unique needs and opportunities of a graying America. Amy is the author of the book *Baby Boomers and Beyond: Tapping the Ministry Talents and Passions of Adults over 50* and regularly teaches gerontology courses to college students. She lives with her family in Council Bluffs, Iowa.

CHAPTER 40

JUST DO SOMETHING

— Chuck Stecker —

All too often we give more power to our circumstances than to God's Word He has spoken to us. That has been the case in my life on several occasions. Tragically, it has happened more than I care to acknowledge. As I have aged, I believe I am more prone to becoming too comfortable in my circumstances as society labels me a senior.

In 1992, when our family was reassigned to Rome, Italy, we left a great community of believers and supporters of what God was doing in our family. There were several areas of ministry I felt we needed to engage in our new home and community. My wife, Billie, and I both felt we wanted to be prepared to be part of a couples' small group.

We were not sure who would be in the group. We had no idea where we would even be attending church. However, filled with unknowns, we purchased small-group materials for couples and took them with us to Rome. Within a very short time, God led us to attend two great churches. Shortly after we settled in, three other couples who lived in the same area of Rome agreed to launch a small group. The group proved to be a very significant time of growth for both me and Billie.

Looking back, I realize one of the keys to success was that when Billie and I clearly heard from God, we decided to do something.

A second area of ministry was that of ministering to and through men. I departed the United states with good intentions but no preparation. As a result, when we arrived in Rome, I saw the obstacles to be greater than the clear Word of God.

In short, because I could not find a place to meet and was unsure if anyone would attend, I did nothing. I gave more power to my circumstances than to God's Word, which I knew had been clearly spoken directly to me.

After our first year in Rome, I was sent back to the United States for meetings. During that trip, I had the opportunity to meet with a couple who had been mentoring and loving on our family for the three years we lived in Fairfax, Virginia. Frank and Doris Burrows are to this day an amazing influence in our lives. They are both in their nineties and live in Pennsylvania. We still see them as often as possible.

During that trip, Frank and I had our normal conversation, which meant talking about what God was doing in my life and what God was calling me to do. I knew the dreaded question would come, and I was prepared with my very logical answer. Then in Frank's quiet, loving voice, he asked me, "So how is the men's ministry going in Rome?"

It is always good to have a great answer ready when you know you are going to be asked about a situation for which you have done nothing. It is good when you can develop an answer with such clarity and sincerity that anyone would understand why you had not done what you know you were sent to do. Fully prepared, I responded by listing all the circumstances preventing me from starting a men's group.

Frank smiled and simply said, "Chuck, *just do something.*" I remember looking at Frank and trying to help him understand there was no place to meet. He had never been to Rome. He had no way of understanding the insurmountable circumstances I was facing. Before I could respond again to help Frank understand, he smiled and said, "God can guide a rolling stone more easily than digging one out of a deep hole in the ground."

And there it was: "Just do something!"

Now determined to "just do something," I told Frank I would do something within the next month.

Within a few days after returning to Rome, I was standing in a familiar place on the sidelines of the soccer field at the American Overseas School of Rome (AOSR), where our sons, Chad and Courtney, attended. Standing next to me was the school's headmaster, who had become a good friend.

The previous year, I had assisted in coaching some of the younger guys who were not old enough for the organized school teams and developed a small intramural program. Now, standing next to the headmaster, I looked around the campus and realized there were many buildings.

I think we've all had those "I don't know what possessed me to ask" moments. This was one of mine. I asked the headmaster, "Is there any chance I could use a room at the school periodically?" He responded with the obvious question: "What for?"

I explained I wanted to start a men's group and needed a room to use two to four times a month. He smiled at me and said, "Come with me, Chuck," and we walked to the main office of the school. We arrived at the desk of his executive assistant, who was a friend of our family. He told her to give me a master key to the entire school. He then told me to be careful with the key because it would open every door, including his office.

After thanking him, I walked outside the building and stood there for a moment looking at the key. In my spirit, I was ready to ask God why He waited so long to get me the key. Before I could ask the question, I heard God ask me, "Why did you wait so long to ask?" The key had been there waiting on me for over a year.

Then my mind went back to Frank Burrows and his words: *Just do something. God can guide a rolling stone more easily than digging one out of a deep hole in the ground.*

Two weeks later, men gathered at that school for our first meeting. Those attending represented men from seven different nations, pastors from several churches, single men, husbands, fathers, and sons. We continued to meet several times a month for the next year.

As many of us have aged, we seem to have begun feeling that if we need to do something, someone should ask us. And, by the way, we want to be asked nicely and with the respect we have earned.

Is it possible we are waiting for a person to ask us to do what we know God has already called us to do?

As seniors, we are better equipped than any generation that has gone before us. Note that I did not say we are better than any previous generation; I said we are better equipped! We are living longer and healthier lives and have greater availability than any generation before us.

James 1:22 makes the point of "doing" very clear: "Do not merely listen to the word, and so deceive yourselves. Do what it says."

Before we waste another day believing that our circumstances are more powerful than what God says to us, I am more than suggesting but rather I am calling you to "just do something. God can guide a rolling stone more easily than digging one out of a deep hole in the ground."

GET TO KNOW THE AUTHOR:

Dr. Chuck Stecker is executive director and founder of A Chosen Generation, which he and his wife, Billie, launched in 1997. After twenty-three years in the US Army, he served on staff of Promise Keepers as regional director in field ministry division for south-central region. Chuck and Billie have three children and nine grandchildren.

FOR PERSONAL REFLECTION OR GROUP DISCUSSION

- What experiences, gifts, talents, possessions, and passions has God given you?
- How can those things be used to further God's kingdom? For example, is there an existing ministry, group, or person you can partner with? Is there a need you can meet? Where can you enter into authentic relationship with others in the church through serving?
- What has God called you to do that you have not started because you believe that you are not capable or that your circumstances are too overwhelming?
- What is holding you back? What will it take for you to "just do something"?
- How can you live more joyfully in the coming months? How will others know of your joy?
- What is one place where you can give of your time, talent, or treasure with a generous heart?
- How can you organize your prayer life in order to make the greatest kingdom impact possible?
- Why is doing "for" often our default?
- How can doing more "with" transform the ministries you've been working for?
- Who can you invite to come along with you?
- Of the three barriers mentioned in chapter 39, which one is the most difficult for you to overcome as you consider leveraging your time, experience, and resources to make an impact for God's kingdom? What other barriers trip you up and keep you from serving?
- Prayerfully consider where you want to leave your heart and what steps you will begin to take to ensure that you invest yourself in things that will affect eternity.

PART 9
FOR PASTORS ONLY

PART 9

FOR PASTORS ONLY

What to Expect

Pastor, the book you hold in your hand is meant to be a resource for you, your seniors, and your leadership team. As we were developing this material, we realized that pastors often hear best from other pastors.

Also, we did not want to develop a book to engage the seniors in a local church and have the pastor blindsided with ideas and even demands of which he or she had no warning or previous knowledge. Our intent is to assist you as pastor and lead where God has placed you.

Bottom line: we want to serve you, and it is our desire that this resource is helpful to you.

In this part, chapters are written *by* pastors *for* pastors. The authors/pastors represent multicampus churches, small emerging churches, and urban and rural churches. The authors have widely diverse ethnic backgrounds from across the country.

We believe there is at least one chapter for every pastor. The questions at the end of this part are meant to help you reflect. It is our hope and fervent prayer that God will bless you and pour out His favor on you and His ministry in and through you.

CHAPTER 41

REPAIRER OF THE BREACH

— Pastor Andy Addis —

Pastor, how do you see yourself?

I'm not talking about that theologically correct, congregation-ally expected response of innate humility we would put down on some form if we were asked this question for publication. I mean how do you see yourself in your own mind's eye?

Maybe if I show my hand first, we can get honest about this.

When the last song is played on Sunday morning and then I step up to preach, I'd love to come on stage to an arena announcer introducing me as if I'm a player in the starting lineup of an NBA game. I even have my theme music picked out: "Frankenstein" by the Edgar Winter Group for home games, and "Don't Stop Believin'" by Journey for away games.

As I step up to the pulpit, my worship pastor meets me half-way across the stage, where we both jump and bump chests before an elaborate fist-bump, handshake routine. The congregation goes wild, holding up signs that read, "Rowdy, Proud, and Baptized" and "World Champs Since AD 33."

Suddenly, I'm kind of sad because I guess I've actually put thought into this.

Still, let's cut through the professional bravado and pseudo humility and ask the question one more time: How do you see yourself?

The way you view yourself as a pastor is essential because you can unknowingly self-limit yourself to the role you have internally assigned. Even if you know the great truths that have "set you free" (John 8:32), believe that you are "in Christ" (2 Corinthians 5:17), and never doubt that He "saved us and called us to a holy calling" (2 Timothy 1:9, ESV), you can still get sideways on what it means to be a pastor.

I have found that most of us see ourselves leaning in one of two directions. Either we view our role as waiters who flit about from table to table refilling glasses of the weekly diners who are constantly evaluating whether or not our service will keep them coming back. Or we see ourselves as sergeants in the midst of battle running ammunition from foxhole to foxhole, telling those young, scared soldiers to stay focused because the battle is ours but the battle is real!

I bet you can guess which direction I think you should be leaning.

A New Title for You

Let me encourage you to start thinking about yourself and your role in terms that will do you and your congregation some good. Let me encourage you to start envisioning your calling and responsibilities from a biblical perspective. Your new title is in this passage from the prophet Isaiah:

> Your ancient ruins shall be rebuilt;
>> you shall raise up the foundations of many generations;
> you shall be called the repairer of the breach,
>> the restorer of streets to dwell in. (58:12, ESV)

Let me encourage you to start thinking of yourself as "The Repairer of the Breach."

We know that the culture has infiltrated the church and the faith. We see it in the gross examples of whole denominations compromising the gospel to pacify politically correct mandates. We experience it in ineffective ministries that have no supernatural power because they are plugged into all the wrong sources.

But those are overt.

The most dangerous infiltrations are subtle changes that are so widely accepted, beliefs so commonly held, that their normalcy causes us to neglect their examination.

One such danger is the deconstruction of church fellowship into age-graded, generationally divided, homogeneously organized "ministries" that have their own meeting times, spaces, and rituals.

We've become so specialized that we no longer have what would actually make us special.

Yes, this is an argument for intergenerational ministry, but, no, I am not suggesting you fire your youth pastor and convert the children's wing into a homeless shelter. There are times when children and students need to meet and learn differently, and there is no doubt there are times when grown-ups need their own "holy" space.

But in the current church culture, we have effectively mirrored modern educational paradigms and siloed our curriculum and classes so that olders never meet youngers, and youngers are kept away from olders. We have bent knees at the altar of consumerism, creating church environments with a multiplicity of options (something for everyone) but rarely providing opportunities for everyone to be together.

When are young men going to figure out how to be older men if all they ever see are other teenage boys? Talk about the blind leading the blind.

When are young women going to learn the strengths of being strong Christian women if all we ever offer is another teen retreat or girl huddle? They get enough of that at school.

How are our older men and women going to pass along all their years of wisdom if there are never any points of contact? They've already paid the dumb tax on things, so why should this generation have to do it as well?

The culture (even the church culture) has been dismantled in many ways, and you, Pastor, have the job, the calling, the privilege of being "The Repairer of the Breach." You can lead your congregation to be a Titus 2 kind of church. Go ahead, read that passage again and see if you don't feel the same conviction I do. It contains specific instructions for how older men are to conduct themselves and train up younger men. It's a detailed guide for older women to rear younger women. It's a clear and challenging teaching for younger men and women.

Without olders and youngers *intentionally* getting together for learning the lessons of life, the truth of the Scriptures, and the walk of faith, there is no hope that these lessons will be passed from one generation to the next.

Olders interacting with youngers is the number one way we can move our church's biblical education from information to transformation. And isn't that the goal?

So, what is an older and what is a younger? Hebrew culture would tell us that we start to consider someone an older man at forty, and we start to consider someone an older woman whenever she tells us to. (See, that's the wisdom of an older man right there.)

With just that bit of information, take a look at your student ministry. If it's like most, it's filled with preteens and teens being led by a twentysomething youth pastor and a small army of volunteers in their twenties or thirties. Why is this a problem?

Go back to Titus 2. Older men are given six instructions, older women are given five, and younger women are given seven!

What about younger men (remember, those under age forty)? They are given just one instruction: self-control. Let me translate the Greek for you there. God has only one instruction for men under forty: get a grip!

It's all they can handle, and we're putting them in charge of raising the next generation?

Don't get me wrong. They are great young men and needed, trusted servants. But they need saints who are forty, fifty, sixty, and seventy years old walking along with them or we're going to have a situation on our hands.

The truth is that we already do have a situation on our hands, but you have been called to be "The Repairer of the Breach."

REPAIRING THE BREACH

As a pastor, I believe this wholeheartedly. I currently serve in the church that I came to fifteen years ago out of seminary. We are in a rural, out-of-the-way town in Kansas called Hutchinson. When we arrived fifteen years ago, it was already a thirty-year-old church in decline. Having seen its heyday in the eighties with attendance in the four hundreds, they had dwindled to 127 and had not been able to entice a pastor for almost two years. Here we are fifteen years later and we are a congregation of about thirty-five hundred with multiple locations across the state of Kansas.

It's been a beautiful thing; it's been a God thing; it's been amazing. But what I think makes it so distinct is that this dying neighborhood church transformed into a church-planting, local-culture-shaping organization not in spite of our seniors but in light of them.

Too many times, I've read articles or gone to conferences where pastors are encouraged to find ways around the seniors who are just "too difficult." But our church found a different path. We invited our olders and our seniors to get back in the game.

We wanted them to work back in the nursery, and not just for the kiddos but to meet the young families dropping off their precious cargo. We wanted them in the student ministry, not for the water-balloon fight but for the truth and insight.

And we wanted our youngers to learn to honor and respect

their elders, even if it was just from the opportunity to watch how they lived out their faith in real time.

Let me give one anecdote to put things in perspective.

John was a World War II veteran, a charter member of the church, and the one person I was warned about before I moved to town. "He's a good guy. Just a little difficult sometimes," they said.

Come on, Pastor. You know the guy I'm talking about, right?

I remember my very first weekend, heading to my office to grab a notebook before the service. As I headed for the door, I nearly head-butted John. It was our first encounter. I was a little shocked that he was coming out of my office, but the only words he spoke to me were, "You left your lights on."

It was clear: he was going to be "that guy."

But our church began to grow. We invested in more than just young families and called upon our senior leaders. We didn't work around them; we worked with them and through them. We now had three services, and I remember one memorable weekend when I had done something a little over the top as a sermon illustration. I had a slight pang of fear that I might be getting a visit from John. Standing in the foyer on that Sunday with young children running around with no shoes on and the worship ministry playing some of that new-fangled music to prep for the next service, I saw him across the room.

He was coming at me like a heat-seeking missile through the crowd. I steeled up and was thinking about how to take a conflict around the corner or to an office, but he didn't come face to face with me. In fact, he came and stood directly beside me but facing the opposite direction.

I remember freezing like an animal worried that a predator might be in the bushes nearby. Then John tugged on my shirt-sleeve, pulling my ear down to where he could whisper into it.

I'll never forget his words: "I'm real proud of you, Pastor. Keep up the good work."

It was a sign that God was bringing unity to our community.

He was creating an intergenerational body that would make a difference in our city and several cities across our state.

I've been asked several times what the "secret sauce" of our growth and model as a church is. We all know that nothing grows without the Lord, but if there is any insight, I would say that the secret is our seniors.

They got in the game. They made sacrifices. They refused to be the obstacles. They led the youngers. They changed the DNA of a dying church to that of a thriving church. They were game changers, and they helped me to repair the breach.

GET TO KNOW THE AUTHOR:

Andy Addis is the lead pastor of CrossPoint Church, a multisite congregation with campuses across Kansas. He has a master's in communication from Fort Hays State University and a master of divinity degree with biblical languages from Southwestern Seminary. Andy is the author of two books, *Reading It Right* and *Blotch*. He married Kathy, his college sweetheart, in 1994, and together they have raised two young men, Noah and Nathan. As a family, they love to play music, take road trips, cheer for the Dallas Mavericks, and play disc golf.

CHAPTER 42

JETHRO:
A GRANDFATHER
PASTOR WHO SAVED
A NATION

— Pastor Jerrel Gilliam —

AT A WEDNESDAY PRAYER GROUP.

In the fifties and sixties, a group of Christians gathered in a small house on McCully Street in the South Hills area of Pittsburgh, Pennsylvania. These prayer warriors, teachers, and leaders fanned flames for the miracles that influenced the height of Kathryn Kuhlman's ministries. Today, more than half a century later, I have the privilege to speak before this powerful group of seniors. They inspire me, encourage me, and challenge me. Every time I go before them I am aware that they are carriers of a prophetic flame from the glory days of Pittsburgh's historic past. Many were firsthand witnesses of God's move in our nation. Yet I know they are not all aware of how powerful they truly are. They carry a wisdom and authority that comes only from decades of testimony and faithful service. Just as this is true for them, the authority to influence is greater for pastors who have given their lives to shepherding the flock. Your longevity has qualified you to speak with power and is validated by decades of service. It is my prayer that this chapter will awaken in you fresh fire for influencing the generations around you through the power of your witness.

It started as a normal day with the grandkids.

The story of Jethro, found in the book of Exodus, holds a wonderful example of how senior leaders can have relevant input for younger generations. We pick up the story in Exodus 18, where Jethro, who is identified as the priest of Midian, is operating in the familiar role of grandfather, finishing a visit with his grandkids. No doubt he was mildly worn out by the boundless energy of youth. As it is with most grandparents, the time for kids to return home holds both a welcomed relief and a dreaded goodbye. After dropping off his daughter and grandkids, Jethro met with his son-in-law to catch up on the events that had transpired since they were apart. As is usually the case, Jethro was unaware that a momentous occasion was unfolding: he was about to save a leader and change the course of a nation. Imagine!

Today may seem like a typical day to you, but can you believe that in one God-ordained moment, you can change the course of a ministry, church, community, or nation through your obedience? Will you dare to believe that God can reveal to you the epic adventure that is already unfolding around you? Life-changing opportunities are often disguised in the mundane routines of life. May God open your eyes to see your world as He does.

Listen, praise, and encourage, and then advise.
Read Exodus 18:1-12.

Jethro models an effective approach for influencing another generation. He first listened, praised, and encouraged and then later advised.

Listen. Jethro listened to Moses's lengthy firsthand retelling of the story of the Israelites and the Egyptians. The Bible speaks of good listening skills as the hallmark of a wise man. "My beloved brethren, let every man be swift to hear, slow to speak, slow to wrath" (James 1:19, KJV). One of the most honoring actions we can do is making time listen. By listening, Jethro honored Moses as he operated in his position as a man of understanding.

Praise. Jethro's response not only was an authentic expression of praise to God but he properly modeled that *all* praise belongs to Him. It is always appropriate to honor God with praise, and it is wise to remind the younger generations that praise should be a lifestyle habit.

Encourage. A unique gift entrusted to senior leaders is affirmation. Jethro acknowledged that God worked through Moses. "Jethro said, Blessed be the LORD, who hath delivered you out of the hand of the Egyptians, and out of the hand of Pharaoh, who hath delivered the people from under the hand of the Egyptians" (Exodus 18:10, KJV). Your words of encouragement carry weight because of your position and experience in the body of Christ. Your words carry power.

Advise. Jethro finally observed an area in Moses's life where he could use some advice. And Moses was ready to receive it.

Remember Psalm 145:4, "One generation shall praise Your works to another, and shall declare Your mighty acts" (NASB). God's kingdom is to be an intergenerational expression of community. The vision requires old, young, experienced, and maturing contributing their parts to the whole. God's plan is simply too big for one generation. It will take different skill sets and levels of expertise to activate God's strategy. He intended there to be a call and response between the generations. One calls, and the other responds. The juniors' questions require the seniors' insights. The seniors' experiences call for the juniors' innovation. Back and forth, one calls to the other. Each generation's response honors the voice of the other, which will ultimately reveal God's complete plan.

WHAT IS NATURAL TO YOU MAY NOT BE OBVIOUS TO OTHERS.

Read: Exodus 18:13–23.

Time and practice are excellent teachers. Jethro had been refined in the crucible of experience through years of being a father and priest. What life experiences have positioned you to shine light for a younger generation seeking direction? Resist limiting your ability to influence, and look for opportunities to be a vessel in the hand of God. It did not take Jethro long to see the problem and to discern a solution. Remember, what may seem natural or obvious to you may not be so to others. Give voice to the inner wisdom God entrusted to you. Your years of practice and experience have honed your sagacity and uniquely qualified you to speak into the lives of other generations. What do you see? What lessons have you learned through life's classroom that would be like cool water to thirsty souls?

JETHRO'S COUNSEL MULTIPLIED MOSES'S LEADERSHIP.

Read: Exodus 18:24–27.

By keeping the baton and staying engaged, Jethro maintained his ordained position of authority to influence Moses and the nation. There is little doubt that if Jethro would have passed his baton and retired to the sidelines, Moses would have burned out, the people would have been in chaos, and the nation likely would not have survived the desert. Notice that after the implementation of Jethro's counsel, not only was order and peace restored to the land but Moses's leadership was multiplied. Moses identified leaders on the bench and activated them to lead. I pray that your eyes will be open to see the "leaders in waiting" in your world who are sitting on the sidelines, waiting for the activating call of a senior leader to encourage them into service.

CONCLUSIONS.

You are more than a pastor, you are an activator of destinies to a new generation of leaders. Your voice is needed. It is impossible to start a bonfire if you give away your torch. Realize that a lifetime of service and practice of shepherding God's people has uniquely qualified you to speak with a voice of authority to ignite a flame in the generations that follow you.

Jethro had a choice: sit idly by and watch a broken system perpetuate frustration, or realize that his position gave him influence to affect change. God has specific people and situations that He has positioned for you to influence for His kingdom. Ask Him for wisdom and strategy to influence others for the good. Prayerfully select those to whom you will mentor and encourage.

Do not minimize the power of your testimony or the wisdom gained through your experience as a pastor. The Enemy attacks what he fears. Revelation records that Satan fears the power of your testimony because it will become a weapon that will result in his defeat. "They overcame him by the blood of the Lamb and by the word of their testimony, and they did not love their lives to the death" (Revelation 12:11, NKJV). Can you see why Satan works so hard to silence your testimony? It reminds him of his future defeat! I declare that his assault against your mind is over, through the power of Christ. Satan has sought to remind you of your failures to bring shame and doubt, but greater is He that is in you than he that is in the world!

Revivalist Dwight L. Moody was greatly influenced by the quote "The world has yet to see what God can do with a man fully consecrated to him." He then added, "By God's help, I will be that man."[1] What could God accomplish through your life if you completely yielded to Him? Take a leap of faith and see what He will do with your life multiplied through the younger generations in your sphere of influence.

---

[1] http://www.christianitytoday.com/history/issues/issue-25/world-has-yet-to-see.html

GET TO KNOW THE AUTHOR:

Pastor Jerrel T. Gilliam is an ordained minister under Bishop Joseph Garlington and Reconciliation! Ministries International. He serves as lead pastor of Shiloh Church, an intergenerational, multicultural church in the South Hills area of Pittsburgh, Pennsylvania. He is also the director of programs for Light of Life Rescue Mission, where he oversees a unique grace-based approach to addiction and recovery. Jerrel and his wife, Shannah, reside in the Pittsburgh area, where they enjoy their blended family of seven wonderful children.

CHAPTER 43

THE LOST TREASURE

— Pastor Chad Stecker —

It has been said that "no man was ever so completely skilled in the conduct of life as not to receive new information from age and experience."[1] We live in a day and age where life experience and those who have it have been devalued and deemed inconsequential.

The culture in which we now live has evolved into something completely different from the era our seniors grew up in. They can't relate to or possibly understand what we are dealing with today. Although this is an understandable thought process within certain areas such as technology, we as a whole have missed a very important truth about seniors: they have lived, and lived well.

The seniors in this generation still have so much to teach, and if pastors would take the time to listen, we would hear seniors expressing a desire to keep learning and living. When a culture maneuvers an entire generation out of sight and mind to ultimately die quietly, the church has a great opportunity to position itself to lead the charge to re-engage a senior generation that can teach us all how to truly live.

As a pastor, I have personally seen that when we allow seniors to

---

[1] Jonathan Swift Quotes. (n.d.). BrainyQuote.com. Retrieved October 4, 2017, from BrainyQuote.com Web site: https://www.brainyquote.com/quotes/quotes/j/jonathansw119963.html

have a sense of purpose and a desire to continue living, it increases the overall well-being of a family, church, and community. Seniors are like a forgotten treasure full of life experience, wisdom, and future potential. All we have to realize and acknowledge as pastors is that the Bible is the map, the gospel is the route, and the church is intended to be the X that marked the spot of where this amazing treasure is found. The church has an awesome opportunity to grab hold and become the place where seniors find purpose again and help the younger generation live fully for the first time.

Before we can answer the question of how we can create this new and beautiful culture within the church, we must understand and re-evaluate three lies that the church has come to believe concerning seniors.

The first lie is that seniors don't understand this generation and today's culture. On the surface this thought process doesn't seem too far fetched or harmful, but when actually looking into this statement, we must first define what seniors are expected to understand to become influential again.

The world wants to invalidate the older generation because that age group might not understand or agree with the new ways of doing things. The way we dress, how we converse, what music we listen to, and the technology we use are all critical barriers blocking understanding from one generation to the next. Most people would even consider a generation who doesn't understand the key areas mentioned useless. I have a question, though: When was there ever a time in history that a younger generation didn't feel that the older generation couldn't possibly understand how they live?

Let me explain. The GI generation didn't understand the music of the boomer generation. The boomer generation still doesn't like the music of Generation X, and we all definitely know how Generation X feels about the millennial generation. When it is all said and done, I don't know of a single generation that fully understood and liked all the practices of the following one.

This is the first lie that must be debunked, because it is at the core of who we are as people. The seniors might not fully understand and agree with this generation's practices or styles, but let us not forget that they do understand how this culture feels. They were once in our position. The reason the first statement is a lie and the church must stop believing it as truth is that this generation does understand people and what our culture is fighting for, even if the style and practices have changed. They fully understand the heart of the issue and the desire to change the world for the better. The Bible says, "Wisdom is with the aged, and understanding in length of days" (Job 12:12, ESV). We might know more than ever before, but without our seniors' understanding, we won't have the wisdom to know what to do with that very knowledge we have gained. The senior generation might not understand our ways, but through the years, they have learned the way toward understanding.

The second lie we have believed is that seniors can't relate with the younger generations concerning temptation. As if it wasn't enough that we have pushed a generation aside for a perceived lack of understanding, we have also improperly judged their ability to relate. This is because the availability and accessibility of pornography has evolved. Pornography has gone from a backroom, embarrassing talking point to a cultural pastime beginning at a very early age. What was once considered adult entertainment is now accepted as cultural lifestyle.

If the church would take a step back, they would realize that although times have changed, the issue of temptation has not. The Bible is filled with stories of men and women dealing with the struggle of temptation. As pastors, we understand this more than any of us want to admit, but we have allowed this issue to become a barrier when it comes to allowing our seniors to be a part of our church community in the way they are intended to be.

Robert Weiss stated in his article "Baby Boomers Gone Wild! Seniors and STDs,"

> According to the Center for Disease Control, among our senior citizen population sexually transmitted diseases (STDs) are spreading like wildfire. Since 2007, incidence of syphilis among seniors is up by 52 percent, with chlamydia up 32 percent. And this isn't merely a phenomenon in the United States, as several recent British studies have produced similar results. So apparently the hippy generation has decided to dust off its slightly musty mantra: *If it feels good, do it.*[2]

This isn't the only study that lets us know that pornography and temptation is not a generational issue. We are dealing with a cultural epidemic because of a human sinful nature. Not only are the studies proving that seniors are dealing with the same issues we are facing culturally, they can relate to the details of the freedom one can have through the love and grace of God. Not only can they relate to us, but if we look close enough, the church can see how we can also relate to them. "All have sinned and fall short of the glory of God" (Romans 3:23, ESV).

The third lie we must stop believing is the belief that it has to be their way or the highway. This one was probably the hardest lie I had to come to terms with as a pastor, because the deeper I looked, the simpler the lie became. We are looking at the last generation that was raised never getting their own way. They were raised to honor and carry out the ways of their parents and other leaders. Our seniors did what they were told or else! It was never about them; it was about what was for the common good of everyone.

2 Robert Weiss, "Baby Boomers Gone Wild! Seniors and STDs," *Psychology Today*, March 5, 2014, https://www.psychologytoday.com/blog/love-and-sex-in-the-digital-age/201403/baby-boomers-gone-wild-seniors-and-stds.

But our current generations think it's all about them.

I found that when seniors in my church disagreed with me, it wasn't coming from a place of selfishness but from a mind-set of what they thought was best for the overall common good of the church and community. Whether they were right or wrong, they were thinking about others, not just themselves. As the pastor, with the responsibilities of others on my shoulders, I began seeing myself fall into the trap of a thought process of "My way or the highway," not the seniors. I have learned from the seniors in my church and in my life that when I have an opinion, the most important part is not the "what" but rather the "why."

Proverbs 16:31 says, "Gray hair is a crown of glory; it is gained in a righteous life" (ESV). If the church would change its thought process, we would realize that the ways of the older generation have something to offer us, even in this day and age. The time they have spent living on this earth has helped bring them to a place of righteousness. Biblical righteousness is defined as "what is deemed right by the Lord" and "what is approved in His eyes."[3] When we change how we see seniors, we will change how we respond to their opinions and wisdom.

We need to stop pointing them to the highway for having an opinion and thought process different from ours and our generation's.

If we can learn to avoid the lies about the seniors in our churches and begin believing the truths God wants to reveal to us through them, we will see a new generation rise up that not only can make a way with new methods but will walk on a foundation laid by the generation before them.

The late president Calvin Coolidge made a profound statement when he said, "No person was ever honored for what he received. Honor has been the reward for what he gave."

---

[3] James Strong, *Strong's Expanded Exhaustive Concordance of the Bible* (Nashville: Thomas Nelson, 2009), s.v. "righteousness."

We have seen a generation that no longer knows how to honor the generation that came before. I believe that is because we have as a culture stopped allowing our seniors to give what they know and pass on the wisdom they have gained. We in the church can make a mighty statement. We can give an opportunity for our seniors to have a platform of influence once again. If that would happen, we would once again see the generation of old finally given the honor and respect it so greatly deserves from the generation of the now.

One of the most vital keys to a healthy and victorious church is in the treasure of our seniors. And once again, the Bible is given as the map, the gospel of Jesus is the route, and the church is intended to be the *X* that marked the spot of where this amazing treasure is found.

My experiences with the now treasured seniors in my life has taught me one of my greatest life lessons: although breath helps us stay alive, it is what we do with those breaths that determines whether or not we truly live.

GET TO KNOW THE AUTHOR:

Pastor Chad Stecker is the lead pastor at Arise Church in Tioga, Louisiana, and a featured speaker to men across the United States. He is part of the faculty of A Chosen Generation and the Center for Intergenerational Ministry. He serves on the advisory board of Louisiana Outpouring and is part of the speaking team for Knights of the 21st Century Men's Ministry.

CHAPTER 44

WHO GAVE THE COMMAND TO "STAND DOWN"?

— Pastor Craig Kirkpatrick —

As one active in pastoral ministry for more than forty years, I find myself saddened that we now have to codify and teach intergenerational ministry. It was not always that way! In the fifties and sixties, both my family and our church were intergenerational, although we never would have thought to call it that! We simply did life together—serving one another, helping one another, and loving one another.

For example, my dad's mom, who was a teen at the close of the nineteenth century, had lived through two world wars and the Great Depression. It seemed like Granny was always there. She blessed us with her eighty-plus years of knowledge, life experience, and wisdom. And she offered a soft place to land when our hearts were hurt, listening to us and loving on us in a manner our folks were often too busy, or focused on parenting, to do.

Church wasn't much different. We were simply an extended family doing life in Christ together. Yes, that meant I sat through the business meetings and learned way young what the reference to "an old-fashioned Baptist bloodletting" meant. But I was also surrounded by godly men and women who were equipped and felt free to "jack me up" if they saw me misbehaving or to dispense the life lessons and biblical wisdom they felt I needed when my childish ignorance was on display. And it never crossed my mind that they were meddling or that I should question their love or intentions.

This pattern extended to my pastor, too. Before I got my driver's license, he was taking me to the Phoenix Rescue Mission to give testimony and to preach. Long before I registered for the draft, he was taking me to the Maricopa County Jail—made infamous by the colorful "Sheriff Joe"—to do cell-to-cell evangelism and Bible studies. It was simply watch one, do one, learn all you can, and do it again.

Through more than fifty years of active ministry and forty-plus years of pastoral ministry, one of the great blessings of my life has been the godly saints who have built into my life and ministry. But when I ran into Chuck Stecker, I had been set adrift and had forgotten things that should not have been forgotten.

That encounter came at a men's ministry leadership conference at Lost Valley Ranch, in Colorado. As I recall, Chuck's was the lone voice focusing on intergenerational ministry—in a not insignificant speakers' panel. But that was not the reason that brief encounter had such a profound effect on me.

I came to the conference battle weary, grieving, and faced with a paradigm shift that I did not want to make. As with every such life-altering moment, there were numerous factors in play, and two were seminal.

First, over the previous five years, I had suffered the loss of every one of the godly men and mentors God had put into my life. This cadence of death had been bookended by the deaths of my two earthly fathers. Each one of these men was of the WWII generation. God had used each of them to mark my life, in incredible ways, beginning with my father and ending with my father-in-law.

From Dad, I received a heart for Jesus, a passion for ministry, and a mind honed to think biblically and theologically. I had also received a deep understanding of what author Sheldon Vanauken called our Father's "severe mercy," a theology of crucifying the flesh and embracing the sufferings of Christ. Dad was the most natural, personal evangelist I have ever known. But he was also an angry and broken man who went to see his Savior before the wound between us was healed.

From my wife's dad, I learned the heart of a gentle and nurturing father. He was the first man I recall ever telling me that he loved me and that he was proud of me. Until the time of his death, Dad Wright was actively building into the generations that followed, for Christ and His kingdom.

Between them were men God brought alongside me for a season to steady the ship of my life and help identify and navigate the course ahead. But there had been another encounter, even more profound. One afternoon as I was holding my newborn second daughter and overwhelmed by the weight of responsibility resting upon my shoulders, my heavenly Father broke into my brooding. In that moment, He was painfully blunt: "You are no longer a stupid kid, and it is time you stopped acting like it!" From that moment forward, my first Father stepped in to directly parent me and mentor me. I became consciously aware that He was guiding my journey into manhood and ministry and that He had been doing so all along. He made it clear that His gifts and His calling were what I had received and that they were irrevocable. He also made it clear that He was calling due the promise I had made to Him many years before: "I will do whatever you ask me to do!"

But now, grieving the loss of every father and mentor—the men who had meant the most to me and who had been used of Him to mark me for the kingdom—I felt adrift and lost. All I knew were the words that had come free form and unbidden when my sister called to tell me that Dad was dead: "I now stand at the head of the generations!" But the men who could have helped me navigate these waters were all gone.

The second factor that was having a powerful effect on the inner landscape of my life, and one that I had been struggling with for quite some time, was a growing sense that I could no longer do ministry. I had been doing it for decades! You see, during WWII, my dad came to salvation through the ministry of The Navigators. I had grown up with a Navigator model of ministry as my "North Star." According to this model, when you were put into the life of a "younger" believer, you offered to disciple him or her. That model was informed by a challenge you issued before you ever began your walk together: "Here is where I am going. If you would like to join me on the journey, great, let's go! If not, let me know if and when you are." Until then, you did not spend a lot of time on that person. I had been raised memorizing the *Topical Memory System* verse packs and doing the Design for Discipleship Bible studies. I had "beta tested" the Nav's Colossians *2:7* discipleship course in our local church. And I fully believed that helping others grow in the knowledge of the Word and in the ministry skills of the kingdom defined my primary calling as a pastor.

But as the years had rolled by, I was increasingly confronted with the disconnect between "biblical knowledge" coupled with "ministry skill" *and* godly character. It seemed that the self-starting, dutiful, and disciplined did well with the Nav model. The other 95 percent, not so much. As I grew more gray hairs and earned pastoral cred, I was increasingly being drawn into the mess of people's lives. It was smelly and ugly and painful! And I often found myself silently screaming—as Bruce Dern did in the 1980 film *Middle Age Crazy*—"I don't want to be the dad! I don't want to be the dad! I don't want to be the *dad*!"

The problem was that real character and genuine godliness are formed in the crucible of real life, not in the study of the Word or the memorizing of Scripture. If the earthly "spiritual director" is going to have an impact on real spiritual formation, he or she will have to be present in the life of the one being helped to grow in life and godliness. And if the pastor/shepherd is to be a pastor and a shepherd, he most certainly must be present in his or her people's lives, especially in the lives of the 95 percent who are not self-starting, dutiful, and disciplined. And that is what I was running from. First, when I was young, I had learned the sinister lesson that people will hurt you and betray you! Better not get too close. Second, being present in the lives of people wasn't just messy and dirty; it hurt at every level. You had to be with them, you had to weep with them, you had to bleed with them, and you had to learn to love them. And what was more, I discovered as I wept for them and bled for them and loved them—even in the dark watches of the night—that it wasn't just excruciating but also exhausting! I was an introvert at heart, so it sucked me dry and left me empty.

Yet not long before the conference, in the normal course of reading the Bible, God had pulled me up short with the words of Judges 5:7: "Until I, Deborah, arose, until I arose, a mother in Israel." In the next instant, He reminded me of my covenant to "do whatever He asked me to do." With that reminder came this command: "I have made you a father, and not just of your four precious children but of many other sons and daughters. I have taught you how to be a dad, and there are many of My kids who need to know My heart for them by knowing the heart of an earthly dad. You will never tell Me again that you do not want to be the dad!"

An aside: Since early in my Christian life, the description of David as "a man after [God's] own heart" (1 Samuel 13:14) had become the longing of my heart. There is a part of David's story, one that lay outside of God's description of David, that I had been intrigued by but had never experienced. It is where we are told of his first encounter with Jonathan. There we read that "the soul of Jonathan was knit to the soul of David" (18:1, ESV).

As I sat at the conference listening to Chuck, everything came crashing in and it all began to come together. He described his journey with his father, and it hit me: this "man's man" knows "the father wound" and that it will never be fully healed until heaven! I began to weep. My emotions were raw as I grieved the loss of so many and so much that really mattered. And my soul was knit to Chuck, even though I doubt he ever knew, as I'd never told him. With that realization came a deep and abiding peace with my heavenly Father being the only father present in my life, till He calls me home. Later that night, as my Father dealt with me in kindness, I surrendered to His will regarding being a father and a shepherd and not just a disciple maker.

I left the conference with my staff, elders, and deacons. As I did so, the Father let me see the incredible band of brothers (sisters, too!) He had placed around me. I found myself so very grateful!

As we began developing our men's ministry, it was natural for it to take on intergenerational DNA from the beginning. The greatest reason was this: as we began wrestling with the form it would take, I realized we already had a great model in place.

For many years, my son and I had been part of a large elk and deer hunting camp. We hunted during the first week of November in the high country of north central Colorado. The camp rarely had less than four or five father/son, grandfather/grandson groups, sometimes nearly twice that many, with ages ranging from ten to over seventy. Together, we had weathered temperatures well below negative twenty degrees and survived blizzards that ran every other camp out of the high valley in which we hunted. Dads and granddads mixed and matched with one another and the various sons and grandsons, biological and "adopted for the hunt." We taught them crafts and about shouldering the various camp responsibilities. We passed on woodworking skills and the care of and survival in the wild and beautiful country we were blessed to hunt. And we passed on the skills and ethics of hunting and harvesting wild game. But we did more! We lived and talked openly about the things of the Lord and His Word. We shared moments of seeing God in the wild place and of worshipping Him in the forest cathedrals. We sought to pass on our faith to our sons, not just our love for the outdoors, hunting, challenging the elements of winter in the high country, and being in fellowship with one another. And we did that as the subtext of everything else, but not in an in-your-face or preachy sort of way.

So the heart of our men's ministry and our efforts to infect every ministry in our midst with the intergenerational virus has been our camping ministry. It began with a father/son camp. A couple of years later, we added a father/daughter camp. (The only difference between the two camps is that the girls get dirtier!) A few years later, we added family camp.

We have worked diligently to see the ethos modeled in our camping ministry penetrate the church and the congregation, and we have seen successes. Some, we have found, run their course and come to an end; others have had the legs to stand the test of time. However, we "type As" are more comfortable talking about our success than about our missteps and failures. But it is our failures and our responses to them that is at the heart of one of the biggest challenges we have faced—that I have faced.

One of our ongoing challenges has been with the generation from which every one of my fathers and mentors had come: The WWII generation ("The Greatest Generation"). With them, I have regularly come up against two issues: an immobilizing sense of having failed in their own families (perhaps a legacy of the rebellion and overt condemnation of their generation by their children, the baby boomers, throughout the sixties and seventies and beyond) and an attitude of retirement entitlement (which usually comes out as "I served my time. I did my duty! Let the younger generations do theirs now!").

To the excruciating sense of failure they express, I usually respond, "Did you learn anything from that?" Almost always, the answer is yes. Normally, I will respond with "Why not pass that on to the generations that follow you?" Yet I wonder if the more tragic answer is this: just as the boomer generation has been marked so deeply by the fallout of the Vietnam War, so also has The Greatest Generation been marked by the enormous amount of disdain and rejection that we heaped upon them. Perhaps we haven't really thought about this because their generation just doesn't complain, as our generation does. God forgive us! I wonder if we will find them truly engaging with the generations that followed theirs before we humble ourselves and ask their forgiveness for our rebellion, scorn, and condemnation.

I think retirement entitlement will be easier to challenge if we take care of the devastation we may have heaped upon them. Imagine winning the war, and saving the world from the scourge of Hitler and the Nazis, only to find two decades later that your best efforts to love and nurture your own children were rejected and condemned. The Greatest Generation cut their teeth on sacrifice and duty. I believe that if we can persuade them that we really have repented and are sorry—that we really do need them, want them, and value them—they will step up!

And we might be able to do that by calling upon their incredible sense of duty and sacrifice. We may just need to ask a few important questions:

"Where in the Scriptures do you see our Father putting His stamp of approval on retirement?" (Taking a Sabbath rest? Absolutely! Retirement? Not a whisper!)

"Who is your Commanding Officer?" (Jesus!)

"What is the mission He gave?" (Storm the gates of hell till He calls you home or returns!)

"Is your tour of duty over?" (If you are still breathing, the answer is no!)

"Then who told you that you could stand down?" (No one who matters!)

GET TO KNOW THE AUTHOR:

Craig Kirkpatrick is senior pastor of the Evangelical Free Church of Eaton, Colorado, where he has served for twenty-three years. He earned his master's in theology from Dallas Theological Seminary and was ordained to the gospel ministry in May of 1979. He also holds ordination within the EFCA and chaired its district board of ministerial standing for seven years. Over his forty-plus years of active ministry, he has planted three churches and pastored four established ones. To date, he has led or served on more than two dozen short-term mission trips on five continents. He considers himself incredibly blessed to have shared love, life, and ministry with his beloved wife, Beccy, for more than forty-two years. Together, they have raised four children and are especially enjoying their ten grandchildren.

CHAPTER 45

WELL DONE!

— Pastor Apolonio "Sonny" Castilleja —

QUESTION: WHEN I MEET JESUS, WILL I HEAR "WELL DONE THY GOOD AND FAITHFUL SERVANT"?

At present, I am sixty-seven years old and in my thirty-fifth year of pastoring a church. Over the past seven years, I have focused on working with Trinity Baptist Church to combine with my previous responsibility of pastoring Agape Christian Church in Longmont, Colorado. The following is the expressed focus of our church effort: to be a "Christ-centered, multiethnic, intergenerational church," which contains a lifetime of submission, prayer, and sensitivity to the leading of God in my life.

BEGINNING

My paternal grandfather, Pastor Jose A. Castilleja, was an uneducated and simple man who, after coming to personally know Jesus Christ as his Savior, was driven by a dedication and passion for pursuing God's will in his life and that of his family.

He began, at age forty and with a wife and already large family, by asking God to teach him to read so that he could then read the Bible and share it with his family and those he would meet and know. He did not realize what God's will or direction was taking but was willing to "seek first His kingdom" so that the other things would then take the direction God would bring into his life.

As he began his spiritual journey with God, he still worked and needed to provide for his family as best he could, which meant traveling from Texas to Colorado and Nebraska in a regular and annual circuit of migrant field work. This involved hard and long hours of work travel and meeting people that helped form his life and ministry. He didn't know what tomorrow would bring and had nothing given to him, but he did have his Bible, faith, and commitment to learning and growing in the life God had drawn for him.

To begin his Christian life, my grandfather became a faithful church member of a Pentecostal church in south Texas, and when he traveled, for months at a time every year, the routine became that he and his family would stay in Colorado for most of the year, spring through early fall, and work. This also caused yearning that came from within his soul to attend church and know, congregate, and fellowship with other believers. The family often traveled long miles and dusty dirt roads to places not otherwise known just to sing, fellowship, and hear God's Word. When that became harder to find, he began to have church services under some big cotton-wood trees in a closed mining camp where he lived, known as Puritan Camp, near Erie, Colorado. There, he and others would meet on Sundays at two in the afternoon to "have church," and then people would travel back to their homes and prepare for long hours of work and hard life (as it seemed to be at that time). That is how he began to fulfill his calling, or desire, to do God's will in his life, as God would lead and provide.

As we all need God to lead us and show us His will, we also need someone to lead and mentor us in this life—with blood, skin, and bones—to share, correct, encourage, and direct our growth. No one is an island, and we all need help to live our lives, learn from our mistakes, and see God's provision and leading in our lives.

In my years of ministry as a pastor in the local church and for several years as part of the dynamic men's movement of Promise Keepers in the nineties, it has become clear that we must be a family of all generations.

This is not a time for the older generations to quit. Never have we needed our seniors more than we do today. It is my belief that if we are to hear the words "Well done thy good and faithful servant," we must minister to all the generations and we need all generations to be engaged.

There is a great work to be done, and God is giving us great opportunities. We will not be able to seize those opportunities if we quit and simply pass the baton.

GET TO KNOW THE AUTHOR:

Sonny Castilleja has been the pastor of Agape Christian Church since June 1982 and has also served Trinity Baptist Church in Longmont, Colorado, since January 2009. His focus has been on building a Christ-centered and multiethnic intergenerational church, therefore blending the two congregations together. Sonny's original church was a Pentecostal Spanish-speaking one that his grandfather pioneered in 1957 that has since become bilingual. It is a blending of heritage, culture, and families under the banner of the Christian faith. Sonny was privileged to serve at Promise Keepers from 1995 to 2000 as Hispanic ministry liaison and finished as global reconciliation manager for Hispanic ministries. He has been married to Nancy for forty years, and they have one daughter and three wonderful grown grandchildren. Sonny's main focus now is health and spiritual maturity to finish strong and faithful to our Lord and Savior.

CHAPTER 46

LEADING SENIORS TO LIVE OUT THEIR CALLINGS

— Reverend Kristi Lemley —

What an honor and privilege it is to be able to speak into the lives of men and women who love the Lord. One of the greatest joys of being a pastor is to see people growing in their walks with the Lord. You are afforded the blessing to work alongside those you do life with in order to reach the lost and hurting.

When the opportunity to write this chapter presented itself, I wondered what I could say to pastors who are in the trenches daily, bombarded with ideas, concepts, and a plethora of information. I do not pastor a church, but daily I help people realize their freedom and full potential. What could I add? Prayer resulted. God has given me a voice to speak His vision with church leaders. What I am about to share from my heart is, I believe, for such a time as this.

I want to encourage you right now to take a deep breath. Are you feeling tired, worn out, frustrated, overwhelmed, or empty? Expectations of what we think things should look like or how they should run zap our strength. We thought the church would have grown by now. That new town we were sent to appeared to be a good move, but in reality, there are more problems than first realized. In addition, oftentimes we arrive at a point of weariness because of others' expectations of us. This or that needs to be changed, someone dislikes the songs, the nursery needs more volunteers, someone complains about where the piano was moved. *You* need to do this! Sound familiar?

Stop and think. Do you have peace, or is it an elusive concept? Do you have passion for ministry, or has it fizzled out? Be honest with yourself. No one is judging you right now. Just be real. Do you have peace and passion for ministry? Take a deep breath, close your eyes, and answer these questions.

So, what did you discover? I would guess you need to be revived. Actually, we all need to be revived. Ministry demands can drain the life out of us. We wonder what it will take to change the situation or to change us. The Lord has provided a solution: *revival.* We are in great need for God to revive us. What is the result of revival? Author Winkie Pratney shares four insights in his book *Revival.* Revival brings (1) a recovery to life from death, (2) a return/recall to activity from a state of languor by bringing a holy shock to apathy and carelessness, (3) a return/recovery from a state of neglect, oblivion, obscurity, or depression by restoring truth and recalling obedience that has been forgotten, and (4) an awakening of people to their spiritual concerns. Revival is necessary to counteract spiritual decline and create spiritual momentum.[1] Oh Lord, send revival! That is my heart's desire for you, and that is the only way to influence our churches and communities for Christ.

We desperately need to return to the Lord as our first love. This will not only cause peace to flow like a river but also ignite our passion. When the pastor's passion is ignited, it spreads. Believe me, people can see your attitude, even when you think you are

---

[1] Winkie Pratney, *Revival: Principles to Change the World* (Pensacola, FL: Christian Life Books, 2002), 12–13.

hiding it. Your passion might not spread overnight, but with a consistent display, it is only a matter of time. Could you imagine people coming up to you wanting to help out or begin new outreaches? Oh Lord, send revival.

What triggers revival? Prayer. Throughout the history of the church, revival began with only a few people praying for more of the Lord. Self-sufficiency pushes revival away, so what would happen if we remembered we are nothing without Him? What would happen if we prayed about every decision? What if our hearts were truly humbled before the Lord on a daily basis? Oh Lord, send revival!

Until revival comes, I encourage you to look at the expectations you place on yourself for ministry. Where do you need to apply grace? Where do you need to step up your game? What expectations are unreachable that you need to reexamine? Pastors have a tendency to give grace better than receiving and applying it.

As I mentioned, people have expectations of you. Most of the time, they are placed on you through no fault of your own. Possibly the previous pastor did things a certain way or the congregation has been taught incorrectly. I want to challenge these expectations and thought processes. Ephesians 4:11–12 explains how the roles of apostle, prophet, evangelist, pastor, and teacher have been given to the church for the edification and equipping of the saints. I do not want to get into a debate over these Scriptures but instead point out that the role of pastor is to equip the saints to do the work of the ministry. Did you catch that? We are to equip *them* to do the work of the ministry.

One way to decrease unrealistic expectations and thought patterns is to return ministry to the people. Pastor and author Geoffrey Thomas reveals, "We get volunteers for the mundane and unglamorous work because we like to regulate everything."[2] In

---

[2] Geoffrey Thomas, *Philip and the Revival in Samaria* (Carlisle, PA: Banner of Truth, 2005), 8.

other words, we do what we think is important, and everything else can be given to others to complete. This creates the mentality that people "help us" instead of us teaching and training people how to do ministry. Author Greg Ogden confirms, "We want pastors who can do it all, so that they *will* do it all. The desire for 'perfect' pastors creates a passivity in the congregation."[3] This creates burnout and frustration for pastors.

So how do we change this? By evaluating how ministries begin and operate. Ogden points out, "Bubble-up ministries are grown out of a permission-giving atmosphere. This means there must be a release of control of ministry from the hands of paid staff and office holders so that ministry can originate at any point in the body."[4] When we are teaching and equipping the saints to do the ministry, a ministry idea can originate within anyone in the church. Yes, there have to be boundaries and leadership within each ministry, but when a congregant comes to us with an idea, we need to listen. Ogden calls this type of leadership idea the "player-coach" mentality.[5]

We undertake ministry to reach out to the hurting and lost and bring them into relationship with Christ. When ministries are born out of people in the congregation, we as pastors do not have to convince people to volunteer; they will hopefully offer themselves when it is prompted by their passion. (Of course, training is vital, and they may need some prompting until people internalize their own calls.) They will recruit their friends and family members to work alongside them. This in turn sets up intergenerational ministry and a diversity of ministries.

The importance of diversity of ministries within the church cannot be overstated. The intergenerational church is essential to

---

3 Greg Ogden, *Unfinished Business: Returning the Ministry to the People of God* (Grand Rapids, MI: Zondervan, 2003), 99.

4 Ogden, *Unfinished Business*, 100.

5 Ogden, *Unfinished Business*, 97.

winning the lost for Christ and living in community. Each age group has certain and specific benefits for the body of believers. God has called and equipped each person with specific gifts that He wants to utilize. It is our responsibility to foster these gifts.

There is a group of individuals who are treasures. These individuals I am referring to are the senior members in your church. Seniors are the greatest untapped group currently. They possess wisdom, experience, and freedom of time.

How do we incorporate seniors and increase intergenerational ministries? Begin to teach on every person being responsible for ministry, not only while preaching, but also in bulletins and newsletters. Ask seniors what their passions are. Encourage them to recognize that the purpose for their lives is not complete as long as they have breath in their body. Have a breakfast or lunch (everyone likes food) and ask for suggestions and ideas. Have the deacons or church leaders host focus groups. Put out a suggestion box requiring a name to be attached to all input. Hold training forums on how to lead a ministry. You get my point. Become creative. Pray about it. We serve a creative God, who I am convinced wants seniors to live out their callings and increase intergenerational ministry.

I pray that the need for revival and to return ministry to the people have stirred your spirit. It has been an honor and privilege to write what the Lord laid on my heart. I pray blessings over your church and the people you serve.

GET TO KNOW THE AUTHOR:

Kristi Lemley is the founder and president of Living in the Light Ministries and Calm Waters Counseling and Resource Center. She is an ordained minister with the Assemblies of God and a licensed clinical social worker in the process of obtaining her doctorate of ministry. Kristi has been in ministry since 2003 and currently serves as assistant presbyter for her section. She resides in Brighton, Illinois, with her husband, Kraig, along with their dog, Kooper, and cat, Kallie.

CHAPTER 47

UNTIL WE DRAW
OUR FINAL BREATH

— Bruce Fong —

She was busy in the kitchen. A cheerful silver-haired woman brought a breakfast feast and set it on the dining room table. Her husband welcomed the food with a bright smile and gave the cook a grateful kiss. She lightly smacked him on his shoulder with a hot pad while they shared a giggle from years of sharing life together.

Then she turned and walked quickly to the stairs while glancing at her wrist watch. Her hand grasped the banister while one foot rested on the first step. Her call was filled with volume and experience: "Hey, sleepyhead! Breakfast is served! Come on down or we will be late for church."

She heard no sounds. Curious, she swiftly ascended the stairs and stopped abruptly at the door of her son's bedroom. He was a young adult, still single, staying at home until he could decide where he wanted to live.

Mom knocked on the door with a hail of raps, intended to startle as well as wake. "Are you awake yet?"

A sleepy groan made her twist her cheerful countenance into the look of a determined messenger. She threw the door wide open to reveal her son still sleeping in bed.

"What are you doing? Get up or we'll be late for church!" she ordered.

"I'm *not* going to church!" sputtered her son, trying to shield his eyes from the light spilling into his room.

"Give me a good reason." Mom uttered those words more a challenge than curiosity.

"I'll give you three reasons. One, I'm tired, so I'm sleeping in. Two, no one there likes me. Three, the sermons are boring!"

"You are getting up and for three very *good* reasons. One, we have always gone to church on Sunday because God wants us to never forsake gathering together with other believers. Two, it doesn't matter if people don't like us; it is up to us to love them. Three, *you* are the pastor!"

Okay, fellow pastors, all of us can relate. We laugh at this joke because we know firsthand the feelings, hurts, and loneliness that have visited our ministry lives too often.

I am one of you. God called me into His service in 1971. Loving the Savior was my life. Whatever and wherever He wanted for my life was my singular passion. We share that ministry calling in common.

Admittedly, I did not know the downside of entering into His service before I signed on the dotted line. Don't get me wrong. I never regretted the decision. I just was surprised that spiritual sheep not only have teeth, but they have sharp teeth. They have no hesitation to bare their fangs, snarl, bite, and tear.

Humanly, it never ceased to shock me that biting sheep always felt justified while attacking God's servants. They believe they are righteous. It's a whole new way of defining good, but they are very proud of their standing up and defending their opinion.

In the meantime, we lie awake wondering what we did wrong. Tears soak our pillows. We smile and warmly shake the hands of our detractors and act publicly as if nothing is wrong. Do you remember those horrible moments?

There is a slow drip of pain inside when a couple whispers about a "special" meeting at Rick and Lisa's house on Friday night, "No, Pastor is not coming, so we can talk freely."

On one of my visits around town, I stopped to meet a pastor in his study during the week. The parking lot was empty when I showed up. I waited for fifteen minutes past our appointment. Just as I started my vehicle, he pulled in and waved me over to the front door of the church. He immediately apologized. Clearly, he was rattled and distracted.

He welcomed me into his office as we both settled down.

"Thanks for seeing me, Pastor. I am just going around town and meeting pastors. How are you doing?"

That's all it took. He looked at me and broke down in tears. Uncontrollable sobs took over. I just waited.

When he gathered his composure, he apologized. He had just met with one of the leading ladies of the church, who informed him that she was calling for a special business meeting. She informed the pastor that she fully intended to call for a vote of "no confidence." She was tired of all the people who were swarming to the new church in the neighborhood with exciting worship, relevant preaching, and sensational youth ministry.

Sound familiar?

But it is not nor ever has been about our sob story. Jesus promised that the gates of Hades would not prevail against His church. Our inconvenience is tenderly cradled in the arms of the Almighty while He directs His army to keep marching on. How does progress continue while we are tempted to lose heart?

Longevity is the goal. How can we contribute to the growth of the church while we are serving and long after our lives are enjoying eternal fellowship with the Savior? There a number of emphases that relate to this endeavor. However, one of the keys is us directing in the intergenerational model.

We can contribute to this model of endurance through several methods. First, make sure we disciple our children. The Scriptures give us a visual model in the Old Testament. Israel was to pass on spiritual truth and lessons to the third and fourth generations. Not only were they to influence their own children with spiritual truth but they were to pour into their grandchildren as well. Be their rock—their confidence that faith really works. Tell them the stories of God's faithfulness in your life. When they sense that you were an eyewitness of truth, their faith will find stability and certainty as well.

Second, make your mark in your local church. Set the example with your active service. Utilize the gifts God has given to you. Mobilize the men to lead the church family. Show them how it is done. Teach them how to study the Bible on their own. Introduce them to rock-solid theology. Give them a chance to break open the Bible to the church family. Teach others to join you in that service.

This is the discipleship model the Savior left for all of us. The numbers do not need to be great, but the selection process is critical.

We won't be able to pour into all the men. Some just won't do it. Look for the ones who are eager to follow the Savior. Invest in them.

In your efforts to pour into faithful men, make sure that a huge part of your training is how they then train others. Walk with them through all of this. Make sure your church is geared up and organized to make opportunities available for all these efforts.

Third, attract younger men to join in the effort. Just as you pour into your children and grandchildren, so you should find the men who need your experience, look up to your example, and hunger for someone they respect to take an interest in their lives. Guide them, challenge them, love on them, and shepherd them and their families.

Remember, they first need to be attracted to follow in your footsteps. Then they also need someone to reach out and walk with them as they grow, strengthen, and live by faith. Finally, when you release them to reproduce, keep on being their example. Model discipleship, win others to Christ, grow them in their faith, teach them how to pray, and let them experience the strength of growing numbers in the Lord.

Keep the intergenerational model going. Its momentum will deliver massive spiritual dividends, multiply impactful leaders, and give each of us spiritual satisfaction at every season of our lives. We are not done serving and loving people. Instead, we will do that until we draw our final breath.

Get to Know the Author:

Dr. Bruce Fong and his wife, Yvonne, have three adult children and multiple grandchildren. Bruce is a speaker, author, and teacher who currently serves as dean at Dallas Theological Seminary in Houston, Texas. He received his PhD from the University of Aberdeen, Scotland, and has previously served on the speaking team for Promise Keepers and in various pastoral roles. He enjoys bicycling, dramas, family time, outdoor sports, musicals, and swimming.

For Personal Reflection or Group Discussion

- Where are the clearest and most significant points of intersection between older and younger believers in your church?
- What are you doing to foster a desire for increased connectivity between generations?
- What is something that needs to happen immediately to "repair the breach" between the generations in the church in America today?
- What are two principles you have learned that you wish you would have learned earlier in your life?
- Make a list of three to five people from a younger generation who are in your sphere of influence and commit to pray for them for thirty days. Follow God's prompting to reach out to the ones most responsive to your input.
- Has passion for ministry decreased or ceased altogether?
- Has a permission-giving atmosphere been cultivated in your church?
- What could you do to heal the hearts of the older generation in your life and congregation, especially in regard to their "parent wound"? When and how are you going to do it?
- Has the "retirement entitlement" bug infected you and your thinking about ministry toward the end of life? Will you repent of such nonsense?
- Where might you have assumed the right to "stand down"? What are you going to do about it?
- What are some things you could do to begin relating more with the seniors in your church and community?
- What are some areas in your life in which you refused to hear advice from others? Why were those areas shut off from others?

APPENDIX A

ADDITIONAL READING

Addis, Andy. *Blotch: A Tale of Forgiveness and Grace*. Nashville, B&H, 2016.

———. *Generation: Repairing the Breach*. www.andyaddis.com.

———. *Reading It Right: Reading the Bible the Way It Should Be Read*. 2015.

Andrews, Andy. *The Noticer: Sometimes, All a Person Needs Is a Little Perspective*. Nashville: Thomas Nelson, 2011.

Barna, George. *Baby Busters: The Disillusioned Generation*. Chicago: Northfield, 1994.

———. *Generation Next: What You Need to Know About Today's Youth*. Ventura, CA: Regal, 1995.

———. *Real Teens: A Contemporary Snapshot of Youth Culture*. Ventura, CA: Regal, 2001.

Batterson, Mark. *All In: You Are One Decision Away from a Totally Different Life*. Grand Rapids, MI: Zondervan, 2013.

Baxter, Jeff. *From Broken to Beautiful: What Repairing Streams Has Taught Me About Healing the Church*. Free Methodist Church USA, fmcusa.org/bookstore, 2017.

———. *Together: Adults and Teenagers Transforming the Church*. (Grand Rapids, MI: Zondervan, 2011.

———. *The Ultimate Guide to Being a Christian in College: Don't Forget to Pack Your Faith*. Grand Rapids, MI: Zondervan, 2012.

Beausay, William, II. *Boys! Shaping Ordinary Boys into Extraordinary Men*. Rev. ed. Nashville: Thomas Nelson, 2002.

Bergstrom, Richard and Leona. *Amazing Grays: Unleashing the Power of Age in Your Congregation*. Edmonds, WA: ChurchHealth, 2000.

———. *Musical Chairs*. DVD. Edmonds, WA: Re-Ignite, https://re-ignite.net.

———. *Third Calling: What Are You Doing the Rest of Your Life?* Edmonds, WA: ChurchHealth, 2016.

———. *Third Calling Study Guide*. Edmonds, WA: ChurchHealth, 2017.

Bevere, John. *Driven by Eternity: Make Your Life Count Today and Forever*. 10th anniversary ed. Palmer Lake, CO: Messenger International, 2016.

Bourgond, Greg. *Papa's Blessings: The Gifts That Keep Giving*. Bloomington, IN: iUniverse, 2011.

———. *Setting Your Course: How to Navigate Your Life's Journey.* Bloomington, IN: iUniverse, 2014.

Brodsky, Jeff. *Stepping into Adulthood: Discovering the Most Significant Event in Your Child's Life.* Conifer, CO: JOY International, 1997.

Buford, Bob. *Beyond Halftime: Practical Wisdom for Your Second Half.* Grand Rapids, MI: Zondervan, 2016.

———. *Finishing Well: The Adventure of Life Beyond Halftime.* Grand Rapids, MI: Zondervan, 2011.

———. *Halftime: Moving from Success to Significance.* Grand Rapids, MI: Zondervan, 2015.

Burton, Jim. *Legacy Builders: Dad, What Does Your Life Say to Your Wife and Children?* Lafayette, LA: Vital Issues, 1996.

Canfield, Ken, PhD. *The Heart of a Father: How You Can Become a Dad of Destiny.* Chicago: Northfield, 2006.

Carnegie, Dale. *How to Win Friends and Influence People.* New York: Simon & Schuster, 1994.

Clinton, J. Robert. *Having a Ministry That Lasts: Becoming a Bible Centered Leader.* Barnabas, 1997.

———. *The Making of a Leader: Recognizing the Lessons and Stages of Leadership Development.* Rev. ed. Colorado Springs, CO: NavPress, 2012.

———. *Strategic Concepts That Clarify a Focused Life.* Barnabas, 2005.

Clinton, J. Robert, and Paul D. Stanley. *Connecting: The Mentoring Relationships You Need to Succeed in Life.* Colorado Springs, CO: NavPress, 1992.

Clinton, Richard, and Paul Leavenworth. *Finishing Well: Establishing a Lasting Legacy.* CreateSpace, 2013.

———. *Living and Leading Well: Navigating Mid-Life Ministry.* CreateSpace, 2013.

———. *Starting Well: Building a Strong Foundation for a Lifetime of Ministry.* Barnabas, 1994.

Covey, Stephen R. *The Seven Habits of Highly Effective People: Powerful Lessons in Personal Change.* 25th anniversary ed. New York: Simon & Schuster, 2013.

Cymbala, Jim, with Dean Merrill. *Fresh Wind, Fresh Fire: What Happens When God's Spirit Invades the Hearts of His People.* Grand Rapids, MI: Zondervan, 2008.

Dalbey, Gordon. *Father and Son: The Wound, the Healing, the Call to Manhood.* Nashville: Thomas Nelson, 1992.

Dees, Robert F. *Resilient Leaders.* San Diego: Creative Team Publishers, 2013.

———. *Resilient Warriors*. San Diego: Creative Team Publishers, 2011.

———. *Resilient Warriors: Advanced Study Guide*. San Diego: Creative Team Publishers, 2012.

DeVries, Mark. *Family-Based Youth Ministry*. Downers Grove, IL: InterVarsity, 2004.

Duewel, Wesley L. *Heroes of the Holy Life*. Grand Rapids, MI: Zondervan, 2002.

Dyet, Jim, and Jim Russell. *The Master's Plan for Your Family*. Lansing, MI: Amy Foundation, 2003.

Eldredge, John. *Wild at Heart: Discovering the Secret of a Man's Soul*. Rev. ed. Nashville: Thomas Nelson, 2011.

Eno, Dr. Nick. *The Orphan Syndrome: Breaking Free and Finding Home*. Enumclaw, WA: Redemption, 2016.

Erickson, Dr. Dan. *God Loves Do-Overs*. Grand Rapids, MI: Credo, 2009.

———. *God Loves Do-Overs: Study Guide*. Grand Rapids, MI: Credo, 2009.

———. *Grandfathering: Live to Leave a Legacy*. Grand Rapids, MI: Credo, 2014.

———. *Ready to Fly: Finding Your Greater Yes*. Nashville: Thomas Nelson, 2006.

———. *Ready to Fly: Study Guide*. Nashville, Thomas Nelson, 2006.

———. *An Unstoppable Force: A Christian Manifesto*. 2011.

Erickson, Dr. Dan, with Rex Tignor. *Why Minister to Men? Learn to Equip and Empower the Men of Your Church*. CreateSpace, 2014.

Faith and Fitness Magazine, http://faithandfitness.net.

Fleece, Esther. *No More Faking Fine: Ending the Pretending*. Grand Rapids, MI: Zondervan, 2017.

Fong, Bruce W. *Determined to Finish Well: More of My Life Is Behind Me Than Ahead of Me, So I Am Doubling My Efforts to Finish Well*. CreateSpace, 2016.

Fouts-Hyatt, Angie. *Nothing Compared*. To be published.

Frost, Jack. *Experiencing the Father's Embrace: Finding Acceptance in the Arms of a Loving God*. Lake Mary, FL: Charisma House, 2002.

Furtick, Steven. *Sun Stand Still: What Happens When You Dare to Ask God for the Impossible*. Colorado Springs, CO: Multnomah, 2010.

Garborg, Rolf. *The Family Blessing: Creating a Spiritual Covering for Your Family's Future*. Lakeland, FL: White Stone, 2003.

Geoffrey, Thomas. *Philip and the Revival in Samaria*. Carlisle, PA: Banner of Truth, 2005.

Handley, Rod. *Character That Counts: Who's Counting Yours? Growing Through Accountability*. Cross Training, 2012.

Handley, Rod, Elliot Johnson, and Gordon Thiessen. *Character Counts for Quiet Time and Small Groups*. Cross Training, 2001.

Hanson, Amy. *Baby Boomers and Beyond: Tapping the Ministry Talents and Passions of Adults over 50*. San Francisco: Jossey-Bass, 2010.

Harder, Hannah. *Exposed: The Raw Thoughts from an Ordinary Life*. Bloomington, IL: WestBow, 2016.

Harris, Alex and Brett Harris. *Do Hard Things: A Teenage Rebellion Against Low Expectations*. Colorado Springs, CO: Multnomah, 2013.

Henslin, Earl R. *Man to Man: Helping Fathers Relate to Sons and Sons Relate to Fathers*. Nashville: Thomas Nelson, 1993.

Holtz, Athena Dean. *Full Circle: Coming Home to the Faithfulness of God*. Enumclaw, WA: Redemption, 2017.

Howe, Neil, and William Strauss. *Millennials Rising: The Next Generation*. New York: Vintage, 2000.

Hunt, Susan. *Heirs of the Covenant: Leaving a Legacy of Faith for the Next Generation*. Wheaton, IL: Crossway, 1998.

Johnson, Greg. *Man in the Making: What You Need to Know as You're Becoming a Man*. Nashville: Broadman & Holman, 1997.

Johnson, Greg, and Mike Yorkey. *Faithful Parents, Faithful Kids*. Wheaton, IL: Tyndale, 1994.

Joy, Donald M. *Becoming A Man: A Celebration of Sexuality, Responsibility, and the Christian Young Man: A Grandfather's Blessing for Grandsons*. Nappanee: Evangel, 2001.

———. *Celebrating the New Woman in the Family*. Anderson, IN: Bristol Books, 1994.

———. *Empower Your Kids to Be Adults*. Nappanee: Evangel, 2000.

Kreider, Larry. *The Cry for Spiritual Fathers and Mothers: Compelling Vision for Authentic, Nurturing Relationships Within Today's Church*. Ephrata, PA: House to House, 2000.

Kricher, Lee. *For a New Generation: A Practical Guide for Revitalizing Your Church*. Grand Rapids, MI: Zondervan, 2016.

Kübler-Ross, Elisabeth, and David Kessler. *On Grief and Grieving: Finding the Meaning of Grief Through the Five Stages of Loss*. New York: Simon & Shuster, 2014.

LeLaCheur, Dan. *Generational Legacy: Breaking the Curse, Starting the Blessing*. Eugene, OR: Family Survival, 1994.

————. *Generational Legacy: Study Guide.* Eugene, OR: Family Survival, 1994.

Lemley, Kristi. *Broken and Transformed: Moving Beyond Life's Difficult Times.* CreateSpace, 2012.

Lewis, C. S. *A Grief Observed.* New York: Harper One, 2009.

Long, Jimmy. *Generating Hope: A Strategy for Reaching the Postmodern Generation.* Downers Grove: IL: InterVarsity, 1997.

Ludy, Mark. *The Flower Man: A Wordless Picture Book.* Scribble & Sons, 2015.

Maples, Nika. *Hunting Hope: Dig Through the Darkness to Find the Light.* Franklin, TN: Worthy, 2016.

McAllister, Dawson. *Saving the Millennial Generation: New Ways to Reach the Kids You Care About in These Uncertain Times.* Nashville: Thomas Nelson, 1999.

McDowell, Josh. *The Disconnected Generation: Saving Our Youth from Self-Destruction.* Nashville: Thomas Nelson, 2000.

McManus, Erwin Raphael. *Chasing Daylight: Seize the Power of Every Moment.* Nashville: Thomas Nelson, 2006.

————. *Seizing Your Divine Moment: Dare to Live a Life of Adventure.* Nashville: Thomas Nelson, 2002.

Menconi, Peter. Aging Well CASA Network Bible Study Series. Centennial, CO: Mt. Sage, 2013.

————. *The Intergenerational Church: Understanding Congregations from WWII to www.com.* CreateSpace, 2010.

Miller, Donald. *A Million Miles in a Thousand Years: What I Learned While Editing My Life.* Nashville: Thomas Nelson, 2009.

Morely, Patrick. *The Man in the Mirror: Solving the Twenty-Four Problems Men Face.* Grand Rapids, MI: Zondervan, 2014.

————. *The Rest of Your Life: A Road Map for Christians Who Want a Deeper Understanding of What to Believe and How to Live It.* Grand Rapids, MI: Zondervan, 1998.

————. *Second Wind for the Second Half: Twenty Ideas to Help You Reinvent Yourself for the Rest of the Journey.* Grand Rapids, MI: Zondervan, 1999.

————. *The Young Man in the Mirror: A Rite of Passage into Manhood.* Nashville: B&H, 2003.

Mowry, Bill. *The Ways of the Alongsider: Growing Disciples Life to Life.* Colorado Springs, CO: NavPress, 2016.

Nouwen, Henri J. M. *The Wounded Healer: Ministry in Contemporary Society.* New York: Image, 2013.

Ogden, Greg. *Unfinished Business: Returning the Ministry to the People of God.* Rev. ed. Grand Rapids, MI: Zondervan, 2003.

Peel, Bill, and Kathy Peel. *Where Is Moses When We Need Him? Teaching Your Kids the Ten Values That Matter Most.* Nashville: Broadman & Holman, 1995.

Pillar, Michele. *Untangled: The Truth Will Set You Free.* Racine, WI: BroadStreet, 2016.

Piper, John. *Don't Waste Your Life.* Wheaton, IL: Crossway, 2003.

Pratney, Winkie. *Revival: Principles to Change the World.* Pensacola, FL: Christian Life, 2002.

Rainer, Thom S., and Eric Geiger. *Simple Church: Returning to God's Process for Making Disciples.* Nashville: B&H, 2011.

Reese, Randy D., and Robert Loane. *Deep Mentoring: Guiding Others on Their Leadership Journey.* Downers Grove, IL: InterVarsity, 2012.

Rhodes, Stephen A. *Where the Nations Meet: The Church in a Multicultural World.* (Downers Grove, IL: IVP, 1998.

Ruchti, Cynthia. *Ragged Hope: Surviving the Fallout of Other People's Choices.* Nashville: Abingdon, 2013.

Schaffer, Dan. *Spiritual Fathers: Restoring the Reproductive Church.* Building Brothers, Littleton, CO. 2006.

Shears, Dr. Jeffrey, and Clarence Shuler. *What All Dads Should Know.* CreateSpace, 2011.

Shuler, Clarence. *The Challenge: Cultivating Disciples That Last.* CreateSpace, 2017.

———. *Experiencing Discipleship: A Small Group Faith-Building Adventure.* Loveland, CO: Group, 2002.

———. *Keeping Your Wife Your Best Friend: A Practical Guide for Husbands.* CreateSpace, 2013.

———. *Single and Free to Be Me.* CreateSpace, 2013.

———. *Winning the Race to Unity: Is Racial Reconciliation Really Working?* Chicago: Moody, 2003.

Smalley, Gary, and John Trent, PhD. *The Blessing.* Nashville: Thomas Nelson, 1986.

Smith, Timothy. *The Seven Cries of Today's Teens: Hearing Their Hearts, Making the Connection.* Brentwood, TN: Integrity, 2003.

Sommers, Christina Hoff. *The War Against Boys: How Misguided Policies Are Harming Our Young Men.* Rev. ed. New York: Simon & Schuster, 2000.

Stecker, Dr. Chuck. *EnCoMentor.* Seismic, 2018.

Story, Laura. *When God Doesn't Fix It: Lessons You Never Wanted to Learn, Truths You Can't Live Without.* Nashville: Thomas Nelson, 2015.

Swindoll, Charles R. *The Quest for Character: Inspiring Thoughts for Becoming More Like Christ*. Grand Rapids, MI: Zondervan, 1993.

Tozer, A. W. *The Root of Righteousness*. Chicago: Moody, 2015.

Walling, Terry B. *Stuck! Navigating Life and Leadership Transitions*. CreateSpace, 2015.

Webber, Robert E. *Ancient-Future Evangelism: Making Your Church a Faith-Forming Community*. Grand Rapids, MI: Baker, 2003.

————. *The Younger Evangelicals: Facing the Challenges of the New World*. Grand Rapids, MI: Baker, 2002.

Wick, Wes. *Half Two: The Quest for a God-Honoring Encore*. November, 2017.

Willard, Dallas. *Renovation of the Heart: Putting On the Character of Christ*. Colorado Springs, CO: NavPress, 2012.

Woll, Mary Beth, and Paul Meier. *Growing Stronger: Twelve Guidelines Designed to Turn Your Darkest Hour into Your Greatest Victory*. New York: Morgan James, 2015.

Wright, Tim. *Searching for Tom Sawyer: How Parents and Congregations Can Stop the Exodus of Boys from Church*. Bloomington, IN: WestBow, 2013.

Zoba, Wendy Murray. *Generation 2K: What Parents and Others Need to Know About the Millennials*. Downers Grove, IL: InterVarsity, 1999.

MINISTRIES AND RESOURCES

SPEAKERS

Truman Abbott was a licensed pastor with The Happy Church and the Foursquare Church. He served one year on the board of the International Christian Accrediting Association (ICAA) and seventeen years as chairman for accreditation teams. He was a frequent speaker for schools going through accreditation and was a presenter of breakout sessions at the Oral Roberts University Educational Fellowship (ORUEF) and Association of Christian Schools International (ACSI) summer seminars. He served as the athletic chairman for the National Christian School Competition at ORUEF for more than twelve years. He can be reached by e-mail at foota@earthlink.net.

Andy Addis is a pastor, speaker, trainer, and author. He has served in the context of church ministry since 1991 and has become recognized as a leader of the pioneering rural multisite movement. Working with the North American Mission Board and national think-tank groups for church planting and multiplication, Andy and his team have experienced numerous opportunities to help churches and church-planting organizations grow and expand. As an author, he regularly publishes articles on discipleship and leadership through his blog (www.CrossEyedlife.com), has self-published Bible-study material called *Reading It Right*, and has published a family resource and children's book called *Blotch* with LifeWay/B&H Kids. Andy also enjoys serving as a trustee for the North American Mission Board and on the Board of Directors for A Chosen Generation Ministries. He is available for speaking and training for church growth/development, revival/discipleship, men's retreats, youth events, and children's camps. He can be reached through www.AndyAddis.com, www.facebook.com/andyaddis, www.instagram.com/andyaddis, or www.twitter.com/andyaddis or via an answering service at (620) 860–2151.

Kathy Addis is proud of her "job" as a full-time wife and mom. She also enjoys speaking to women's small Bible-study groups as well as large gatherings of ladies. She is an annual session leader at Renew Women's Conference and has spoken for the SHINE Girls' Conference and many other women's events. Kathy regularly posts articles at www.kathyaddis.com and can be reached at kathyaddis@me.com and 620-665-8983.

Noah Addis currently serves as an intern at his home church, CrossPoint Church in Hutchinson, Kansas. He leads worship for the youth and college groups as well as weekend services and helps with the tech team each week. Noah spends much of his time in the summer helping lead worship for several youth and children's camps in Kansas and Texas. He can be reached at Instagram.com/noahaddis1110, facebook.com/noah.addis.9, noah@crosseyedlife.com, and (620) 860-2151.

Dr. Jeff Baxter spends his time living for Jesus with his beautiful family. He leads River Church, investing in all generations, feeding the congregation through passionate and relevant teaching, and reaching into the local community with love and service. He also is a Christian-book writer and speaker at conferences, churches, and events. Please check out his blog at SacredOutfitter.blogspot.com and his church's website at riverchurchmovement.org. He can be reached through social media at facebook.com/drjeffmbaxter, twitter.com/drjeffmbaxter, and Instagram.com/pastorjeffbaxter.

Dr. Richard and **Leona Bergstrom** are coauthors of the book *Third Calling: What Are You Doing the Rest of Your Life?* Together, they directed the national older-adult ministry for their denomination for a decade and also led midlife and older-adult ministries in a local church. Through their ministry of *Re-Ignite*, they write, speak, facilitate retreats, and coach individuals in living their calling throughout the various stages of life. Contact them at Re-Ignite.net or by e-mail at info@chonline.org.

Greg Bourgond is a leader, teacher, author, speaker, consultant, and mentor. His experience in the military, commercial enterprises, the defense industry, and the church inform his leadership activities. His ministry, Heart of a Warrior, seeks to help men live with integrity and honor under God's authority. Greg has a passion for developing leaders. He is a frequent speaker at men's events, churches, and various organizations. He can be reached at HOAWAdvance@aol.com, www.heartofawarrior.org, and (651) 308-1530.

Jamey Bridges is a speaker, pastor, and coach. He combines years of ministry experience and athletics to help churches, teams, groups, and ministries empower and release a new generation of leaders. Please contact him at Jamey@lifeillinois.org, www.lifeillinois.org, (618) 610-5444, or Facebook/Instagram/Twitter: jameybridges.

Bob Dees, Major General, US Army, Retired, is an author, ministry leader, mentor, and nationally recognized speaker on faith-based resilience, leadership, and national security. To access Resilience Resources or schedule Bob for a speaking event, contact him at (202) 257-4292, www.ResilienceGodStyle.com, contact@ResilienceGodStyle.com, or author@ResilienceTrilogy.com.

Cheryl Eichman is a writer, photographer, speaker, and mentor. She taps into her experience of being a youth pastor, managing an overseas missions program, and speaking to youth and adults in order to help people live out the knowledge that Jesus loves them deeply and has a great story for them to be a part of. She can be reached by e-mail at Ceichy24@hotmail.com, Instagram: Gloryphotoco, and Twitter: CherylEichman.

Cathy Erickson was a co-minister with Dr. Dan Erickson, an author, and a ministry leader. She has led groups of children in Christian education, youth, Mothers of Preschoolers (MOPS), and various ministries. She started a ministry to single-mom families and worked with Kids Matter Ministry in Joplin, Missouri, to bring hope and necessities to the children there. She coauthored the book *God Loves Do-Overs* with her late husband, Dr. Dan Erickson.

Bruce Fong is a speaker, author, and teacher. He currently serves as dean at Dallas Theological Seminary in Houston and has served in various pastoral roles since 1973. Dr. Fong was part of the Promise Keepers speaking team from 1996–2007 and has authored numerous books. Please see his website at www.brucefong.com and his blog at brucefong.wordpress.com. He can be reached by e-mail at bruce@brucefong.com.

Jerrel Gilliam has more than thirty years of ministry experience, including serving as national manager of worship for Promise Keepers and manager of urban praise for Integrity Music. He conducts seminars for men's ministry and worship-leader workshops and is an international speaker with a special calling to Latvia and Africa. He has a passion for intergenerational ministries and for people experiencing the love of God through divine encounters in worship. His e-mail address is mosaicprez@hotmail.com.

Scott Haima's lifelong passion is intergenerational, gender-specific, discipleship. He combines forty-five years of experience with twenty-seven years of military and business to help churches equip their men to serve in a masculine context of mentoring and discipling boys and young men. He conducts seminars, trains men, and speaks at various men's events. CSB Ministries (Christian Service Brigade) partners with local churches to see all men take responsibility to lead, equip, and disciple each generation. Please contact him at shaima@csbministries.org, www.csbministries.org, or (800) 815-5573.

Rod Handley is a speaker and the founder and president of Character That Counts, a ministry that was established in 2000. He served as senior vice president and CEO/CFO of the Fellowship for Christian Athletes until May 2000 and has published more than twenty books, including *Character That Counts: Who's Counting Yours?*, which details how to begin the process of being accountable to one another. Rod is a popular retreat and banquet speaker for men's and women's groups. Please contact him through the website www .characterthatcounts.org or by e-mail at rhandley@kc.rr.com.

Amy Hanson, PhD, leads a speaking, writing, and consulting ministry that equips the church for ministry with the new old. She speaks throughout the US with pastors, church leaders, health-care professionals, and older adults about the unique needs and opportunities of a graying America. She is the author of the book *Baby Boomers and Beyond: Tapping the Ministry Talents and Passions of Adults over 50* and regularly teaches gerontology courses to college students. You can read more about her ministry and follow her blog at www.amyhanson.org.

Hannah Harder is a writer and speaker who has written a devotional called *Exposed: The Raw Thoughts from an Ordinary Life*, a daily devotional of quick reads. She has launched her own ministry called Purpose Generation, which is a company that seeks to propel people into their God-given purpose. Contact her at www.purposegeneration.com.

Maddison Hardin is a published author who lives in Nashville. You can contact her at maddisonhardin@gmail.com.

Terry Hoggard is a missionary, pastor, networker, coach, and author. He has served as European missionary since 1984 and has spent a lifetime building relationships, nurturing life-giving connections, creating teams, resolving conflict, and seeking to make a difference. Terry travels extensively, passionately engaging with progressive leaders to inspire better performance at every level. He does this by crafting strategies, coaching synergy, and creating solutions. He can be contacted through the websites www.terryhoggard.com and www .convoyofhope.com and his e-mail address, thoggard@convoyofhope.com.

Athena Dean Holtz is a speaker, author, former radio host, publisher, and pastor's wife. She is a cult survivor, twice over: once in Scientology before knowing Jesus, and again after having known Him for thirteen years being lured into a legalistic, toxic, and abusive cult. Her incredible story of being deceived, losing everything, and then escaping will elicit tears and cheers as you watch her life transformed and redeemed by the Lover of her soul. She has been speaking to groups large and small for more than thirty years and has written four books, including her memoir *Full Circle: Coming Home to the Faithfulness of God*. Her passion is to declare the faithfulness of God and instill hope in those who've been deceived, betrayed, or wounded, equipping believers to recognize the tactics of the Enemy and guard their hearts. She can be reached at athena @athenadeanholtz.com, www.athenadeanholtz.com, and (360) 226-3488.

Geoffrey Ross Holtz is a pastor, speaker, and author. Ross has been in ministry for more than forty years, having served three churches in that time. He believes that the church is the hope of the world and that men are the hope of the church. Ross has a heart for ministries for men in the local church and for pastors and men's ministries leaders. He authored *Are You in the Game or in the Way? A Question for Pastors and Men's Ministry Leaders* to help overcome obstacles in developing ministries for men. He has been a frequent speaker at men's events. Please contact him at revholtz@gmail.com, www.rossholtz.com, or (253) 951-2179.

Reverend R. Craig Kirkpatrick is the senior pastor of the Evangelical Free Church in Eaton, Colorado, and is a lover of Jesus and God's Word. He also is a counselor (Fellow, APA), Bible-conference teacher, mission field conference speaker, chaplain (CMC, ABCMC), husband, father, grandfather, and spiritual father. Craig pursues his heavenly Father and is willing to do whatever He asks. He is a two-time cancer survivor who seeks to live, love, and minister in light of his mortality, convinced of the truth the apostle Paul proclaimed in Philippians 1:21–25 and 3:14.

Kristi Lemley is an author, speaker, counselor, television host, and ministry leader. She combines twenty-one years of experience as a counselor with her ministry platform to assist listeners in living in freedom and to their fullest God-given potential. She speaks at women's events, churches, and organizations, as well as on her television program, *Living in the Light*, which is viewed around the world. She can be contacted at Kristi@KristiLemley.com, www .LivingintheLight.tv, and (618) 557-2676.

Marni Mrazik's greatest desire is to see people come to know Jesus and grow in relationship with Him. She combines her passion for God and for people with her teaching and ministry experience to encourage, empower, and equip others to serve, bless, and disciple those in their spheres of influence. She has led multiple seminars on parenting, baby dedications, blessing, and rite of passage. She can be reached by e-mail at marni@tcchurch.ca.

Sid Overton is a speaker, author, attorney, and ministry leader. He has been engaged in the private practice of law in Colorado for fifty years, in the areas of real estate and estate planning, and has been an attorney for more than twenty nonprofit corporations and organizations in Colorado. He served as the original incorporator and attorney for Promise Keepers and as a board member and executive officer of the organization for eleven years. Sid has also served as a teacher/ leader of a men's Bible-study fellowship for twenty-seven years. He was engaged in a limited teaching assignment with Cru on a mission trip to Albania in 2016. He can be contacted by e-mail at sidoverton@oalaw.net or (303) 779-5900.

Toby Quirk is a chaplain, author, and speaker who writes and speaks with a passion for encouraging Christian disciples to grow deeper in their walk with the Lord. His message points to the inextricable bond linking spiritual training with physical training. He also writes fiction and has had short stories published and has a novel in the works. Toby is frequently invited to speak at Christian men's groups and at patriotic events. Check out his website at www.tobyquirk .com and his Facebook page at https://www.facebook.com/authortobyquirk/.

Dr. Clarence Shuler is an author, speaker, life and relationship coach, and counselor who heals individuals, couples, and organizations wounded by pornography, affairs, and diversity by taking the BLuR out of their struggling relationships. He speaks at his own Building Lasting Relationships family and marriage conferences and for FamilyLife and Gary Chapman's (*Five Love Languages* author) marriage conferences. He also speaks at family, marriage, and men's retreats; at singles', youth, and women's events; and NFL chapels. Clarence has written six books, with three more to be released. He can be contacted at clarencefs@gmail.com, www.clarenceshuler.com, or (719) 282-1340.

Chad Stecker's life mission is to be a motivated, personal warrior and servant for the Lord. His desire is for people to know what they believe and why as well as be successful at applying their faith where they live, work, and play. In ministry, he emphasizes discipling people to understand who they are in Christ as a son or daughter of our Father in heaven. Chad has been the featured speaker at conferences across the country.

Ward Tanneberg has served as a denominational youth director, a Christian-college public-relations director, a guest lecturer and adjunct professor, a writer and novelist, and pastor in three churches, including five years as pastor of the Assembly of God in Forks, Washington; twenty-three years as senior pastor of Valley Christian Center in Dublin, California; and seven years as executive pastor/pastoral care of the nondenominational Westminister Chapel in Bellevue, Washington. He served as executive director of CASA 50+ Network from 2008 to 2014. His interests and ministry have taken him to more than fifty countries of the world. Please visit his website at www.wardtanneberg.com or e-mail him at ward@wardtanneberg.com.

Joel Thomas brings more than twenty years of ministry and leadership experience to speaking, presenting, coaching, and community-development mentoring. He speaks often at men's events, camps, churches, and community events. You can contact and/or follow him at joel@harborchurchco.org, harbor churchco.org, and facebook.com/harborchurchco.

Julie Thomas is a speaker, writer, and pastor's wife. Her passion is for women to believe God for all He is and walk out their one and only life in truth, strength, and love. Please check out the website WomenWhoBelieve.com, a resource for Bible studies and encouragement. Julie can be reached by e-mail at julie @womewhobelieve.com.

MINISTRIES

Building Brothers helps local churches develop a leadership core of men who are pursuing God and becoming spiritual fathers and are capable of reproducing that pursuit in the lives of other men. The reproduction process includes creating a clear "path" that leads men from spiritual immaturity to spiritual fatherhood. This reproductive process develops leaders who become spiritual fathers who then create meaningful legacies, make impacts in their churches and communities, and experience true significance in their lives.

Flowers in the Desert is a treatment program that helps women who have experienced the devastation of a husband's infidelity find counseling, resources, and a road map for traveling a path to redemption. See their website at www .revolutioncounseling.com.

Resilience God Style (www.ResilienceGodStyle.com) is a campaign to restore faith-based resilience at individual, leader, and national levels. Resources include books, video series, resilience board games, and speaking for conferences, churches, and men's groups. For more information, e-mail contact @ResilienceGodStyle.com or call (202) 257-4292.

Second Half Coaching helps people fifty-five years and older navigate the remainder of their days. For more information, contact Peter Menconi at peter menconi@msn.com.

Shiloh House offers nurturing, therapeutic, and educational services to empower youth and families to overcome the impact of abuse, neglect, and trauma. Through guidance, clinical intervention, and advocacy, Shiloh House meets the needs of the community while respecting the diversity of youth and families. Shiloh House is located in Littleton, Colorado. Please see their website at www.shilohhouse.org.

With help from all generations, **YES! Young Enough to Serve** inspires adults over age fifty to become more intentional in praying, serving, and making disciples. In addition to providing direct serving opportunities, YES! is passionate about helping churches break through peer-only bubbles, bringing stronger unity to the body of Christ. Visit yestoserve.org/ted for an innovative three-minute plunge into the world of YES! More information can be found at www.yestoserve.org.

A CHOSEN GENERATION MINISTRY AND SEMINARS

You are a chosen generation, a royal priesthood, a holy nation, His own special people, that you may proclaim the praises of Him who called you out of darkness into His marvelous light.

1 Peter 2:9 (NKJV)

Vision

The vision of A Chosen Generation is to see an explosion of dynamic intergenerational churches reproducing among God's people.

Ministry Purpose

A Chosen Generation is a Christ-centered ministry that exists to equip and train leaders with strategic vision, passion, concepts, and resources for intergenerational ministry.

Mission Statement

The mission of A Chosen Generation is to provide leaders with training, resources, and strategies in order to strengthen the intergenerational culture and spiritual continuity of the church, thus helping each person grow in spiritual maturity as a reproducing disciple.

Contact Information

A CHOSEN GENERATION
PMB #355
11757 W. Ken Caryl Avenue, F
Littleton, Colorado 80127

Tel: 303-948-1112
info@achosengeneration.org
www.achosengeneration.org

Ministries and Training of A Chosen Generation
Men of Honor Women of Virtue

Weekend seminar that culminates in ceremonial rites of passage for young men and women to be recognized as adults in the community of adult believers. Normally presented to a single church.

Target: entire church congregations

Anchor Points Seminar

Strategies for intergenerational ministry.
A graduate-level training day for leaders at all levels of the church. This training positions the church to begin communicating with all ministries with the same terminology and begin the process of shaping their strategy based on developing a clear intergenerational community.

Target: pastor, church and ministry leaders

The Power of Rites of Passage

The power, significance, and need for church families to conduct rites of passage for all the young men and women of the church. This day equips leaders with the materials and strategy to implement rites of passage in their local church.

Target: pastor, church and ministry leaders

If You Passed Your Baton . . . TAKE IT BACK

Churches across America are struggling with how to engage their older members. Many churches have chosen to marginalize them instead of empower them. The greatest asset most churches have within their church family is going untapped.

Target: pastor, church and ministry leaders, and seniors

Never *Just* Babysit Your Grandkids

Grandparents should never become $15-an-hour hirelings.
Grandparenting is a gift from God, and every moment between grandparents and grandchildren should be cherished and viewed as an opportunity to shape families for generations yet to be born.

Target: Pastor, church and ministry leaders, parents, and grandparents

EnCoMentor

Finding and Becoming an EnCoMentor (Encourager, Coach, Mentor)
Two of the most critical things you can do to increase your likelihood of finding fulfillment as well as passionately pursuing your purpose and destiny is to find an EnCoMentor and then learn to EnCoMentor another. We must ask ourselves, who have I given permission to "walk alongside me"? and Who am I "walking alongside"?

Target: pastor, church and ministry leaders, entire church congregations